ANTHROPOLOGICAL PAPERS OF
THE UNIVERSITY OF ARIZONA
NUMBER 34

THE
DURANGO SOUTH
PROJECT

Archaeological Salvage of Two Late
Basketmaker III Sites in the
Durango District

JOHN D. GOODING
editor

with contributions by

Elaine Anderson

Lorraine Dobra

Priscilla B. Ellwood

O D Hand

Signa Larralde

Barbara Love-dePeyer

Edward J. Rowen III

Susan K. Short

THE UNIVERSITY OF ARIZONA PRESS
TUCSON, ARIZONA
1980

Library of Congress Cataloging in Publication Data

Main entry under title:

The Durango South project.

    (Anthropological papers of the University of
Arizona; no. 34)
      Bibliography: p.
      Includes index.
      1. Basket-Maker Indians—Antiquities. 2. Durango
region, Colo.—Antiquities. 3. Excavations (Archae-
ology)—Colorado—Durango region. 4. Colorado—
Antiquities. I. Gooding, John D. II. Anderson, Elaine.
III. Series: Arizona. University. Anthropological
papers; no. 34.
E99.B37D87   978.8′29   80-16361

ISBN 0-8165-0705-8

Contents

FIGURES

iv

TABLES

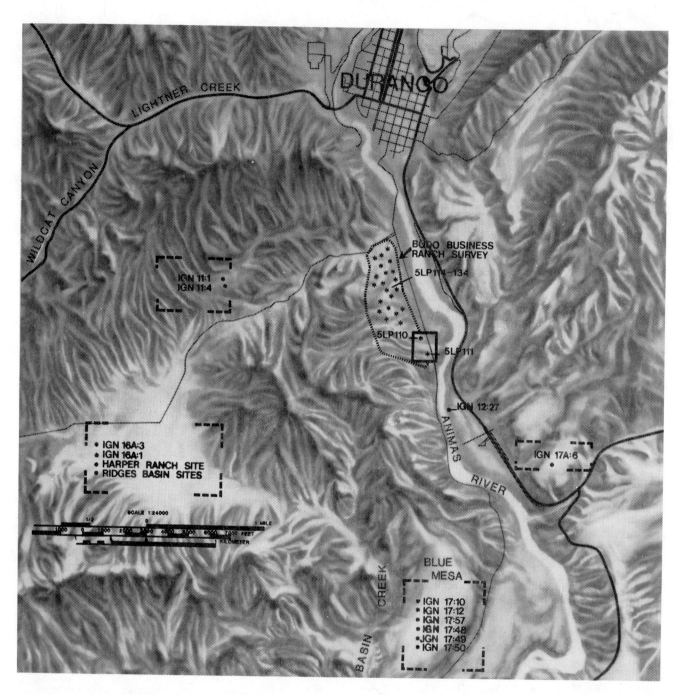

Figure 1. Shaded relief map showing 5LP110 and 5LP111 as well as other archaeological sites south and west of Durango.

Preface and Acknowledgments

Archaeological salvage of two Basketmaker III sites south of Durango was conducted in October and November of 1976 in conjunction with the relocation of U.S. Highway 550/160. Three pit structures and one surface area were excavated. The archaeological data recovered from these excavations are employed in defining: 1. the geographical, temporal, and cultural limits of the Durango District; 2. a local variety of an established ceramic type, Twin Trees Black-on-white; 3. multiple functional classes that exist within the single formal artifact class "bone awl"; 4. a broadened spectrum of the faunal resources exploited by Basketmaker III people. The two sites at Durango South can be interpreted as part of the terminal Basketmaker III occupation prior to the general abandonment of the district at approximately A.D. 800.

This report is based on the proposition that archaeological research designs are only as valuable as the quality of the personnel that participate in the project. This is especially true when the scope and nature of the archaeology to be undertaken is determined by nonacademic factors. In this regard I feel that the Colorado Department of Highways has been extremely fortunate with this salvage project. The table of contents illustrates the variety of tasks that resulted from a simply designed clearance procedure that attempted to address general questions of cultural affiliation, technology and economy. I believe that the contributions of the authors cannot be understated. All participated in the numerous menial chores that are necessary in generating a report of this complexity, and although each piece of analysis represents an individual effort, each also represents a spirit of cooperation and a continuing interest in the larger story that the total document represents.

On behalf of myself and the contributing authors I wish to extend my gratitude to C.A. Morain, James Mayfield, Coy D. Sweat, and Carl Watson of the Highway Department District 5 Office for their understanding and support of this project as the official sponsors.

It was my pleasure to work in Durango with the finest group of field personnel in my experience. Field foremen Tommy Fulgham and O D Hand provided numerous suggestions for the rapid and accurate excavation of the sites as well as thorough and complete notes and observations. Two excavation crew members made significant contributions to the speed and quality of the

excavation: Jim Rancier provided outstanding stratigraphic interpretations and cartographic expertise; the profiles, architectural, and artifact location maps contained in the report are his. Joel Brisbin was invaluable in the architectural interpretations of both sites.

The excavation crew must be commended for their willingness to work long hours through some inclement weather. They include: Larry Biedle, Tom Bridge, Stephen F. Chapman, Pat Comer, Lorraine Dobra, Jeff Indeck, J. Steven Meyer, Jan Von Nieda and Doug Wells.

The field laboratory was operated by Barbara Love-dePeyer and Priscilla Ellwood. Their efforts kept the laboratory within days and sometimes hours of the excavation. The transfer of the mass of data and artifacts to the laboratory in Boulder is a tribute to their organizational abilities. I wish to thank Randy Bacus of Durango for his talented and sensitive work as our backhoe operator. He saved many, many hours of backbreaking labor. Digging test pits and clearing overburden from archaeological sites with heavy equipment can often be counterproductive, but he proved that it can be done with an absolute minimum of destruction to the archaeology. I wish also to thank the graphics section of the Department of Highways staff for building all the camera ready figures. The photographic catalogue from this site is thorough and detailed. For that I wish to thank Tommy Fulgham, Curtis Martin, and Bertrand dePeyer.

Special acknowledgement for expertise in dating the sites is due to Richard L. Warren of the Laboratory of Tree-Ring Research, Tucson, Arizona and Robert L. DuBois of the Earth Sciences Observatory, Norman, Oklahoma. I am indebted to Joe Ben Wheat of the University of Colorado Museum and David A. Breternitz of the Department of Anthropology, University of Colorado, for observation, suggestions and unpublished data that contributed to most of the subjects dealt with in the report.

Finally I wish to express my special thanks to Barbara Love-dePeyer and Signa Larralde, for without their continued questioning, points of clarification, and lively debate with all authors, this document would have attempted little and accomplished less.

John D. Gooding

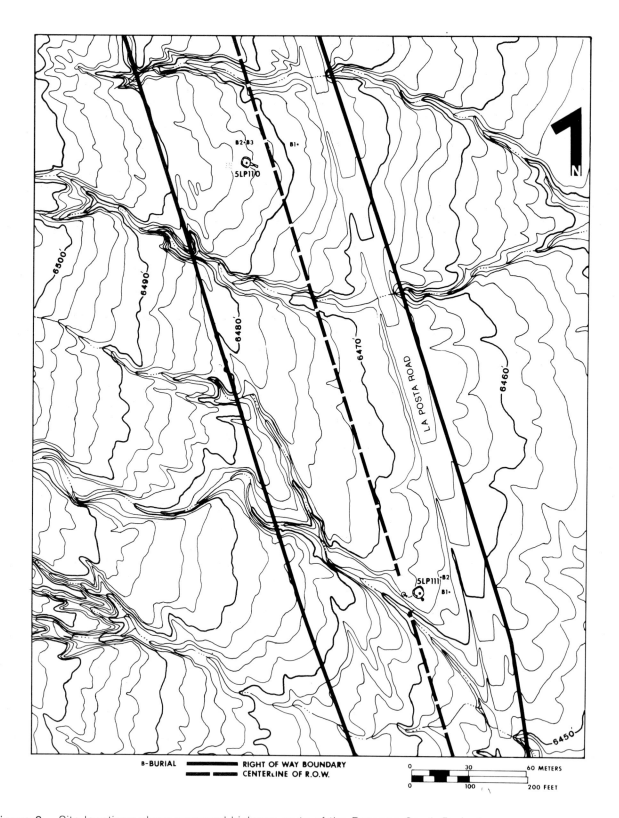

Figure 2. Site locations along proposed highway route of the Durango South Project.

I. The Sites In Context

by John D. Gooding

Introduction

In October and November of 1976, a Colorado Department of Highways archaeological field crew directed by John D. Gooding conducted clearance excavations of two sites recorded during a preliminary survey (Schaafsma and Gooding 1974). Upon excavation, both sites proved to be of the Basketmaker III culture period: Site 5LP110 was a pithouse (Feature 1) with an attendant surface room and a ramada (Feature 2); Site 5LP111 consisted of two pit structures (Features 1 and 2). Both sites were situated near the centerline of the proposed highway route (Fig. 2) and were the only identified archaeological remains that would have suffered direct adverse impact as a result of highway construction. The sites were located approximately 2.5 km south of the city of Durango along La Posta Road in the NE¼, NW¼, Section 5, Township 34 North, Range 9 West, N.M.P.M. Loma Linda Quadrangle.

An additional survey in the immediate area (Applegarth 1974) and amateur excavations by Homer Root (1965-1967) and others suggest that these sites were subsidiary to a large rancheria type village or two immediately neighboring villages.

The surface characteristics of 5LP110 included a crescent-shaped rubble mound consisting of sandstone slabs, sherds, lithic debris and burned clay. Southwest of the rubble mound was a level area which proved to be the location of the pithouse.

5LP111 was situated at the edge of an arroyo with partially exposed cultural debris near the surface. There was no suggestion that pit structures were present or that there was substantial depth to the cultural deposits. Exploratory tests conducted in June 1976 did not confirm the presence of any architectural remains. However, through extensive testing efforts with a backhoe over the entire area, the structures were located and excavated.

The Setting

The sites are located on the lower (eastern) periphery of a large alluvial fan (Fig. 3), as were all the sites recorded on the Bodo Business Ranch Survey (Applegarth 1974). The fan is at the base of Sliding Mountain and terminates on the first terrace above the Animas River. Geologically, it is made up of decomposed Lewis Shale and Cliff House Sandstone which together comprise Santana Loam (U.S. Soil Conservation Service 1976). The soil is a Loamy A 11 horizon that grades into a light Clay Loam A 12 horizon with carbonate deposits, at a depth of 10 cm. This overlies a Clay Loam B 2 horizon which varies in depth from three meters or more at the base of the mountain to a few centimeters at the Animas River. Underlying the Santana Loam are the tilted Cliff House Sandstone and Pleistocene outwash gravels. The soil in the alluvial fan is thus predominantly clay, making excavation difficult even in pithouse fill. Initial construction of the pithouses in this soil must have been laborious but certainly resulted in structures with strong walls and smooth, hard interior features.

The average annual precipitation of 46 cm occurs mostly in the form of snow during the winter months, and rain which falls typically as late afternoon showers in the spring and summer (Environmental Data Service 1977). This quantity of precipitation, when viewed from the dendroclimatic record provides a most interesting contrast between the recent climate in the vicinity of Durango and that of twelve hundred years ago (Dean and Robinson 1977). The departures from the norm for precipitation and temperature are as follows:

Decade	Departure	Decade	Departure
760-769	+1.20	1930-1939	-0.50
770-779	-1.90	1940-1949	-1.00
780-789	+1.90	1950-1959	-4.00
790-799	-0.30	1960-1969	-0.80
800-809	-2.90		

The long term averages suggest that the climate around Durango was slightly cooler and wetter during the Basketmaker occupation than it is today. Currently there is an average of 120 frost-free days and an average annual temperature of 48° F. An exception to this generalization is the decade 800-809 which appears to have been significant and is discussed below.

Within the last 70 years, overgrazing has resulted in a general denuding of the area and has initiated the present arroyo cutting. The list of local flora in Table 18 reflects the present ecological setting of the site in the pinyon-juniper vegetation zone. After flotation and pollen analysis of some of the internal features of the pithouses, it was found that some of the present plant species also occurred prehistorically at the site (see Pollen, Seed Remains, Chapter IV).

Fauna indigenous to the Durango area are typical of areas of contact of the mountain, piedmont and

3

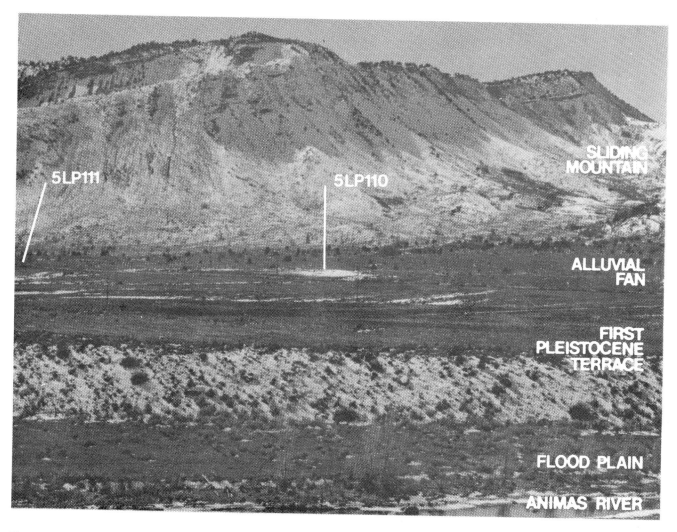

Figure 3. Location of sites on Bodo Business Ranch, as viewed from east of the Animas River.

desert zones. Analysis of the faunal remains from the two sites provides a list of the faunal resources available to the prehistoric inhabitants (see Fauna, Chapter IV).

Previous
Archaeological Investigations

It has long been known that the upper Animas valley in the vicinity of Durango contains a wealth of archaeological sites (Morris and Burgh 1954, Carlson 1963); though much of it has been recorded, little has been published. In 1974 and 1975, surveys were conducted by various academic institutions which broaden the geographical range of what was tentatively defined as the Durango District (Bullard 1962). This recent work, coupled with earlier amateur efforts, elucidates the prehistoric context of the Durango South sites.

An archaeological survey conducted by Fort Lewis College (Applegarth 1974) on the Bodo Business Ranch industrial property revealed 20 sites immediately north and west of 5LP110 and 5LP111. All of the sites contained one or more pithouses. The topographic location of the sites suggests that at least four of the sites could be grouped together as a village, while two others may form another village.

Barry Hibbets (1975) conducted a survey on Blue Mesa, 9.6 km south of Durango. He recorded 41 sites including five large villages which had been previously recorded by Flora and reported by Gladwin (1957). All of these sites exhibit evidence of the presence of one or more pithouses.

A survey crew from the University of Colorado Mesa Verde Research Center recorded 23 sites with pithouses in the proposed Ridges Basin Reservoir, 4.3 km southwest of Durango (Leidy 1976). They also found nine sites with possible pithouses and six sherd and lithic scatters.

These three surveys covered an almost continuous 26 square km area south and west of Durango (Fig. 1). In all, 95 pithouse sites were recorded. Among these, at least six village sites were recognized, but it is impossible to determine exactly how many sites or groups of pithouses may be villages. Dean (1975) reports another 23 sites, surveyed primarily by Flora, north and west of Durango, one of which was a large village, and four sites on the Florida River east of Durango.

Although there are many other known archaeological sites in the upper Animas valley, few have been professionally excavated. Talus Village is from the Basketmaker II period which in the Durango area is dated as third century B.C. to third century A.D. (Morris and Burgh 1954), while another group of sites is a Basketmaker III village dated at the eighth century A.D. (Carlson 1963). Other professional reports include Dean's (1975) analysis of tree-ring information from the Durango area and Gladwin's (1957) description of one excavated pithouse and several large villages.

More recently, the Anthropology Department at Fort Lewis College excavated several sites in the vicinity. John C. Ives (personal communication) has conducted investigations in the Blue Mesa region. Barry Hibbets (1976) salvaged a site (5LP115) which had been partially destroyed by the industrial activity on the Bodo Business Ranches. This site, dated near the end of the eighth century A.D., was located approximately 600 m north of 5LP110. Bill Biggs and Susan Applegarth (personal communication) partially excavated a site (5LP135) occupied after A.D. 586 on the campus of Fort Lewis College.

The extensive amateur work in the region has been poorly documented and was often based on arbitrary and misinformed archaeological judgments which resulted in patently incorrect and unsubstantiated interpretations. Much of this work illustrates the enduring detrimental effects pothunting can have on retrieval of archaeological data. One amateur, I.F. "Zeke" Flora, brought the Durango area to the attention of professional archaeologists through his desire to establish a tree-ring chart for this area. He trenched no less than 35 sites searching for tree-ring samples. Few of these excavations are well recorded (for example, see Flora 1941a).

Another amateur, Helen Sloan Daniels, excavated several Basketmaker III sites in Griffith Heights on North Durango Mesa. The National Youth Administration Museum Project of the Durango Public Library sponsored this work during the late 1930's. Since the primary purpose was to collect artifacts for exhibit, information was often poorly recorded (Daniels, Lee and Allen 1938; Daniels 1938, 1941; Lee 1938). The NYA also dug three other sites which are best described by Dean (1975:55, 62-63). These are IGN 12:23 (GP), IGN 12:58 (GP), and IGN 12:59 (GP). Helen S. Daniels (1941) also partially excavated two additional sites, IGN 7:25 (GP) and IGN 7:36 (GP). Excavation was completed by Earl Morris and reported by Carlson (1963).

Amateur excavations were carried out at Ridges Basin by Homer Root (1965-1967), curator for the Center of Southwest Studies at Fort Lewis College. In 1965 Root uncovered an isolated pithouse on the Bodo Ranch in the Ridges Basin Region. It was round, 8.2 m across, and had a full bench. There were eight major support posts set in the bench about halfway between the back wall and the bench face. The vent shaft was in the southeast portion of the house. Twelve surface rooms arranged in two rows of six rooms each were also excavated. They were of adobe and pole construction with a row of rocks at the bottom. The only tree-ring sample had a noncutting date of A.D. 749 (Dean 1975).

The 1966 project involved three small pithouses, associated surface rooms, and extensive trash deposits. All three pithouses were constructed with four support posts set into the floor; none had a bench. The central firepits in all three pithouses were filled with clean sand which contained small sandstone spalls. A sandstone slab covered one firepit.

On the floor of the first pithouse lay the skeleton of a man with skull missing and both arms and legs broken. There were nine surface rooms with this pithouse. A circular floor with a large center post and a post wall on the south uphill side was associated with the pithouse. The second pithouse had seven surface rooms in two rows, and the third pithouse had six associated rooms.

The site map drawn by Homer Root shows eight additional rows of surface rooms scattered within 60 m of the excavated houses, indicating that this was a large site. The trash deposits yielded numerous burials with associated grave goods. The skeleton in the first pithouse along with the lack of artifacts in any of the pithouses led Homer Root to assume that all three pithouses had been abandoned and intentionally burned. Tree-ring dates from this site indicate a late seventh century A.D. occupation (Dean 1975:78-79).

In 1967 another isolated pithouse with surface rooms was excavated. It was round, approximately 7.3 m in diameter and had seven roof support posts set in the bench face. There were two vent openings which were above the floor, similar to pithouses A, D and E at Jeddito 264 (Daifuku 1961). The central firepit was filled with clean sand and small sandstone spalls. Eighteen whole vessels, three pipes and various stone implements were on the

floor of the pithouse. Five metates were leaning on end against the bench. In all probability this pithouse was occupied at the time of its destruction by fire. Post patterns on the surface indicated nine contiguous rooms of adobe and pole construction.

Although the information from the above list of excavations is incomplete, the data base is adequate for the postulation of an archaeological district that covers a substantial geographical area, displays consistent cultural elements, and is bounded by distinct temporal limits.

Definition of the Durango District

The Durango District, first described by Bullard (1962:59), lacked geographic boundaries and was misclassified as predominantly Pueblo I. However, accumulated tree-ring dates from *Colorado W* (Dean 1975) provide a basic (Basketmaker) time frame for the occupation of the district.

The definition of the Durango District is based on the homogeneity of architectural and artifactual remains, all of which belong to Basketmaker II and Basketmaker III culture periods beginning as early as the third century B.C. (Dean 1975) and terminating at approximately A.D. 800 (5LP111, Durango South). These remains are distinct from those of other districts in the Northern San Juan Region, which were defined by Kidder (Bullard 1962:56). Type sites for the district are Talus Village (Morris and Burgh 1954), the type site for Basketmaker II, and the Basketmaker III Hidden Valley sites north of Durango, also excavated by Morris (Carlson 1963). Talus Village represents the range of variation for Basketmaker II artifacts and architecture in this district. The Basketmaker II occupation terminates in the fourth century A.D. Transition dates from Basketmaker II to Basketmaker III are very sparse and are not cutting dates. The florescence of Basketmaker III begins in the sixth century A.D., and is reflected in a different settlement strategy with a preference for flatter, more open country and an increased reliance on agriculture. Basketmaker III is also characterized by considerable architectural variation between villages and some degree of homogeniety within villages (e.g. Hidden Valley vs. Bodo Ranch). Basketmaker III sites from the sixth through the eighth centuries A.D. are numerous.

The district is bounded by the drainages of the Animas, Florida and Los Pinos Rivers (Fig. 4). Specifically, the western boundary of the Durango

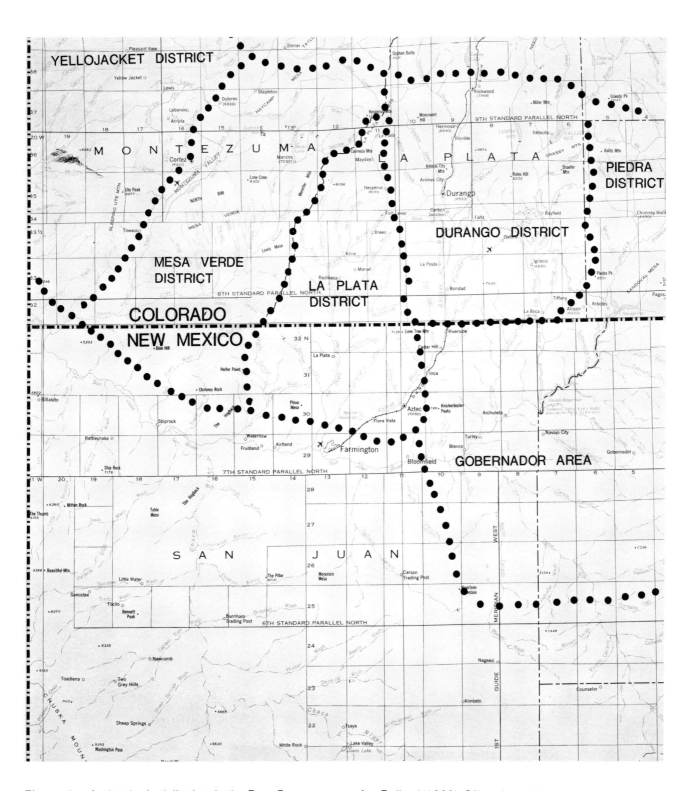

Figure 4. Archaelogical districts in the Four Corners area, after Bullard (1962), Gillespie (1976), and Dean (1975).

FIGURE 5

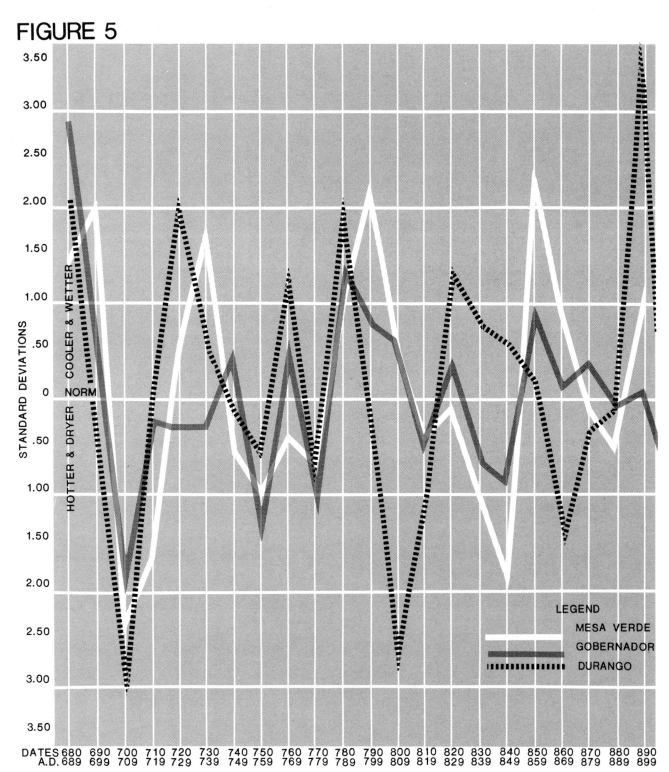

Figure 5. Dendroclimatic variability in the Mesa Verde, Gobernador and Durango Districts, A.D. 680 - A.D. 960 (Dean and Robinson 1977: Appendix 2).

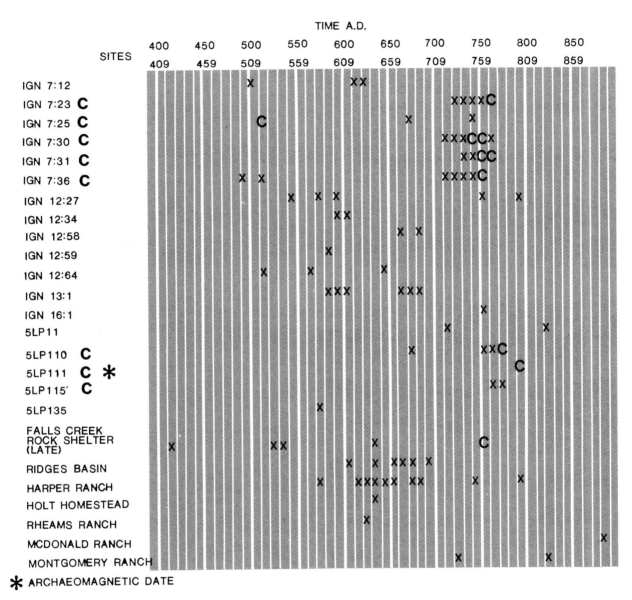

Figure 6. Tree ring dates from all Basketmaker III sites tested in the Durango District. "X" indicates one or more dates within a ten year period. "C" indicates cutting dates.

9

District is the La Plata District (Morris 1939). To the east the district is defined by sites along both sides of the Los Pinos, including Holt Homestead, La Boca pithouses at LA 4573, and 5LP11. Two possibly later sites along this boundary are McDonald #1 and Montgomery Ranch, since Pueblo I ceramics are present at these two sites. The boundary between the Durango District and the Chimney Rock and Stollsteimer Mesa Districts (Eddy 1977, Adams 1975) within the Piedra District is best defined by the divide between the Piedra and Animas Rivers. To the south in the Los Pinos drainage, the Durango District is bounded by the Navajo Reservoir District (Dittert, Hester and Eddy 1961) at the Colorado-New Mexico border. This portion of the boundary is reflected in the dates of the following sites, which all show cultural development after A.D. 800 and are thus outside the district: Cueva Grande, Simon Canyon Cave, Grotto Cave, Mesa Mountains Cave, Cox Canyon Cave, and Site H (Mesa Mountains). The district is bounded on the north by the La Plata and San Juan Mountains, which also mark the northern boundary of the Northern San Juan Region (Fig. 4).

The Durango District does not provide substantive data for the approximately 400 year period separating Basketmaker II and Basketmaker III. The noncutting dates from IGN 7:12, IGN 12:1, IGN 12:10, IGN 12:27, IGN 12:34, IGN 12:58, IGN 12:59, IGN 12:64, IGN 13:1, IGN 16:1, Harper Ranch, Ridges Basin, and 5LP11 (Fig. 6, Dean 1975) strongly suggest occupational activity but cannot be construed as definitive evidence of late Basketmaker II - early Basketmaker III manifestations. The accumulated data also suggest no cultural development later than Basketmaker III. At the end of the eighth century A.D. there was a general abandonment of the upper Animas River, Florida Creek, and the upper Los Pinos River. Reasons for abandonment of this area at the end of the eighth century are unknown. The dendroclimatic variability for this district (Dean and Robinson 1977) indicated in Figure 5 suggests that in general the climatic patterns in the vicinity of Durango were less stable than in neighboring areas from which similar data were collected.

Figure 5 illustrates variation of annual tree growth around the mean growth for dated specimens in the study areas. There is a high correlation between annual tree growth patterns and precipitation and temperature (Dean and Robinson 1977:7-8). In Figure 5 standard deviations are divided in half to provide a detailed view of dendroclimatic

differences between the Durango District, Mesa Verde to the west, and the Gobernador area to the south. Most of the fluctuations are minor, but according to Dean and Robinson (1977:7):

> Variation that exceeds two standard deviation units in either direction is considered to be significant in the sense that such departures are sufficiently rare to have had potential adaptive consequences for plant, animal, and human populations.

Figure 5 indicates that a large drought hit the three areas between A.D. 690 and A.D. 710 and was most severe in the Durango District. It is apparent that the Durango District recovered from this drought more rapidly than the surrounding areas; by A.D. 710 the climate was normative and for the following two decades, it was cooler and wetter than the norm in the district. By A.D. 750 the three areas again underwent a warmer and dryer period; the Durango District was least affected and recovered most rapidly. This rapid recovery reflects a building cycle in the Durango District beginning in the middle of the 8th century.

There was a third warm and dry cycle in the three areas from A.D. 770 through A.D. 779. Again, however, the change in climate was less than one standard deviation in the Durango District and this district recovered faster than Mesa Verde or the Gobernador. The number of tree-ring dates collected from this period indicates that building activity in the later half of the eighth century was slower than the first half. This may suggest that the population was relatively stable.

A local drought occurred in the Durango District between A.D. 800 and A.D. 809. This drought had no effect on the Mesa Verde or the Gobernador where precipitation and temperature patterns remained cooler and wetter. The drought in the Durango District was severe and is believed to have been the cause of the general abandonment of the area.

The relatively small number (six) of tree-ring dates after A.D. 800 around Durango and the lack of clustering between them suggest the hypothesis that this local drought forced a mass migration out of the Durango District, which was never reoccupied except for a few isolated sites representing extremely small populations. This may be the result of a more erratic local climate here from A.D. 800 through A.D. 890 than in the neighboring districts.

The abandonment of the Durango District can be

correlated with site frequencies and related demographic inferences in neighboring districts. On Wetherill Mesa there are nine known La Plata Phase (ca A.D. 450-750) sites and 138 known Piedra Phase (ca A.D. 750-990) sites (Hayes 1964:89-91). This is an increase of 1533% in known sites. In the Gobernador area, tree-ring dates indicate that there was little occupation before ca A.D. 800. However some sites that were occupied at or shortly after A.D. 800 are Cox Canyon Cave, LA2121, LA2122, Salt Point, and Site H (Mesa Mountains). In the Navajo Reservoir District, the Rosa Phase (A.D. 700-850) parallels the above developments (Dittert, Hester and Eddy 1961). In the discussion of this phase Eddy (1966:484) states, "The increase of the number of sites was so dramatic after A.D. 750 that natural biological reproduction could hardly account for the expansion." Sambrito Village and the Uells Site represent whole villages that sprang up abruptly during this period. To the east in the Piedra District there is also an increase in site frequency at A.D. 800 or shortly thereafter. The Sanchez Site and Sandoval Village are part of the beginning of a general population increase for the Piedra District. In parts of this district, the population increased 23% from the Rosa Phase (A.D. 750-850) to the Piedra Phase (A.D. 850-950) (Adams 1975:159).

Basketmaker III was thus the terminal indigenous cultural occupation for the Durango District. Sites 5LP110 and 5LP111 date to the last quarter of the eighth century and were a part of the terminal occupation.

II. The Site Descriptions

by
John D. Gooding
and O D Hand

Excavation Procedure

Datum points were established for each site on the northwest edge of the cultural debris, at an elevation of 1977.76 m for 5LP110 and at an elevation of 1971.53 m for 5LP111. All vertical and horizontal measurements were made from these points. Two subdatum points were later established for 5LP110, one at 34E 8S, elevation 1975.55 m, the other at 24E 36S, elevation 1976.45 m. These subdatum points were used for recording vertical provenience only. At both 5LP110 and 5LP111, baselines for the grid system were aligned with true north and were staked at four meter intervals south and east of datum.

Vegetation on the sites was cleared by hand. A road grader was used to clear vegetation from areas surrounding the sites. The surface of these areas was scraped to a depth of 3 to 4 cm at 5LP110 and to 10 cm in 2 to 3 cm intervals at 5LP111, in an attempt to locate surface features and burials. One burial partially covered with a sandstone slab was found at 5LP110 east of the pithouse.

A backhoe was used to define the limits of structures, to test for hidden features and to remove loose fill. At 5LP110, Trenches A, B and C were dug in the pithouse depression and extended approximately 5 m to the east. At a depth of 1.8 m the pithouse floor was uncovered. The trench was then extended to the west at a depth just above the floor until the west wall was exposed in the profile. Trench B started in the center of the depression at Trench A and extended north until the north wall was visible in the profile. Trench C extended southward from Trench A. It was placed 2 m to the east of center in order to avoid hitting the vent shaft and other features found in the southern part of most pithouses. Outside walls were not visible in either the east end of Trench A or the south end of Trench C. Trench D cross-sectioned the surface mound from the southeast to the northwest (Fig. 7).

Trenches E through I were excavated by backhoe in an attempt to locate other pithouses. All were found to be sterile 10 to 20 cm below the scraped surface and were immediately backfilled.

In the part of the pithouse north of Trench A, fill was cleared to within 1 m of the back wall, bench faces, and floor with the backhoe. Excavation of the remaining fill was accomplished with picks and shovels to the bottom of the roof fall and then with hand picks and trowels the remaining distance to the bench and floor. Here and in Feature 1, 5LP111, a portion of the lower fill was screened through ¼ inch mesh hardware cloth, but this process proved to be unproductive and was discontinued. The south wall of Trench A was photographed and profiled before it was removed with picks and shovels to the bottom of the roof fall. Hand picks and trowels were used to expose the bench surface and floor.

The architectural profile of Feature 1 bisects the structure through the vestibule, antechamber, partition wall and firepit (Fig. 11). Since all of these subfeatures are aligned from east to west, the profile line is considered the north-south boundary for artifact and subfeature locations. A hypothetical line following magnetic north and bisecting the firepit was drawn through the pithouse to serve as the east-west boundary. Artifact and subfeature locations within the pithouse are discussed in quadrants from magnetic north: northeast, southeast, southwest, northwest. In contrast to the pithouse, the excavated surface room areas were quite shallow. Consequently, artifacts and subfeatures are located by grid designations.

At 5LP111, a backhoe was used to remove loose fill from an eroded area along the north face of the arroyo where charcoal and other cultural debris were noticeable. Fill removal was discontinued when the floor and firepit of Feature 1 were discovered. Backhoe Trench A was excavated from the arroyo edge north, in what was thought to be the center of the pithouse (Fig. 8). Feature 1 was much smaller than anticipated and the west wall was destroyed.

After Feature 1 was isolated with the backhoe, the remaining fill was excavated wholly with small hand picks and trowels, and artifacts above the floor were mapped and collected by natural levels. Floor artifacts were located both horizontally and vertically and a sketch map was drawn of the profile.

Trench B was parallel to Trench A and 8 m east of it. It proved to be sterile and was backfilled immediately. Trench C was excavated parallel to and 10 m east of Trench A. An occupational surface (presumed to be the bench surface) was exposed in the west wall of Trench C, 1.25 m below the surface and 8 m north of the arroyo. Because of the presence of this surface, it was felt that Feature 2 must lie east of Trench C.

Trench D was excavated from the center of Trench

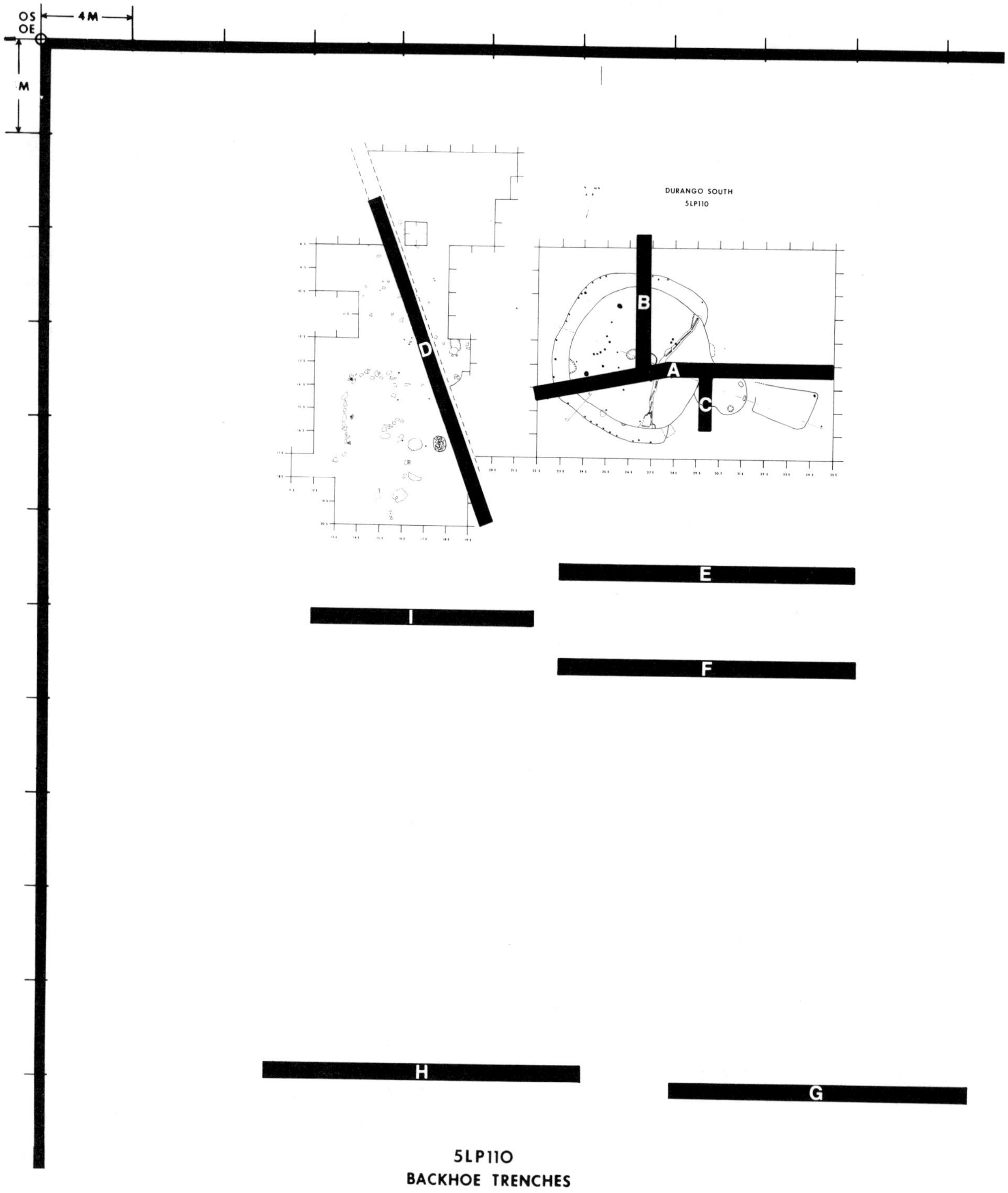

OS
OE

4M

M

DURANGO SOUTH
5LP110

D

B

A

C

E

I

F

H

G

5LP110
BACKHOE TRENCHES

Figure 7.   Backhoe trenches excavated at 5LP110.

C, and extended 9 m to the east. The first vertical 1.8 m was removed by backhoe. Excavation was continued with hand picks another 30 cm where the floor of Feature 2 was encountered. No outside walls were visible in either Trench C or Trench D.

Removal of the upper fill was accomplished with the backhoe. Excavation of the remaining fill between bench top and floor was accomplished with hand picks and trowels, exposing the floor from Trench D to the circumference of the pithouse. Walls and bench faces were almost impossible to find; the only indication of their existence was deterioration or disappearance of the floor.

Feature 2 at 5LP111 proved to be an unburned structure, apparently abandoned as a result of a flood. The timber had been confiscated for construction in some other area. The lack of typical pithouse fill (abundant charcoal, burned adobe and artifact fragments) made the existence of the structure uncertain until the first bench surface was encountered in Trench C. Without the aid of the backhoe this postulated structure would most likely have been given up as nonexistent.

Feature 1 at 5LP111 was not divided into quadrants for discussion of artifacts or subfeature proveniences because of the relatively small size of the structure. At Feature 2 the profile A-A' (Fig. 18) is 11° west of true north. As at 5LP110, (Fig. 18), a hypothetical line bisecting the center of the firepit was drawn perpendicular to the profile. All artifact and subfeature locations are discussed by quadrant from magnetic north: north, east, south and west.

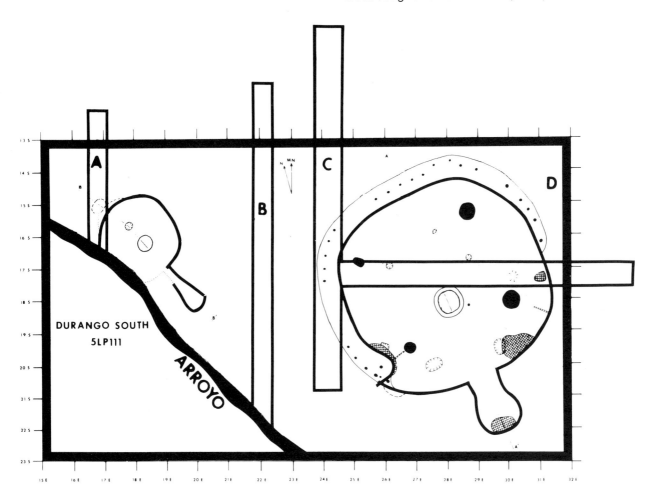

Figure 8.   Backhoe trenches excavated at 5LP111.

At both 5LP110 and 5LP111, all artifacts were given field specimen numbers and their vertical proveniences were determined. In addition, those artifacts found in contact with an architectural feature were replaced by flagged pins which were later mapped along with the architectural features using a plane table and alidade. Flotation and pollen samples were taken from all floor features as they were excavated. Most of the artifacts were photographed *in situ*.

5LP110, Feature 1 (The Pithouse) and Feature 2 (The Surface Areas)

The pithouse at 5LP110 was excavated in natural levels, as established from the profile of Trench A (Fig. 9). The surface was designated Level 1. Level 2 extended from the surface to the top of roof fall (27.5 cm). All of the fill from the top of roof fall to the floor was designated Level 3 (33 cm). Architectural surfaces were called Level 4.

Few tools were found in Level 2 and all these were fragmentary. This material probably represents trash from the surface.

Level 3, lower fill, represents roofing material of the pithouse: burned and unburned adobe, charred wood, and sandstone slabs. This level was excavated entirely by hand; consequently, the artifact collection was somewhat more complete than that in upper fill.

A secondary occupation was encountered in Level 3 which consisted of a slab-lined storage cist and a slab-lined hearth (Fig. 10). The storage cist was situated in the center of the pithouse above the firepit and had been constructed by digging into the roofing debris. It was 63 cm in diameter with upright side slabs 33 cm high leaning outward at the top. Nothing was found in the cist. However, a small fire had been built on the bottom and the ashes cleaned out before this occupation was abandoned.

The hearth was constructed against the southeast wall 22 cm above the floor. The bottom slab, a broken overturned metate, measured 31 cm by 36 cm. The upright slabs, 19 cm high, were tilted outward at the top. Charcoal and ash filled the hearth and the sandstone slabs had been heavily burned.

There was no preparation of the secondary

occupational surface and it was difficult to separate the debris of this occupation from debris which may have been on the roof of the pithouse when it collapsed. Fifty-seven cm northwest of the intrusive cist was a small concentration of broken sandstone slabs and other debris which is also thought to be associated with the secondary occupation. Included in this debris was part of a small globular grayware vessel and a metate fragment, which was part of the metate that had been used as the bottom of the fire hearth. Near the west wall a polished grayware bowl (Fig. 48c) was found. Also thought to be associated with the secondary occupation was a small Lino Gray jar (Fig. 45e) located close to the bench on the north side of the pithouse. On the west side of the pithouse near the wall, a second jar (Fig. 49d), a bowl (Fig 47d), and two floor polishers were found together.

A secondary occupation in the depression of an abandoned pithouse is an unusual phenomenon. However, it seems unlikely that the above architectural features were constructed in the roof and fell intact when the roof collapsed. On the other hand, the number and variety of artifacts located in Level 3 could easily represent artifacts that were resting on the roof when it collapsed. The ceramics of Level 3 do not reflect a culturally different occupation. Therefore, it seems plausible that within a few years after the collapse of the structure, new occupants slightly modified the pit depression by incorporating a cist and a small hearth, and utilized the depression as an extramural storage unit.

At 5LP115, 200 m to the northwest, Hibbets (1975:46) described a storage cist constructed in the roof fall, similar to the one found at 5LP110. He was able to recognize a thin discontinuous sheet of sherds which he attributed to this secondary utilization of the pithouse depression. There was no preparation of the living surface. A roof was postulated based on the presence of burned wood and adobe. Unfortunately, only half of 5LP115 was excavated so it was impossible to determine if there were any other features associated with the secondary occupation. At 5LP110 the bottom 10 cm of the roofing debris and floor contact was arbitrarily designated as Level 4. This level included all architectural surfaces. Burned logs and adobe were abundant and some evidence of several functionally specific areas was present.

At the completion of excavation, the pithouse at 5LP110 proved to be subrectangular with a ¾ bench.

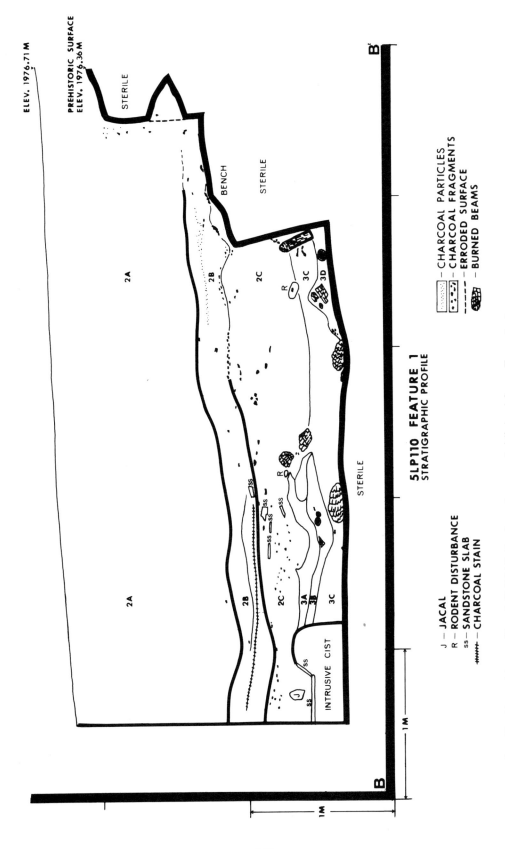

Figure 9.   Stratigraphic profile of 5LP110 Feature 1, as established from Trench A.

Figure 10. Slab-lined storage cist and slab-lined hearth from secondary occupation, 5LP110 Feature 1

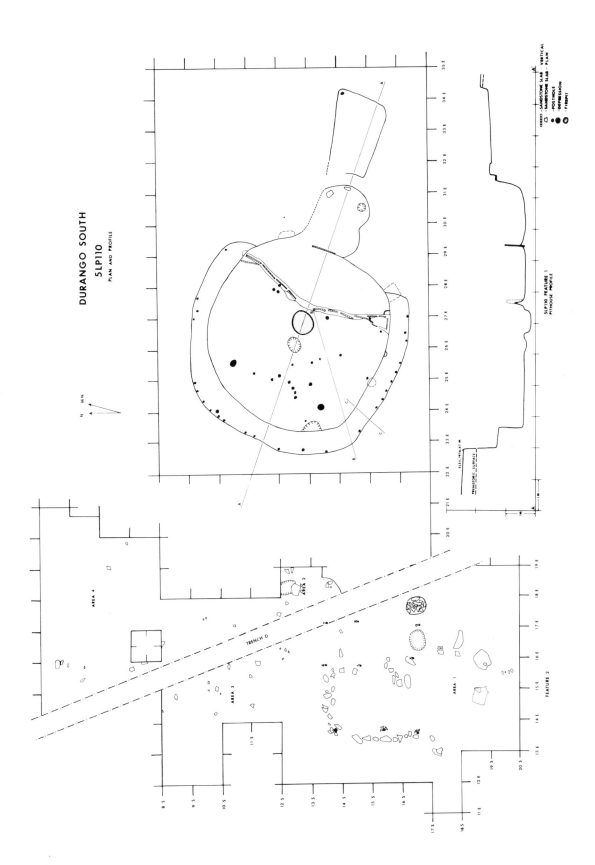

DURANGO SOUTH
5LP110
PLAN AND PROFILE

Figure 11. Site 5LP110, showing Feature 1, the pithouse, and Feature 2. Surface areas. A-A' profile of Feature 1 is beneath the plan view of the feature.

21

Figures 11 and 15 show architectural features and artifacts *in situ*. The pithouse measured 5.8 m by 5.8 m at the base of the bench and 6.45 m by 7.1 m at the back wall with the main axis oriented east-southeast. It had been destroyed by fire.

From the abundant burned logs on and near the floor, 15 samples were selected for dating by the Laboratory of Tree-ring Research in Tucson. The outside rings on ten samples were dated between A.D. 752 and A.D. 776 (Table 1). Although none of the dates are bark dates, the tight clusters at A.D. 765-A.D. 766 and A.D. 774-A.D. 776 indicate a probable roof construction date of A.D. 776. The one sample collected from the surface room was dated at A.D. 675.

The disparity between the only date from the surface structure and the relatively tight cluster of dates from the pithouse can be attributed to one of two possibilities: 1. the dated ring is from the interior and does not represent a cutting date; 2. since reclamation of structural wood is known to have

been practiced at other sites, this particular sample could easily have been a post reclaimed from an earlier structure.

A partition wall, which divided the main room, was continuous across the pithouse. It was composed of eight sandstone slabs and two worn out metates set upright on the floor and plastered on both sides. The center of the wall in front of the firepit was partially destroyed by Trench A and did not contain a slab. Only a remnant of plaster remained on the floor at that point.

The height of the slabs varied from 65 to 70 cm, while the plaster was 4 to 6 cm thick on either side and terminated below the top of the wall. The partition was heavily burned by beams which had fallen directly on the slabs. The plaster may have completely covered the slabs, if so the fire and falling beams reduced it to its current level.

At the north end, 48 cm from the bench face, the top of the partition wall sloped downward at a 45° angle

Table 1.   Tree Ring Dates from 5LP110

	Lab Number	Species	Inside Date	Outside Date
Pithouse	DUR-104	juniper	666fp	752vv
	DUR-95	pinyon pine	732p	765vv
	DUR-96	pinyon pine	699p	765vv
	DUR-99	pinyon pine	733p	766vv
	DUR-106	pinyon pine	728fp	766r
	DUR-94	pinyon pine	743fp	774vv
	DUR-97	pinyon pine	731p	774vv
	DUR-91	pinyon pine	721p	775v
	DUR-98	pinyon pine	724p	776v
	DUR-103	pinyon pine	727p	776vv
Surface Room	DUR-100	juniper	557fp	675vv

Key (Dean 1975:9-10):

Inside Date:
    p   pith ring present
    fp curvature of inside ring indicates that it is far from the pith

Outside Date:
    r   less than a full section present, but outermost ring is continuous around available circumference

    v   no direct evidence of true outside of specimen, but date is judged to be within a very few years of cutting date

    vv no way of estimating how far the last ring is from the true outside

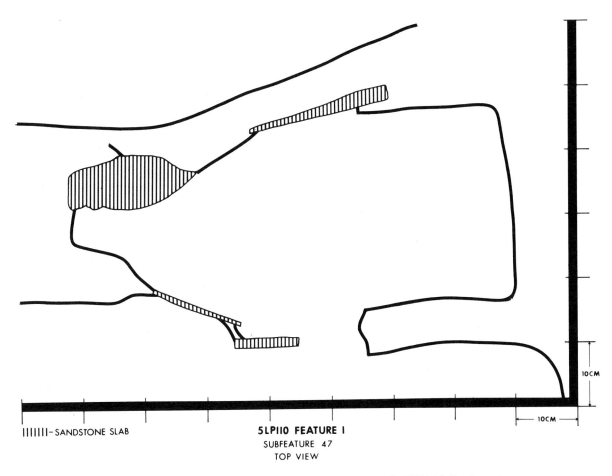

I||||||- SANDSTONE SLAB

5LPIIO FEATURE I
SUBFEATURE 47
TOP VIEW

10CM

10CM

Figure 12. Triangular storage bin at southern end of partition wall, 5LP110 Feature 1.

to a height of 12 cm, thus terminating the wall 8 cm from the bench face. A subrectangular sandstone slab, 60 by 52 cm, covered the gap between the bench and partition. A second slab in the partition 60 cm north of the firepit had also not been plastered, but was socketed on an oval shelf of adobe which extended 17 cm west of the partition wall 23 cm above the floor. The gap created by moving either slab probably functioned as a doorway in the wall between the two portions of the pithouse. Both of the slabs were movable and could have been used as deflectors.

The southern end of the partition wall served as one side of a triangular storage bin (Fig. 12). Sandstone slabs lined all three sides and the bottom. The walls had not been plastered on the inside, but the floor of the bin had a covering of adobe, which made it 5 cm higher than the floor in the surrounding room. Bins of this type are apparently limited to the Northern San Juan Region (Bullard 1962:171).

Joined to the east wall of the bin and the south bench face was a small adobe shelf. It measured 16 cm wide, 25 cm long, 9 cm thick, and was 49 cm above the floor.

The floor of the pithouse was slightly bowl-shaped, with a maximum difference in elevation of 14 cm from the west bench face to the central firepit. One coat of plaster 1 - 2 cm thick covered the entire floor. Near the northwest bench this plaster coat had been disturbed by rodent activity.

The floor east of the partition wall was 9 cm higher than the floor of the main room and had also been plastered with a 1 cm coat of adobe. The center of the main floor was covered with a 2 to 3 cm layer of compacted ash and charcoal. This layer became thinner in all directions, disappearing at the eastern margin of the pithouse.

The firepit was located east of center, next to the partition wall. Its shape, circular with a flat bottom and sloping sides, is common in the Northern San Juan Region (Bullard 1962:158). It was 79 cm wide, lined with plaster, and extended from floor level down 17 cm. The top 4 to 5 cm of fill consisted of charcoal and ash, while the bottom 12 cm was compacted ash.

At the base of the bench on the west side of the pithouse was another oval depression; a heating pit (Bullard 1962:163). It measured 60 cm long, 45 cm wide, and 13 cm deep with inward sloping sides. The fill consisted of large pieces of charcoal and ash.

Thirteen small pole sockets were concentrated in the western portion of the pithouse. Their measurements ranged from 6 to 13 cm in diameter and from 5 to 18 cm deep. Eleven were filled with clean brown sand; five of these were capped by up to 4 cm of adobe. One of the holes had a small sandstone slab at the bottom and was completely filled with adobe. The small postholes appeared to be in two alignments. One row of four, oriented in a north-south direction, was located 90 cm west of the firepit and marked the western boundary of an ashy white area. Carlson (1963:7) thought that a floor discoloration similar in size at IGN 7:23 was the result of a pile of burned mats. With that hypothesis in mind, the row of posts may be the remains of a short partition wall/storage feature. The other alignment was a semicircle of six postholes open toward the bench and located midway between the firepit and the bench. This may represent a post-and-adobe structure which served as a storage bin built on the floor. The adobe plugs in most of the holes suggest that these features were eliminated as part of a remodeling effort.

Sixteen centimeters west of the firepit was a large ovoid depression. It measured 49 cm on the long axis, was 9 cm deep, and was filled with ash and small pieces of charcoal. Depressions of this shape and size have generally been called ash pits (Brew 1946:155; Bullard 1962:159). Roberts (1929:26, 38; 1939:254-255) describes similar depressions in both Chaco and Whitewater houses. He suggests that they functioned as entrance ladder rests. Although most ash pits are located between the ventilator and the firepit, the ash pits in two houses at the Cerro Colorado site (Bullard 1962:161), as well as in 5LP110, were located behind the firepit. Four main roof supports were present: two of these were incorporated into the partition wall and two were on the west side of the pithouse. The roof

support on the northeast side of the house consisted of three small posts arranged in triangular fashion within 10 cm of one another and plastered into the partition. All were 10 cm in diameter and were butted against the floor rather than having been placed in holes. The southeast roof support post, 12 cm in diameter, rested on the floor. It was plastered into the partition wall close to the firepit.

Two additional postholes were found in the floor, one located in front of a wall niche in the southern part of the pithouse and the other located west of the bin built into the partition. Both were 5 cm in diameter and nearly 8 cm deep.

The ¾ bench of the pithouse was 64 cm below original ground surface. The top of the bench averaged 65 cm wide and 73 cm above the floor at the front. It was 3 to 7 cm higher at the back wall. Only patches of plaster remained on the bench surface. The bench face sloped inward at the bottom, creating an average 14 cm overhang between the floor and the top. South of the southwest support post the edge of the bench had a raised plaster lip extending 1.22 m (Fig. 13). The bench at structure 3, MV 1937 on Wetherill Mesa, had a similar lip around its entire edge (Birkedal 1976:76).

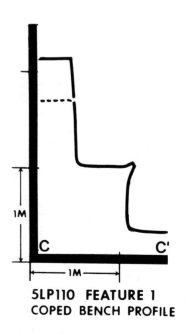

5LP110 FEATURE 1
COPED BENCH PROFILE

Figure 13.   Bench profile showing plaster lip, 5LP110 Feature 1.

Twenty-four wall post sockets were found on the bench. Their positions ranged from 3 cm in front of the back wall to 2 cm within the wall. Most of the post sockets were less than 5 cm deep and had an average diameter of 6 cm. Given an average of 32 cm measured between eight posts, it can be postulated that a total of 52 posts were once present. In the northwest section of the bench an adobe coping 5 cm high was found in front of the postholes. The coping probably circled the entire back wall at one time, but has since largely eroded.

Directly west of the two main support posts in the floor on the west side of the pithouse, two large posts were set into the bench. Both posts had diameters of 12 cm and were set 15 cm from the back wall. They may have functioned as buttresses for the tops of the main support posts.

Two niches were located in the bench face; three others were located in the wall east of the partition. One niche located in the bench face 60 cm west of the partition wall had been plugged and plastered over before abandonment. It was 54 cm above the floor and 15 cm deep, angling down into the bench. Plaster had been added on the bottom edge to form a sill 5 cm high.

The other niche in the bench face was located 1.5 m west of the partition wall at the base of the bench on the south side of the pithouse. It extended 24 cm into the bench face with a maximum interior width of 35 cm. Maximum depth was 28 cm, 11 cm of which extended below the floor. The eastern edge of the niche had been plastered, decreasing the opening to 23 cm.

East of the partition wall in the southeast corner of the pithouse was a large wall niche. It was placed 18 cm above the floor at the end of the bench. The subrectangular niche measured 58 by 41 cm and extended 21 cm into the wall. Niches of this size and position are thought to be storage bins (Bullard 1962:171) and are not uncommon in the Mesa Verde Region (Lancaster and Watson 1943; O'Bryan 1950).

Another subrectangular niche was built into the wall at the junction of the wall and the north end of the partition (the partition actually ended 8 cm from the wall). This niche was 17 cm high, 18 cm deep, and 64 cm wide, with 32 cm extending on either side of the partition. Therefore, access was possible from either side when the slab covering the gap between the wall and the bench was removed.

The third wall niche west of the partition was partially destroyed by the backhoe. It was in the east wall next to the doorway into the antechamber, 50 cm above the floor, 50 cm long, and 20 cm deep; the width was no longer measurable. It probably would have been comparable in size to the niche in the southeast corner of the room.

Trenches A and C cut through major portions of the wall features in this corner of the pithouse; consequently features of the antechamber are for the most part reconstructed. The antechamber was ovoid, approximately 2.17 m long and 1.8 m wide. Neither the floor nor the walls had been plastered. Unlike the rest of the pithouse, there was no evidence of burning. Morris (1939:64) observed this at Site 19 in the La Plata District and interpreted it as an indication that the antechamber had not been roofed. An alternate explanation is that the draft for the fire entered through the door and antechamber; the pithouse could thus have been severely burned only at the back, leaving the antechamber itself untouched.

On the other hand, the lack of charred remains and artifactual material in the antechamber suggests that the antechamber may not have been in use at the time of the fire. There is some possibility that it had been remodeled into a vent shaft and tunnel to the main room at the east wall. Isolated pockets of burned debris in the otherwise sterile fill of the antechamber are the only evidence of this hypothetical arrangement. Alteration of antechambers into vent shafts was noted at pithouses B and C, Site 1, Ackmen-Lowry (Martin and Rinaldo 1939:342-349) and is discussed by Brew (1946:209) as an example of remodeling practices at Alkali Ridge.

There were two stone steps on the east side of the antechamber, one placed 20 cm and the other 82 cm below present ground surface. They may have been steps leading into the antechamber; however, the distance between them (62 cm) would seem too large for this purpose. No other entrance was located. The only floor feature in the antechamber was a cist in the southeast corner which was 27 cm in diameter and 16 cm deep.

Adjacent to the east side of the antechamber was a roughly rectangular surface area 2.1 m long and 1.7 m wide. The builders excavated this area 10 cm into the soil. The floor had not been plastered but consisted of heavily burned, compact soil. One posthole, 11 cm in diameter and 6 cm deep, was found in the northwest corner. This slightly subsurface area is strongly reminiscent of the vestibule at IGN 7:23 (Carlson 1963:5) in orientation as well as in room arrangement. The location of the stone steps discussed above also suggests that this area was a vestibule or ramada entry.

A slight rise in contour just west of the pithouse depression indicated the presence of above-ground features at 5LP 110. The area was bladed with a road grader to 10-15 cm below the present surface level. Burned jacal and an increased amount of charcoal were present at this depth. Re-excavation of backhoe Trench D (Figs. 7, 11), originally dug to test the site, provided further evidence of the occupational level indicated by a gray compact soil layer interspersed with charcoal specks at a depth of 30-35 cm. As the soil dried, a crack developed along the base of this level, separating it from the lower clay.

The surface area was gridded into 4 m squares, subdivided into 1 m segments and excavated as two levels: lower fill and floor. Units could not be distinguished in the lower fill since the sparse evidence of roof fall was concentrated in small areas. Evidence of occupational surface varied abruptly from well-defined to poorly defined to nonexistent. Water-deposited layers, rodent activity, and damp soil caused by daily ground thaw added to the difficulties of defining the elusive floor.

Four large sandstone slabs were found in the fill above the floor approximately 2 m north of Feature 2 and 14 cm above the occupational level. They may be associated with the structure.

Excavations at 5LP110 revealed one surface structure and ramada (Fig. 14) 5 m west of Feature 1, the pithouse. As determined by the placement of post sockets, the area including the room plus the ramada was square, and measured 3.57 m east-west by 3.42 m north-south (see Figs. 11, 14, 23, 28, 54 for architectural details and placement of artifacts).

The floor of the structure consisted of hard-packed soil that has since been riddled with rodent activity. In the eastern half of the structure the floor was the relatively flat original ground surface, but in the western half a shallow basin had been dug. The basin reached a maximum depth of 16 cm near the western wall, and sloped up to the original occupational level on the north, south and east.

On the floor southeast of the basin was a cluster of eight small horizontal sandstone slabs, measuring 32 by 164 cm. Previous excavations in the Durango area established the use of similar slabs in wall construction (Carlson 1963). The only floor feature within the structure was a small oval pit 55 by 70 cm, averaging 8 cm in depth.

There was only very fragmentary evidence of walls. The lower portion of the west wall (the footing) of the surface structure was still partially intact. It was constructed at the time the basin was dug, and is composed of hard-packed dirt which slopes sharply to the east where it merges with the floor. This footing was an average of 10 cm below the original occupational level. Upon the footing lies a well defined row of 12 rough sandstone blocks 3.19 m long. There is less evidence of wall construction in other areas of Feature 2. However, the position of various large slabs close to the structure on the north, south, and along the central post row suggests that walls made of slabs were once present (Joe Ben Wheat, personal communication).

The superstructure was supported by nine posts in three parallel rows of three posts each, oriented north-south. The first and most obvious row was located to the west along the wall remnant. All three of the posts in this row were large, ranging from 10 to 15 cm in diameter, while the remaining six post remnants measured 6 cm in diameter. Post 1 was located on the east side of the stone wall and was braced between the wall and a small sandstone block. Directly south 1.59 m was post 2 to the east of the wall in the floor, supported by two sandstone slabs placed in the 26 cm deep post socket and by a small sandstone block. Post 3, 1.15 m further south, was also located on the east side of the wall but south of the basin and floor area. Post 3 was supported by the wall and by two sandstone slabs placed within the socket. Only posts 1 and 2 had upper surfaces burned as a result of the structure's destruction. Post 2 was the only specimen in this feature intact enough to be extracted for a tree-ring date (Table 1).

The remaining six posts were located on an average of 2.37 and 3.47 m east of the first row. The position of the central row places it in close association with the previously mentioned sandstone cluster, possibly indicating the location of a wall. The placement of a sandstone block near each of the central row posts suggests that blocks were used as braces. The two end blocks were substantially larger than the central block. Structures similar to

Figure 14.   5LP110 Feature 2, excavated living surface of room block. Note alignment of stone slabs.

this one are found north of Durango with "four corners reinforced by foundation stones" (Carlson 1963:20).

The presence of large braced posts, a basin floor area, and a single wall remnant strongly suggest that the western portion of Feature 2 was the main body of the structure. The presence of nine large sandstone slabs, six of which were shaped fragments, within 1.5 m of the structure indicates a vertical slab foundation. Previous work in the Durango area has documented the utilization of vertical as well as horizontal slabs in the construction of surface structures (Carlson 1963). The foundation was constructed by plastering the slabs to the ground (Joe Ben Wheat, personal communication). The destruction of the plaster, probably by weathering, caused later displacement of the slabs. Similar deterioration was noted by Carlson (1963:24).

The slabs were part of the foundation or protected the base of the structure. The remainder of the wall was probably of post and adobe construction. The placement of the stone slabs suggests that the east and west walls were vertical and the north and south walls sloped inward towards the main support posts. Burned jacal is the only indication of the method of construction of the roof. There was no evidence of an entrance.

The part of the structure east of the central row of posts may have been a ramada. It is unlikely that a wall extended through the hearth between the southern-most posts of the central and eastern post rows. Also, the third row of posts is composed of smaller uprights than those braced by the western wall; it may have only supported a roof.

It appears that the main body (i.e., the western section) of the structure was used for storage, food preparation, and perhaps some chipping activity, based on cultural debris found there.

The firepit was located on the occupational level 40 cm east of post 9 in the structure. It could easily have been tended by those using the ramada as a work area. A shallow (4 cm deep) ovate basin, it covered an area 49 by 59 cm. This hearth was lined with ten sandstone slabs ranging in size from 10 by 10 cm to 17 by 18 cm, all with scorched surfaces and fire cracks. Charcoal was found only in those areas protected by intrusive stones, and the amounts recovered were too small for carbon 14 dating.

The structure seems to have been abandoned before it was burned. During excavation only small amounts of burned jacal were recovered, in all cases above the fill protecting the floor.

Further excavations within the area produced no evidence of additional structures. No large contiguous habitational surface could be discerned. However, four areas had hard-packed surfaces, all of which were within 4 vertical cm of the previously defined occupational level. The first area was located south of the surface room. It was irregular in shape, 4 m by 2.3 m. Located in this area were a number of sandstone slabs of various sizes, both in the occupational level and in the fill above this level. These slabs are possibly related to the wall construction of the surface room.

The second area was located to the northeast of Trench D and was approximately 6 m by 2 m. Although irregularities in the surface varied as much as 7 cm vertically within a meter distance, the level averaged 39 cm below the present ground surface. A small ovate depression was partially exposed 2 m northeast of post socket 7. It was 45 cm wide by 50 cm long. The depression was 10 cm deep and contained one undecorated sherd and a large slab on the southeast side. The purpose of the basin could not be determined.

The third area, 2 m by 4 m, was situated north of the structure. Only Trench D separated this area from the second area; however, differences did exist. The surface of the third area was more level, with patches of burned red-orange soil, particularly in the northern section. Little charcoal or ash was found on the occupational surface.

The fourth area, located northeast of the other areas, was irregular in shape, measuring 5.5 m by 4 m. The floor sloped slightly towards the south, becoming steeper as it approached the southern edge of the area. Test excavations within the lowest part of the surface showed that it extended 15 cm below the previously defined occupational level. The presence of grinding implements on this occupational surface (two metates, one mano, one mortar and a polishing stone) suggests a specialized activity area.

Interpretations

The pithouse at 5LP110 (Fig. 15) produced a wealth of artifactual and faunal remains. This array of material indicates that the structure was a habitation in use at the time of a fire and involuntarily abandoned. Although the floor artifacts were not strictly segregated by function, certain artifact classes clustered in various locations in the structure suggesting the possibility of functionally specific areas. The metates were located on both sides of the partition wall but most were clustered at the north end, near the bench. Other ground stone artifacts such as metate supports, manos, and pounding/polishing stones were distributed throughout the structure. Only one metate was set up as if in use; the remainder were turned face down with manos under them or were stacked against the wall in the northeast quadrant. The inordinate number of metates in temporary storage (seven) suggests that at least on occasion grinding was the principal activity in the structure.

The chipped stone was evenly distributed in the pithouse and was not an abundant class of floor artifacts. Chipped stone remains include three projectile points, one knife, one biface, a drill, two cores, two utilized flakes and several debitage flakes that were located on or near the bench. It seems likely that the bench was a locus of chipping activity. It is interesting to note that many more of the utilized and non-utilized flakes were located in the upper fill and lower fill than were found on the floor of this structure. It is thought that these fill artifacts were originally floor artifacts that floated into upper levels with the subsequent filling of the structure after abandonment. It appears that chipped stone tools were used in the structure with some regularity and that their use was not localized in any specific area. However, in contrast to Feature 2, activities involving use of chipped stone tools were not centered around this structure.

The ceramics from this pithouse are discussed in detail in Chapter III. Functionally they portray a variety of activities that revolve around storage, cooking and eating. The largest functional class of ceramic artifacts was small jars. The presence of heavy charring on many of these vessels suggests that they were culinary wares. One group of such jars was found in association with butchered and cooked bone. Vessels 13a, 13b, 17 (Fig. 45d) and 18 (Fig. 49c) were located on the bench and floor in the southwest corner of the pithouse. The bone found in association with the vessels was abundant and included specimens of cottontail, jackrabbit, wolf, unidentifiable canids, deer, elk, voles, pocket gophers, assorted mice, unidentifiable mammals and unidentifiable birds. The proximity of these remains

to the heating pit at the base of the bench in the southwest corner leaves little doubt that this was the principal cooking pit and that the southwest quadrant of the pithouse was the food preparation area, even preferred over the central firepit for cooking. One of the jars, Vessel 17 (Fig. 45d), contained a charred corn cob and a knot of cordage. On the bench above the pit was an unclassifiable jar base that contained over 200 fragments of two small canid skulls which had been cooked.

Two restorable ollas and one jar base were located on the floor in the west half of the house. One olla, Vessel 12 (Fig. 46a), was located near the firepit. The other, Vessel 22 (Fig. 46b), was located very near the bench at the west wall. The jar base, Vessel 39, was on the floor beside two bowls. The large size of the ollas suggests that they were used for storage. Although capacity measurements were not taken, it is clear that the ollas would have been extremely cumbersome when filled. The location of the ollas at the perimeter of the cooking area, away from the cooking pit, would seem inconvenient.

The southwest corner also produced a mortar (Fig. 34b), four manos, an axe head (Fig. 38a), and the antler shaft (Fig. 84b). A broken antler wrench (Fig. 85) was plastered into the face of the bench in this corner with one protruding tine that probably functioned as a hook or peg.

In the northwest quadrant two adjacent bowls, Vessel 24 and Vessel 6 (Fig 47d), were located near the center of the floor and at the perimeter of the cooking area. A third bowl, Vessel 19 (Fig. 50c), was a highly polished Twin Trees Black-on-white which may have been associated with fragments of matting that also came from that corner.

East of the partition wall the ceramics were not clustered or immediately associated with other artifacts, with the exception of a broken Lino Gray jar (Vessel 15, Fig. 47a) possibly containing a projectile point (Type 2, Fig. 25f) located near the metates.

Bone tools from the pithouse were more common in Level 3 than in Level 4. Here again, it is postulated that these artifacts floated to some extent as the cavities in the collapsed structure were filled. The tools seemed to be evenly distributed with the exception of the bone awls which were all located in the southern quadrants.

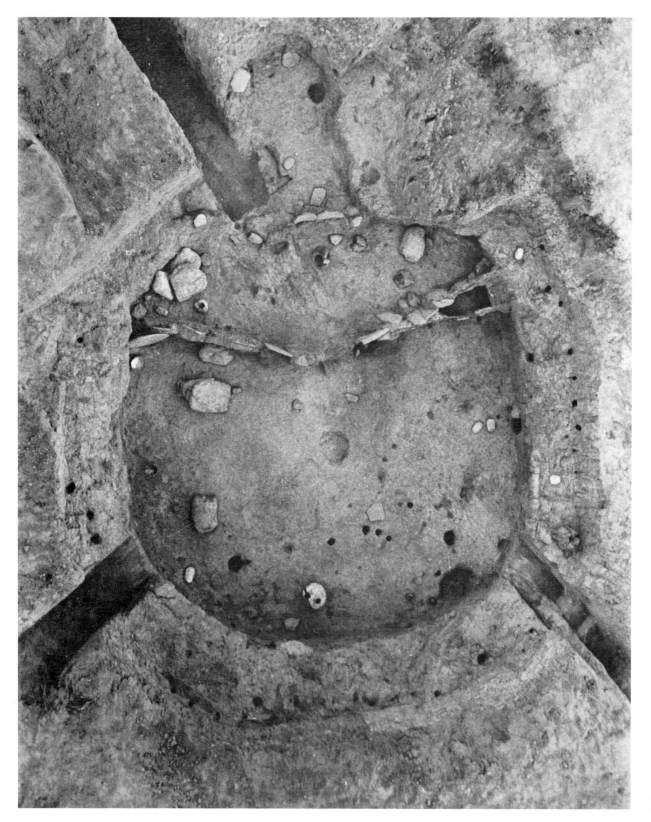

Figure 15. 5LP110 Feature 1, excavated pithouse with reconstructed ceramic vessels and ground stone.

The artifact assemblages of Feature 2, the surface area, differs from but complements material found in the pithouse. Eight metates and metate fragments were located in this area. One of the specimens was located within the walls of the surface room. Here again the 11 manos were distributed across the area.

Six hammerstones were located north of the surface with three of them in a loose cluster near the north wall. It is obvious that this was the principal chipping area for the site. Feature 2 also produced 14 cores, 149 debitage flakes, 37 scraping tools, including utilized flakes, six biface blades, one knife, two drills and one projectile point. These numbers represent artifacts from all levels but it must be remembered that the maximum depth at this feature is 39 cm.

Ceramics were considerably less numerous in the surface area than in the pithouse. Only four specimens were retrieved from Feature 2: a Lino Gray pitcher (Vessel 20, Fig. 48b), a Lino Gray jar (Vessel 16), and two unclassifiable bases.

Some unique bone artifacts are present in the assemblage at this feature. The only bone pin, the only spatulate awl, and the only bodkin (Figs. 73c, d, e) retrieved from the excavations were found here.

The faunal remains at Feature 2 were not as abundant as in the pithouse. Remains of canids, cervids and sciurids, including *Marmota* and *Cynomys*, were present, along with unidentifiable birds.

These observations at site 5LP110 reflect its character as a habitation that displays most attributes common to such structures including storage facilities, cooking facilities, preliminary food processing areas, and tool manufacturing and maintenance areas. Artifacts representing all these activities were scattered throughout the site but clustered in preferred areas for specific tasks.

Burials at 5LP110

Two burials containing the remains of three individuals were located at 5LP110. In Burial 1 (Fig. 16) were the remains of a female, aged 25-30 years. This burial was exposed by a road grader during clearing operations. The grave, an extremely shallow pit, was located 22 m east of Feature 1. The body was in a semiflexed position on its left side. The skull faced east and the arms were extended toward the knees. Immediately north of the skull was a small Lino Gray seed jar and a large Lino Black-on-gray bowl sherd (Fig. 49b). Two sandstone slabs covered this burial and preserved it almost totally intact.

Burials 2 and 3 were located in the same grave 9 m north of the pithouse at 5LP110. The maximum depth of this grave was 38 cm; it was the deepest grave at either site. The grave was lined on three sides by a natural sandstone outcrop which had been modified to incorporate it. The east side of the grave was lined with upright sandstone slabs. Burial 2, the disarticulated skeleton of a child aged two to four years, had been placed in the soft fill. Below the infant skeleton was mortuary furniture including a Lino Gray bowl (Fig. 45a) and a large Lino Gray sherd, which were located on the skull of Burial 3. It is impossible to conclusively determine which burial they were associated with. Burial 3 proved to be the complete skeleton of an adult male (Fig. 17) in a flexed position with the upper torso on its back, flexed legs propped against the slabs and right arm extended along the side. The left arm was flexed to the right shoulder. Placed on the chest in the crook of the elbow was a large Lino Gray jar (Fig. 44b). Around the right wrist was an *Olivella* shell bracelet consisting of 27 beads (Fig. 57a). Also scattered throughout the burial cist were 20 additional *Olivella* shell beads which may have belonged to either or both burials. These two individuals may have been a joint burial or the infant may have been a subsequent burial placed in a known grave site.

5LP111, Feature 1 (A Small Pithouse) and Feature 2 (Domestic-Ceremonial House)

Feature 1 at 5LP111 (Fig. 18) was a small subterranean room 5 m west of Feature 2. The main axis of the room was oriented toward the southeast, 138° east of magnetic north. Although partially destroyed by the arroyo cutting through it on the south and by a subsequent backhoe trench dug by the investigators, enough of Feature 1 remained to indicate general size and shape. The fill was almost indistinguishable from the surrounding sterile soil.

Figure 16.   Burial 1, 5LP110.

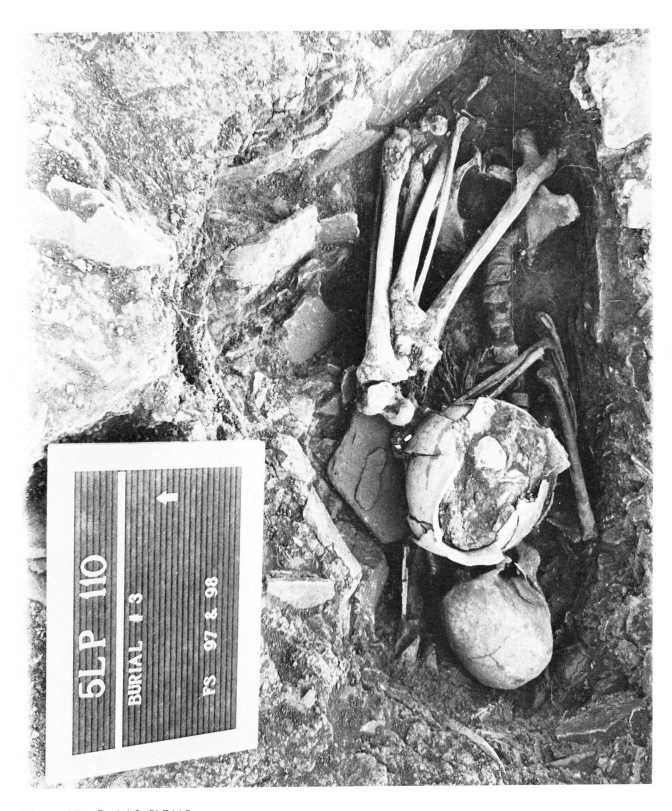

Figure 17. Burial 3, 5LP110.

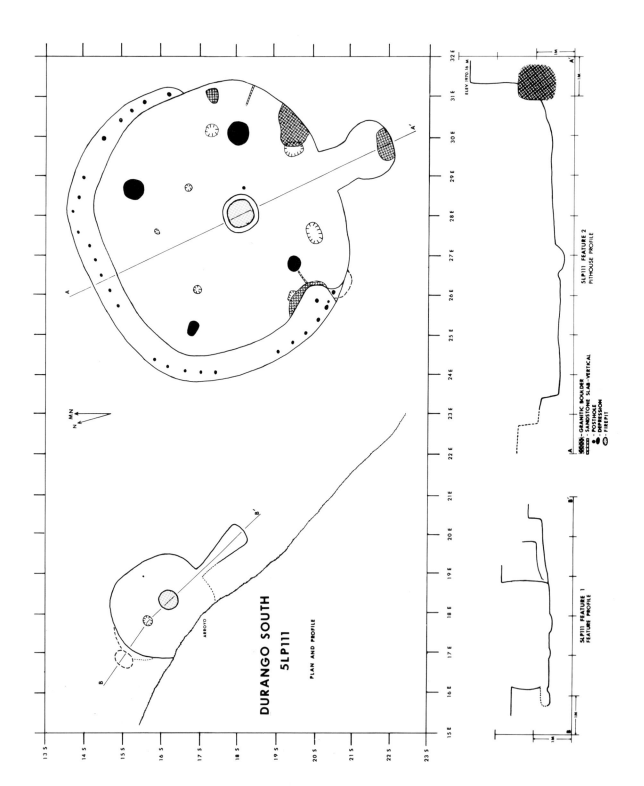

Figure 18. Site 5LP111, showing Feature 1, the small pit structure and Feature 2, the larger pithouse. Profiles are shown beneath the plan views of each feature.

Differentiation between the pithouse walls and the fill was best made only after completely exposing the limits of the floor.

Feature 1 was excavated in four natural levels from surface to floor; Levels 2 and 3 were further subdivided into a total of five units (Fig. 19). The cultural debris in Levels 2 and 3 of the pithouse consisted largely of sherds, flakes and fragmentary pounding tools.

Level 4, the floor of Feature 1, was 1.2 m below the present ground surface and measured 2.6 m in diameter. The flat, unplastered floor curved up to merge with the walls. The north and east walls were the only remaining details from which to determine the shape of the room. These walls bowed out at the center (Fig. 19) with a 9 cm overhang at the top, and had not been plastered. In the northwest wall, which had been partially destroyed by the backhoe, was a wall niche 48 cm deep. It was placed 6 cm above the floor, with an opening 1.2 m wide which tapered to 52 cm at the back. A bowl-shaped firepit, 50 cm in diameter and 8 cm deep, was located southeast of the center of the room. The top of the firepit was level with the floor. The bottom was lined with a layer of clean brown sand about 1 cm thick. Forty cm northwest of the firepit was a shallow bowl-like depression. It was 23 cm in diameter, 2 cm deep, and contained fill but no artifacts. The function of this depression is not known but it could be an ash pit as described by Bullard (1962:159). A small posthole 10 cm in diameter and 7 cm deep was located 60 cm northeast of the firepit, close to the wall.

To the southeast of the firepit was a vent shaft and connecting tunnel. Both had been extensively damaged by the arroyo. The base of the vent shaft was 50 cm in diameter and terminated 18 cm above the floor in the room. The diameter of the tunnel was greater than 23 cm, but erosion prevented more accurate measurements. The 1 m long tunnel sloped gently downward toward the main room. It was impossible to determine size, shape or location of the tunnel opening in the wall. A large, shaped sandstone slab lay just inside the wall near where the opening should have been. It may have functioned as a vent cover.

There was no evidence of roofing debris in the fill, nor any indication of the surface, as to the method of roof construction. However, it would seem that if a vent shaft was present, there must have been a roof. The small posthole in the floor may represent the remnant of a prop for a sagging roof. A cribbed roof constructed like those described by Morris and Burgh (1954:50) at Talus Village could have been present. There was no sign of exterior postholes to suggest a conical roof. Evidence of cribbed roofs constructed within similar small pithouse depressions has recently been discovered in the vicinity of St. John's, Arizona (James Bradford, Museum of Northern Arizona, personal communication).

Feature 1 was devoid of wood and the firepit was in such poor condition that it was impossible to obtain an archaeomagnetic sample. Consequently a definitive date for this structure is not available. The spatial relationship of the structure to 5LP111 Feature 2 and the cultural material retrieved from it indicate that it was contemporaneous with Feature 2.

Miniature pithouses like this one are roughly analogous to the small pit structures at the Stevenson Site, 5MT1 (Wheat MS). They have also been described in areas to the southwest (Bullard 1962:123; James Bradford, personal communication) in association with Basketmaker III and Pueblo I sites. The interpretation of their function has varied from protokiva to remodeled entry for an adjacent pithouse. The distance of Feature 1 from the other pithouse at this site definitely indicates that it was intended as an independent structure and not as an attachment.

Observations during the backhoe trenching of Feature 2, a subrectangular pithouse, indicated that the fill was virtually homogeneous from the surface down to floor level. This suggests that deposition in the pithouse may have occurred rapidly.

The surface was designated Level 1. Mechanical removal of the upper fill (Level 2) in Feature 2 undoubtedly included some artifacts. Backhoe operations were halted 1.2 m below the surface when a Twin Trees Plain platter (Fig. 47c) and a decorated bowl (Fig. 50d) were uncovered. The area around these vessels was investigated but no occupational surface could be isolated. The vessels are assumed to have been on the roof when it collapsed. An antler burnisher (Fig. 86) and a large sherd were found near the vessels. Over the bench in the southern portion of the house a trough metate was found; this is also thought to have been left on the roof.

The fill between the vessels and floor was arbitrarily called Level 3 for recording purposes and was

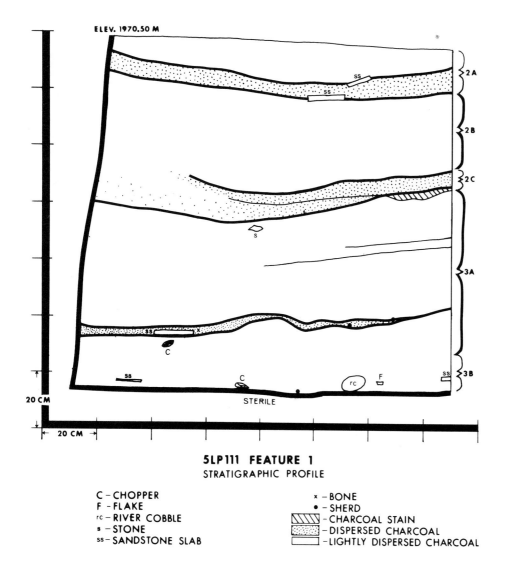

ELEV. 1970.50 M

2A

2B

2C

3A

3B

STERILE

20 CM

20 CM

5LP 111 FEATURE 1
STRATIGRAPHIC PROFILE

C – CHOPPER
F – FLAKE
rc – RIVER COBBLE
s – STONE
ss – SANDSTONE SLAB

x – BONE
• – SHERD
⧄ – CHARCOAL STAIN
▒ – DISPERSED CHARCOAL
▭ – LIGHTLY DISPERSED CHARCOAL

Figure 19.   Stratigraphic profile of 5LP111 Feature 1.

excavated with hand tools. A number of non-utilized flakes were recovered from this level along with a few cores and pounding tools. Since the roofing debris could not be definitely identified, all of these items could have been on the roof.

The pithouse measured 6.1 by 6.5 m at the base of the bench. Orientation of the principal axis was towards the south-southeast (Fig. 18).

The basin-shaped firepit was located on the major axis, southeast of center. It was 70 cm in diameter and 19 cm deep, with bottom and sides unplastered. Lining the firepit was a 2 cm layer of clean brown

sand. On top of this was 7 cm of compacted ash which was covered with another layer of clean brown sand. The top layer was an additional 7 cm of compacted ash. A plaster collar 5 cm high and 14 cm wide had been added around the circumference of the firepit. The firepit produced an archaeomagnetic date of A.D. 720 plus or minus 23 years (Robert L. Dubois, University of Oklahoma, personal communication). This date indicates that 5LP111 was a contemporaneous occupation with 5LP110.

There was no partition wall standing at the time of excavation. The only visible suggestions of a wall were two small sandstone slabs abutting the outside walls on either side of the pithouse. A small posthole 16 cm east of the firepit may indicate that an adobe and pole deflector was once placed directly in front of the firepit.

A rock 87 cm north of the eastern wing wall slab was connected to the east wall of the pithouse by a ridge of plaster. This may be the remnant of the north wall of a bin. However, there is no evidence of other connecting walls.

The four main support posts were all 60 cm to 1 m from the walls. The two on the south side were incorporated into the wing walls and were 23 cm and 25 cm in diameter. The hole for the southeast post was started 30 cm north of where the post was finally placed but was moved because of the rocks beneath the floor. The northwest posthole had also been modified, because of subsurface rocks, into a bell-shaped hole 25 cm in maximum diameter. The northeast posthole had been damaged by rodents; measurements were therefore impossible to make. All of the postholes had a lining of clean brown sand which had been used as packing for the posts. In addition, there were five green schist stones in the bottom of the northwest posthole. The depth of the postholes was between 55 and 62 cm.

The floor was 2.1 m below present ground surface. The presence of several large boulders on the floor dictated the depth of the pithouse. The floor was slightly bowl-shaped, sloping down from the bench face and outer wall towards the firepit with a maximum vertical difference of 15 cm. One coat of puddled adobe plaster 1 to 1.5 cm thick covered the entire floor area as well as several large exposed boulders.

Four small and three large cists were located in the floor. Three of the small cists were in the northern half of the house. One was conical in cross-section, 20 cm in diameter, 19 cm deep, and filled with an ashy brown sand. The second cist was 13 cm in diameter and 4 cm deep. On the bottom was 2 cm of clean gray sand which had been capped with 2 cm of charcoal flecked adobe. The third cist was 7 cm deep with a 16 by 12 cm rectangular opening. It had been filled with adobe. The fourth small cist was located in the east-central area of the floor and was 35 cm in diameter, 10 cm deep, and lined with a 2 cm thick layer of clean brown sand. No cultural material was recovered from these cists.

A large oval cist was located at the base of the boulder extending into the southeast portion of the house. It measured 26 by 48 cm at the top and narrowed toward the bottom. The cist was started next to the boulder but because of a large rock 7 cm below the floor, it was extended underneath the boulder to a final depth of 50 cm. On the bottom was a 5 cm layer of ash covered by a 35 cm level of soft brown soil mixed with charcoal, and other debris and capped with a 10 cm layer of ash. Included in the brown soil layer were five choppers, a hammerstone, a mano and a round concretion. South of the wing wall, in the western portion of the house, was a second large oval cist which had been filled with adobe before the pithouse was abandoned. It was 36 cm wide, 55 cm long at the top, and 18 cm deep. The third large cist at the base of the boulder on the south end of the bench was 28 cm long, 11 cm wide and 8 cm deep and filled with loose dark brown soil. No specific function could be assigned to any of the large cists.

The pithouse had a ¾ bench 1.6 m below the present ground surface. The bench began on the southwest side of the house and extended around to the east side. A large boulder in the southwest portion of the pithouse was incorporated into the bench at this depth. The bench averaged 50 cm high at the front with a gentle rise to the back wall. The slope is thought to be the effect of erosion rather than to have been a construction characteristic. The back wall was only identified intermittently. The bench averaged 62 cm in width where measurements were possible.

Twenty-five wall post sockets were identified around the periphery of the bench. At an average of 45 cm apart, there would have been room for six more posts, bringing the total to 31. The post sockets averaged 11 cm in diameter and 9 cm deep. On the south side on top of the boulder, two holes had been plugged with adobe and probably represent a repair of a broken wall. A round sandstone ball, a flake, and four bone fragments were recovered from a neighboring pole socket. There was another small posthole 30 cm in front of the replacement socket which may represent an attempt to shore up a weak spot in the roof.

At the south end of the bench near the boulder was a wall niche 53 cm wide, 25 cm high, extending into the wall 32 cm. The floor directly in front of the niche sloped up steeply to the wall, placing the niche 5 cm above floor level. One of the two fully articulated dog skeletons (Fig. 20) found in Feature 2 was found in this niche. The dog lay on the right side with its

Figure 20.   Fully articulated dog skeleton FS 139 in wall niche, 5LP111 Feature 2.

head toward the opening and its tail toward the back of the niche. The spine was curved and the feet and legs were pulled together. There was no conclusive evidence to suggest the manner in which the dog died, but the head, atlas, and axis were not in proper alignment with the rest of the vertebral column indicating a possible broken neck. There was no attempt to fill the niche or cover the dog after it had been placed there.

The other dog skeleton (Fig. 21) was 1.5 m east of the wall niche and 50 cm north of the south wall. It was lying on its left side with the head toward the west and spine toward the back wall. The cranium of this dog had a depression fracture, suggesting that it may have been killed by a blow on the head. A small remnant of plaster south of the head was the only suggestion that the dog had been buried.

The vent shaft was located 70 cm southeast of the pithouse. It was 1.3 m in diameter and extended down to the floor level in the main room. The connecting shaft was 40 cm in diameter and opened at floor level. It is possible that the final size of the vent shaft was determined by the boulders encountered during construction.

Interpretations

Even though Feature 1 at 5LP111 was unique in size, some of the artifacts and artifact relationships suggest that it was a habitation, perhaps with some special functions. However, the house could not have been a comfortable habitation for more than two people and probably housed only one (Kluckhohn and Leighton 1962:100-104; Basso 1969:12; Shepardson and Hammond 1970:15; Dobyns and Euler 1970:13; Cook 1972:15). If one follows Bullard's (1962:124) estimates, Feature 1 could have housed three individuals but the 1.5 square meter estimate per individual is based on structures housing at least six people.

The ground stone assemblage included four manos. Other large stone artifacts consisted of 12 choppers and four hammerstones. Many of these were in a cache in the ventilator but five, along with a maul, were dispersed on the floor. In contrast to this, the only chipped stone artifacts retrieved from the floor were two cores and a utilized flake; there was no debitage on the floor. There may have been some reduction of cryptocrystalline material for small tool manufacturing, but the greatest number of heavy percussion implements in this structure were quartzite cobbles that did not display wear; these must represent a cache.

Six specimens constitute the ceramic assemblage: one Lino Gray platter (Vessel 37, Fig. 47c), one Lino Black-on-gray bowl (Vessel 33c), two Twin Trees Black-on-white bowls (Vessel 33a and Vessel 38, Fig. 50d), and two Lino Gray jars (Vessel 40, Fig. 44a; and fragmentary vessel 33b, Fig. 45f). The modified bone assemblage was limited to bead fragments and one antler rubbing tool (Fig. 86). The faunal assemblage retrieved from the structure includes canids, cervids, leproids, sciurids and unidentifiable birds. The presence of these last three classes indicates that culinary activities occurred here.

Feature 2 at 5LP111 (Fig. 22) was roughly equivalent in size and in architecture to the pithouse at 5LP110. However, the artifact assemblages at the two pithouses differed considerably. The assemblage at Feature 2, 5LP111 suggests that this structure was functionally different from Feature 1, 5LP110, and may have occasionally been used as a kiva.

As an initial point of contrast, only one metate and five manos were on the floor at Feature 2, 5LP111. In addition, 12 choppers and five hammerstones were concentrated in the southeast corner. The function of this abundance of choppers has not been determined. Although ethnographic evidence suggests use of choppers in butchering large animals (Bonnichsen 1973), the bone assemblage from this area does not necessarily support this hypothesized activity. Both structures at this site were devoid of perishables, including hides or leather.

Chipped stone artifacts were more abundant on the floor of this pithouse than on the floors of the other pithouses. The floor inventory is comprised of two knives, four biface blades, ten scraping tools (including utilized flakes), six cores, and 34 pieces of debitage. Two of the pieces of debitage were refitted to one of the cores. The dispersal of the chipped stone reflects the distribution pattern at 5LP110 Feature 1 in that much of the debitage and the tools are concentrated on or near the bench. The lack of projectile points in this assemblage is noteworthy.

The ceramics represent another point of contrast between this structure and 5LP110 Feature 1. Only four specimens were located on the floor here: a Lino Gray miniature bowl (Vessel 30, Fig. 45c), a Lino Gray jar (Vessel 34, Fig. 47b), a Lino Gray seed jar (Vessel 36), and one unclassifiable jar (Vessel 41). None are charred or otherwise appear to have been used in cooking. The comparatively small number of sherds (83) recovered from the floor of this structure suggests that there never was extensive use of ceramic vessels during its occupation.

A third point of contrast is in modified bone artifacts. A total of 20 specimens were recovered from the floor of the structure, including awls, drills, punches, a matting tool, a reamer, antler burnishing tools, canid beads and a bear tooth pendant. Ten of the bone tools commonly called awls were clustered in the northwest quadrant of the structure and were in association with two biface blades and a scraper. This cluster of artifacts is assumed to have been a kit (see Modification Attributes of Bone Tools, Chapter III). However, the lack of perishable material in association with the bone artifacts precludes the definition of a functional area. The tools could have simply been a cache that was dispersed at the time of collapse and abandonment of the structure. The presence of the kit plus additional bone tools located in upper levels does strongly suggest that utilization of such tools for working leather or other pliable materials was common in this structure.

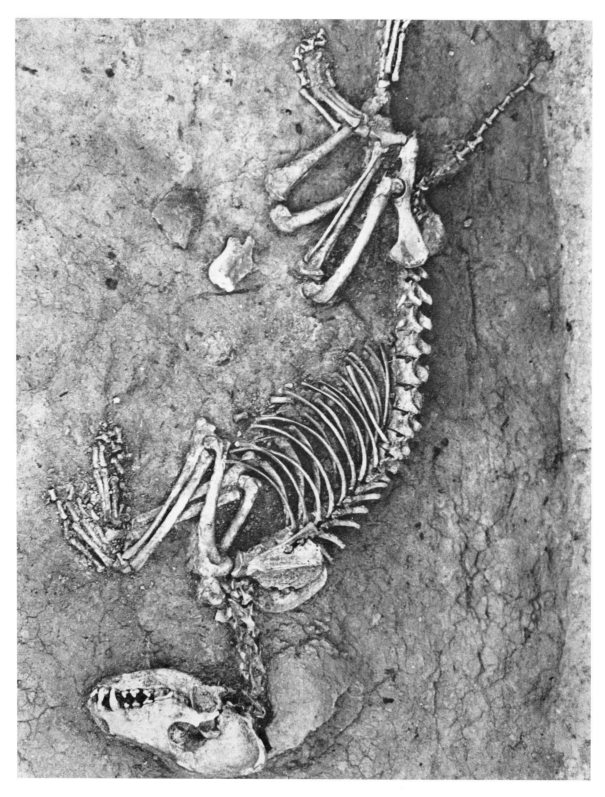

Figure 21. Fully articulated dog skeleton FS 91 on floor, 5LP111 Feature 2.

Figure 22. 5LP111 Feature 2, excavated pithouse. Wall niche with articulated dog skeleton FS 139 is located in upper left corner.

The faunal assemblage includes avids, canids, cervids, leporids, sciurids, geomyids and cricetids plus numerous unidentifiable mammals. At this structure, most of the bone was fragmentary and only 2% was burned. This would suggest that very little cooking or at least very little burning occurred at any stage in the processing. The salient faunal remains at Feature 2 are the two articulated dog skeletons which appear to have been killed and perhaps interred in the structure. Gillespie (1975:93) points to the ceremonial disposal of animals as a distinguishing characteristic of kivas.

To summarize, in line with the definition of kivas put forth by Gillespie (1975:93), the artifactual evidence supporting occasional use of this structure as a kiva includes the following characteristics: abundance of chipped stone, abundance of bone tools, fragmentary and unburned condition of faunal remains, presence of articulated canid skeletons, reduced number of ceramics and lack of culinary vessels, and reduced amount of ground stone. Architectural features supporting this function consist of an orientation closer to north-south than to east-west; lack of or removal of the partition wall; absence of the numerous postholes in the floor, present at 5LP110, that are characteristic of habitations (Bullard 1962:173); and more circular shape of the structure. A critical architectural feature that is missing is, of course, the sipapu.

Sipapus are not a distinguishing characteristic of Basketmaker III structures in the Durango District. None were observed by Morris as discussed by Carlson (1963) nor were any present at either 5LP110 or 5LP111. Hibbets (1976:50) describes a sipapu at 5LP115. However, this description is based on excavation of only half the structure, and the sipapu in question was filled with brown sand which was typical of the packing for almost all postholes at 5LP110 and 5LP111. On the basis of the evidence, it is uncertain whether or not a sipapu was present at 5LP115.

In contrast, sipapus were common at La Plata Phase pithouses in the Mesa Verde area. Sipapus were found at MV1824-71 (Nordby and Breternitz 1972:10), pithouses A and B at the Twin Trees Site (Lancaster and Watson 1954:11), pithouse G at site 1644 (Hayes and Lancaster 1975:9), MV1937 structures 2 and 3, MV1938, and MV1940 (Birkedal 1976:36, 78, 113, 132). On the other hand, there were structures in that area that lacked sipapus: MV 1944 pithouse A, MV1676 pithouse G and protokiva C (Hayes and Lancaster 1975:6-23), and MV1990

(Hallisey 1972:5). Sipapus were also located in the early village, Unit Village 1 and Unit Village II at 5MT1 (Wheat MS).

The sipapu is not a necessary requirement for a structure to be defined as a protokiva or to be assigned kiva functions. Cases in point are protokivas 3, 4, 5 and 7 in the La Plata District (Morris 1939:59-81).

The autonomy of nuclear family units in a "settled band" level of social organization is well defended by Birkedal (1976:460-470). This autonomy probably accounts for the architectural diversity of Basketmaker III structures, which can be viewed as individualistic expressions of common needs in a loosely structured band-level society. It is commonly assumed that the religious activities during Basketmaker III times took place in habitations (Roberts 1929:81-90). The logical extension of this argument (Smith 1952:154-165) is that all Basketmaker III pit structures are habitations unless they have radically different architectural features as in the great kiva at Shabik'eshchee Village (Roberts 1929:73-81), or Protokiva House immediately outside the village (Roberts 1929:62-68), or the great kiva circle at Broken Flute Cave (Morris 1959: 112-116). This interpretation is supported in the San Juan Region by the different architectural classes of structures at Unit Village I and Unit Village II at 5MT1 (Wheat MS), where the central pithouse (protokiva) is substantially larger than other structures with clear evidence of habitation features. However, in most Basketmaker III sites such architectural distinctions are not clear and it seems useful to attempt other modes of definition. In an analysis of pithouse-kiva transitions, Gillespie (1976:88-98) applies the term "activity loci" which focuses attention away from non-diagnostic architectural variability common to Basketmaker III pithouses and toward the artifact assemblages. It is obvious that the true kiva is a rare phenomenon in Basketmaker III sites in the San Juan Region. But if kiva functions can be attributed to structures on the basis of artifact assemblages, then there is a very good possibility that Feature 2 at 5LP111 possessed those functions. The principal weakness in this mode of interpretation is that artifact assemblages only reflect the last functional activities in a structure prior to its destruction. If a structure is cleaned or reorganized prior to replacement of domicilary equipment all or most of the evidence of ceremonial activities may be wiped away, and the discovery of such "activity loci" is fortuitous. Therefore this structure can best be described as a domestic-ceremonial house.

There is little doubt that both structures at 5LP111 were involuntarily abandoned. The volume of clean fill that covered the cultural deposits, as well as the surprisingly large number of artifacts on the floor of Feature 2, makes a strong case for a flood as the cause for abandonment. Flood damage to the architecture and to the artifact assemblage would probably be much the same as fire damage, with the addition of deterioration of the plaster and increased probability of the rotting of perishables. Structural timber would sustain considerably less damage in a flood, making reclamation of the timbers a very likely possibility. If not moved over a long period of time, the timbers would be more prone to rot. In either case the possibility of dating the structure through dendrochronology is eliminated.

The principal difference between the effects of flood and fire on pithouses is that floods mask the ground surface. The features at 5LP111 were difficult to locate, not because of the lack of artifacts, but because of the lack of typical pithouse fill (charcoal, burned adobe, fire cracked rock, etc.) and the lack of the characteristic pithouse depression. Initial tests at the site supported the assumption that the surface artifacts were in sheet wash from a neighboring site 20m uphill on the alluvial fan. This original assumption was disproven only through extensive subsurface testing with a backhoe, too time-consuming to attempt by hand. The discovery of the structures at 5LP111 strongly implies the presence of at least twice as many pit structures in the area of Bodo Ranch as have been recorded.

Burials at 5LP111

The human remains were clustered in three localities southeast of Feature 2, 5LP111. At least three and possibly four individuals are represented by these remains. The practice of burying the dead in extremely shallow graves probably accounts for both the fragmentary condition of the bone and the lack of mortuary furniture. The remains are analyzed in detail in Human Skeletal Remains, Chapter V.

III. Material Culture

Chipped Stone Tools

by
Barbara Love-dePeyer

Relatively few (169) chipped stone tools and only 428 flakes of non-utilized debitage were recovered at 5LP110 and 5LP111 (see Table 2 and Figures 23 and 24 for stratigraphy and distribution). The tools were classified in general terms according to their probable uses (such as projectile points, knives, scrapers, etc.) although there is evidence to suggest that several of the tools were used for a variety of purposes.

The limited sample of projectile points found at the sites was quite distinct from the larger bifacially flaked specimens classed as knives. This classification does not, however, deny the fact that some projectile points also show wear patterns indicating use as cutting or perforating tools. Knives were separated from scrapers using Kidder's (1932:14) definition of a knife as "a tool whose cutting edges have been produced by chipping from both sides; a scraper one whose edges are chipped from one side only." Drills were classified on the basis of their relatively thick cross-sections as well as bit shape and wear patterns. Flake tools with intentional edge retouch, such as biface blades or unifacial scraper facets, were distinguished from utilized flakes whose naturally sharp cutting edges had been used without prior retouch.

Due to the paucity of specimens in each artifact category (Table 2) distinct typologies were difficult to establish. However, tools in each classification with shared morphological or utilization features were grouped together and then compared with similar specimens in other published reports.

The inhabitants of Durango South used a variety of chalcedonies, cherts, quartzites, petrified woods, obsidians and other silica-rich materials for their lithic tools. As Morris and Burgh (1954:54) indicate, "quartzites and chalcedonies occur abundantly in the Durango vicinity as cobblestones in glacial moraines and stream beds." Particularly high percentages of these two materials, 47% and 30% respectively, dominate the lithic assemblage from the sites, although quartzite and chalcedony occur most frequently as large utilized flakes, cores, and debitage. Other lithic materials, including petrified wood and obsidian, comprise smaller portions of the total lithic collection, but make up 80% of the smaller more finely flaked tools such as projectile points, drills, and knives. These tools appear to have been manufactured elsewhere and transported to the area in their finished form or as preforms.

The following section defines and discusses in detail the different types of chipped stone tools found at 5LP110 and 5LP111.

Projectile Points (N=12)

Type 1: (5 specimens, Fig. 25 a-e) Small triangular points with deep corner notches and asymmetrical bases.

Blade outline: Straight and sharply pointed. Secondary retouch on opposing lateral edges near the tip gives the blade a slight bevel.

Stem: Expanding asymmetrically.

Base: Straight to slightly convex, with asymmetrical corners. Narrower than the blade.

Flaking: Unpatterned, bifacial thinning of an interior flake. Figure 25a exhibits some serrations along the lateral edges. All specimens have bifacial secondary retouch along the blade edges.

Use/Wear: Two specimens, Figure 25a with worn serrations, and Figure 25d with step fractures along the blade edges, may have been used secondarily as cutting tools. Figure 25c has wear polish on the tip and unifacial attrition on the beveled blade edges near the tip, as though used in a rotary, piercing motion.

Comment: Morris and Burgh (1954:56) indicate points of this description came in with the bow and arrow.

Comparison: Hall 1944:47, Fig. 31; Hayes and Lancaster 1975: Fig. 179a; Hibbets 1975:21; Kidder 1932:18, Fig 3aa; Morris and Burgh 1954:56, Fig. 106i; O'Bryan 1950: Plate 27 row a.

Type 2: (2 specimens, Fig. 25 f-g) Small triangular points with shallow corner to basal notches, small bases, and triangular cross-sections.

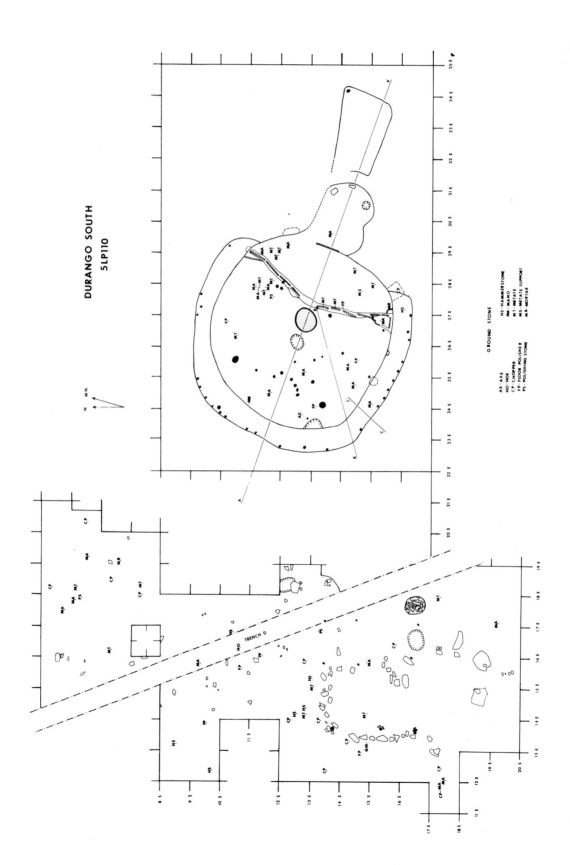

Figure 23. Chipped stone artifact distribution, 5LP110 Features 1 and 2, floor.

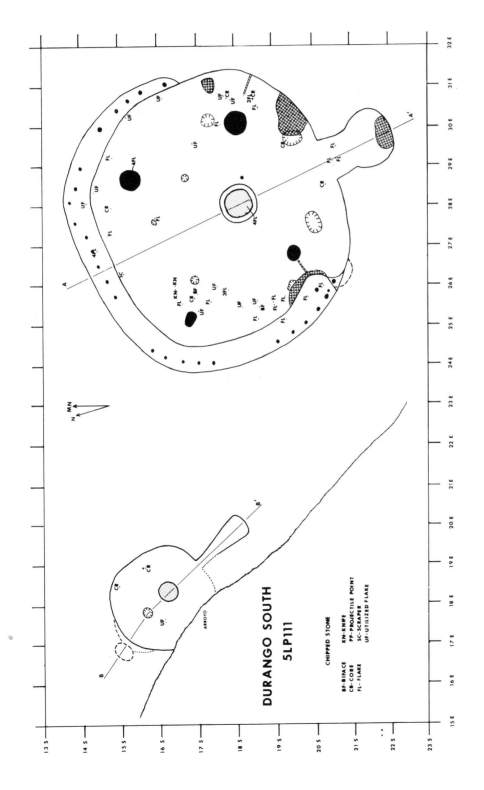

Figure 24. Chipped stone artifact distribution, 5LP111 Features 1 and 2, floor.

49

Table 2. Chipped Stone Tool Summary

Tool Type/Site	Site	F1 L1	F1 L2	F1 L3	F1 L4	F2 L1	F2 L2	F2 L3	F2 L4	Chalcedony	Chert	Obsidian	Petrified Wood	Quartzite	Jasper	Basalt	Rhyolite	Siltstone	Granite	Schist	Sandstone	Quartz	Copper Carbonate	L Max	L Min	W Max	W Min	Th Max	Th Min	Totals	Figure
Projectile Points Type 1	5LP110	2			1					1			1		1									20	17	12	8	2	2	3	
Type 1	5LP111		1	1								1			1									21	15	14	10	3	2	2	Fig. 25a-e
Type 2	5LP110				2					2														18	13	11	9	3	2	2	Fig. 25f-g
Type 3	5LP111						1								1									12		9		2		1	Fig. 25h
Type 4	5LP110	1											1											18		10		2		1	Fig. 25i
Type 5	5LP110	1														1								25		14		4		1	Fig. 25j
Type 6	5LP110							1						1										27		18		3		1	Fig. 25k
Type 7	5LP110	1												1										frag		19		3		1	Fig. 25l
Drills Type 1	5LP111							1				1												15		8		2		1	Fig. 25m
Type 2	5LP110							1					1											24		13		3		1	Fig. 25n
Type 3	5LP110							1					1											frag		11		4		1	Fig. 25o
Type 4	5LP110				1								1											27		12		4		1	Fig. 25p
Type 5	5LP111							1					1											50		18		13		1	Fig. 25q
Knives Type 1	5LP110				1								1											64		34		9		1	Fig. 25y
Type 1	5LP111						1							1										72		34		7		1	Fig. 25x
Type 2	5LP111						1						1											69		23		4		1	Fig. 25z
Type 3	5LP111							1					1											65		16		6		1	Fig. 25aa
Type 4	5LP111							1					1											29		11		5		1	Fig. 25bb
Type 5	5LP110							1												1				40		23		6		1	Fig. 25v
Type 5	5LP111							1					1											30		32		6		1	Fig. 25w
Biface Blades Type 1	5LP111							1	1	1	1													17	13	18	14	4	4	2	Fig. 25r-s
Type 2	5LP110				1			4		1	1	2	1											50	20	46	22	16	6	5	
Type 2	5LP111					1	3	1					5											48	42	45	22	11	4	5	Fig. 25t-u
Type 3	5LP110		1					2				2		1										34	14	51	17	21	4	3	
Type 3	5LP111		1				1		2			1	1	2										40	14	44	12	13	1	4	Fig. 25cc-gg
Scraping Tools Type 1	5LP110	1		2		1		2				2	1	3										69	39	58	32	23	8	6	
Type 1	5LP111						1					1												58		35		12		1	Fig. 26a-d
Type 2	5LP110	1	1					3		1		1		3										70	34	43	23	28	6	5	Fig. 26e-g
Type 3	5LP110	1	3	1		1	6	1				2		10				1						68	26	62	29	22	8	13	
Type 3	5LP111		1		1	1		2						5										66	28	74	29	14	8	5	
Type 4	5LP110	1	4	5	1	1	21	1		2		20	2	5	4			1						67	17	63	13	21	2	34	
Type 4	5LP111	1	1	3			3	7		2	2	2	1	4	5	1								70	17	50	14	29	3	15	
Cores Type 1	5LP110	2	2	1	1		8			8				5				1						126	29	88	25	67	15	14	
Type 1	5LP111	3		1	1	2	3	4		4		2		6				1	1					137	29	87	32	75	12	14	
Type 2	5LP110		1	1			4			1	1			2	1			1						64	20	63	20	38	18	6	
Type 2	5LP111		1			1	1	1						4										73	48	62	26	27	15	4	
Type 3	5LP110	1	2				2							4							1			82	40	101	47	59	25	5	
Type 3	5LP111							1						1										89		64		62		1	Fig. 26i-j
Type 4	5LP110	1		1						1				1										58	50	59	51	34	22	2	
Type 4	5LP111				1									1										89		78		66		1	Fig. 26h
Non-Utilized Flakes	5LP110	1	24	36	8			147	2	3	67		9	120	1	3		9	3		3									218	
	5LP111	18	31	25			39	63	34	13	38	4	41	104	1			4		5										210	
Concretions	5LP110		4	5				12																						21	
	5LP111						2	1																						3	Fig. 27a-d
Stone bead	5LP111		1																				1	13		12		3		1	Fig. 27e
Stone ball	5LP111			1																		1		7		7		7		1	
Copper Carbonate	5LP110							1															1	21		16		12		1	
Totals	5LP110	11	39	56	18	2	1	216	4	10	104	4	23	155	4	4	1	13	3	1	3	0	1							347	
	5LP111	22	36	32	3	0	47	81	56	15	47	9	59	126	4	0	0	6	1	5	0	1	1							277	

Blade outline: Straight and sharply tapering. Minimal secondary retouch on opposing lateral edges.

Stem: Parallel sided.

Base: Straight to slightly convex. Much narrower than blade.

Flaking: Minimal unifacial thinning with secondary edge retouch creating the notches and blade outline.

Use/Wear: Little or no wear was visible on either specimen. The size, crudeness of manufacture, and lack of wear suggest that these points were probably not attached to projectiles.

Comment: The face that both points were found within ceramic vessels on the floor of the pithouse at 5LP110 may suggest their function was more symbolic than practical.

Comparison: O'Bryan 1950: Plate xxvii-a. No reference was found as to the use of projectile points in any but a purely functional manner and O'Bryan's illustration resembles these points only in outline.

Type 3: (1 specimen, Fig. 25h) Small triangular point with shallow lateral indentations.

Blade outline: Recurvate, tapering to a sharp tip.

Stem: Slightly expanding.

Base: Convex.

Flaking: Irregular bifacial thinning with steep retouch on opposing lateral edges, giving the blade a slight bevel. The tool is oriented at an oblique angle to the original flake, and the original striking platform remains on one side of the base.

Use/Wear: Shearing and step fractures along the blade edges.

Comment: The blade appears to have been reworked and sharpened near the tip, suggesting possible use as a drill. This

point was found on the surface and may not be directly related to the pithouse at 5LP111.

Comparison: No similar specimens were found in other publications.

Type 4: (1 specimen, Fig. 25i) Small triangular point with rounded shoulders and a short wide stem. Blade edges are serrated.

Blade outline: Straight, serrated blade tapering to a sharp tip. The serrations are formed by minimal bifacial edge retouch.

Stem: Parallel sided.

Base: Convex.

Flaking: Minimal thinning on dorsal surface. The point was manufactured at an oblique angle to the longitudinal axis of the original flake. The shape is derived from light bifacial retouch around the periphery.

Use/Wear: Worn serrations and lateral step fractures indicate the point may have been used for cutting or sawing.

Comment: This point is made from an unusually homogeneous and translucent type of obsidian. The only other example of this material was a drill recovered from 5LP111 (Fig. 25m).

Comparison: Hayes and Lancaster (1975:Fig. 179t) describe a larger, thicker, dart point which resembles this specimen in basal configuration and serrated blade. No closer comparisons were found in the literature.

Type 5: (1 specimen, Fig. 25j) Triangular point with long parallel sided stem and angular shoulders.

Blade outline: Short, slightly concave blade terminating in a blunt tip.

Stem: Long, nearly half the length of the point, parallel sided.

Base: Convex.

Flaking: Regular bifacial thinning. Blade edges appear to have been reworked.

Use/Wear: Occasional step fractures along the blade edges.

Comment: No other tools of this material were found at either site. This point, like point Type 3, was found on the surface and may not be directly associated with the two sites.

Comparison: Carlson (1963:39, Plate 19m-o) mentions points made from similar material but with shorter stems and sharper tips, which "could have been tips for either arrows or darts." The point also resembles a dart point illustrated by Hayes and Lancaster (1975:154, Fig. 179u) and another found in Woodbury (1954:Fig. 27h).

Type 6: (1 specimen, Fig. 25k) Moderate sized, broad side-notched point with straight base and serrated blade.

Blade outline: Slightly convex and serrated.

Stem: Expanding.

Base: Straight. Slightly narrower than blade.

Flaking: Long, oblique basal thinning of ventral surface, irregular thinning on dorsal surface. Ventral side of blade is the original flake surface. Serrations are unifacial on one blade edge, bifacial on other. Tip has been retouched to a sharp point.

Use/Wear: Slightly worn serrations on one blade edge.

Comment: This was the only point found at Feature 2, 5LP110. It is also the only point made of quartzite.

Comparison: Woodbury (1954:Fig. 26s) illustrates a similar but unserrated point.

Type 7: (1 specimen, Fig. 25 l) Midsection fragment of a large corner-notched transverse-flaked point with serrated blade edges.

Blade outline: Straight, almost parallel sided, serrated blade.

Stem: Broken in a hinge fracture.

Base: Unknown.

Flaking: Regular transverse bifacial thinning with edges serrated by small bifacial retouch flakes.

Use/Wear: Worn serrations on both edge facets. Haft and tip are both broken by hinge fractures.

Comment: This is the largest and most carefully flaked point recovered from either site.

Comparison: Shows some similarities to a point illustrated by Kidder (1932:23, Fig. 8b or c).

Drills (N=5)

Five perforating or incising tools were recovered. They have been divided into types on the basis of the differences in their haft elements and general morphology. It is interesting to note that of the five tools, one was made from a small obsidian flake while the other four were all made from differing qualities of petrified wood (ranging from fine grained and translucent to coarse and opaque).

Type 1: (1 specimen, Fig. 25m) Small triangular point with shallow side notches, straight base, and concave blade edges.

Blade outline: Concave with blunt tip and relatively thick triangular cross-section.

Stem: Expanding, narrower than blade.

Base: Straight.

Flaking: Bifacial edge retouch which shapes and notches the tool by a series of steep pressure flakes. The tool is oriented laterally with respect to the original interior flake.

Use/Wear: The blade and tip are worn by

step fractures and shearing with some polish. The notches and base have step fractures and crushed edges.

Comment: This tool could have served as a projectile point; however, the wear patterns, the short thick blade, and the blunt tip indicate its main use as a perforator.

Comparison: Woodbury (1954:141) suggests drills were probably used on wood, horn, shell, bone, and small stone ornaments. Perforated bone, antler, and stone artifacts which could have been pierced with such a tool were recovered at Durango South. Woodbury also discusses drills found at other sites which were hafted in wooden shafts or handles.

Type 2: (1 specimen, Fig. 25n) Triangular drill with expanding haft element merging with a tapering, sharply pointed blade.

Blade outline: Straight, rapidly tapering. Longitudinal cross-section is concavo-convex.

Haft element: Sub-rectangular, with straight base and one straight and one convex lateral edge. Wider than blade.

Flaking: Regular bifacial thinning with steep unifacial retouch on dorsal lateral blade edges.

Use/Wear: Slight unifacial shearing on tip and lateral blade edges. Not heavily used.

Comparison: Hayes and Lancaster 1975:146, Fig. 181b; Kidder 1932:29, Fig. 11g; Woodbury 1954:141.

Type 3: (1 fragmentary specimen, Fig. 25o) Parallel sided drill with shallow lateral indentations setting off a stem and rounded base.

Blade outline: Blade is mostly missing. Proximal portions suggest it was straight and gradually tapered.

Haft element: Shallow, asymmetrical lateral indentations form small shoulders

at their juncture with the blade and terminate proximally in a convex base, slightly narrower than the blade.

Flaking: Steep bifacial retouch along the edges of blade and haft. Original surface of the flake is visible in the central portions of both dorsal and ventral surfaces.

Use/Wear: Edge crushing and step fractures on lateral edges of haft element. Blade is broken off in a hinge fracture.

Comparison: Hayes and Lancaster 1975:146, Fig. 181c.

Type 4: (1 specimen, Fig. 25p) Pinnate drill with short, blunt tip and ovoid haft element.

Blade outline: Straight, parallel sided. Convexo-triangular cross-section; concavo-convex longitudinal-section.

Haft element: Convex lateral edges flair slightly out from the blade and merge in a convex base.

Flaking: Minimal bifacial edge retouch. Flakes are steeper on the dorsal surface of the blade edges.

Use/Wear: Base and lateral edges of haft are ground and striated and the ventral surface has areas of high polish from contact with haft socket. The blade tip is crushed and appears to have been heavily used.

Comparison: No similar specimens were found in other publications.

Type 5: (1 specimen, Fig. 25q) Thick, pinnate blade with square base and shallow lateral indentations.

Blade outline: Convex outline, blunt tip, triangular cross-section.

Haft element: Parallel lateral edges with shallow indentations near juncture with blade. Straight base, narrower than blade.

Flaking: Irregular bifacial edge retouch, with irregular thinning on tip and haft element. The dorsal ridge has been bifacially retouched, so the blade tapering to the tip is triangular in cross-section.

Use/Wear: The lateral edges and dorsal ridge show shearing, step fractures and polish due to utilization. The tip has been fractured, but the flake facets leading to the fracture show shearing and polish on the ridges between the flake scars. The proximal end and square base have been crushed through contact with a haft socket.

Comment: The wear patterns and polish on the distal end of the tool suggest use in incising or perforating a relatively soft material, such as wood or fiber (Kidder 1932:24).

Comparison: Kidder 1932:24, Subtype a: "Large, heavy drills," Fig. 10s.

Knives (N=7)

Type 1: (2 specimens, Fig. 25x-y) Broad, sub-rectangular blade with asymmetrical shoulders and tapered haft element.

Blade outline: Parallel sided with broad, convex distal end.

Haft: Narrower than blade, one straight and one convex lateral edge tapering to a convex base. Approximately one-third the length of the tool.

Flaking: Unpatterned large bifacial thinning flakes, with secondary edge retouch shaping the blade, shoulders, and haft.

Use/Wear: The tool from 5LP110 (Fig. 25x) has been heavily utilized, with extensive step fractures and shearing on the distal end and along one blade edge. While the haft elements on both specimens are of comparable length, the blade on this tool is 12mm shorter, and appears to have been reduced by heavy use in chopping and cutting.

The specimen from 5LP111 (Fig. 25y) had little or no use and was found with another blade (Type 2, Fig. 25t) and several bone

awls. It is possible that these tools were part of a tool kit.

Comment: Figure 25x illustrates the original shape of this distinctive type of knife, while Figure 25y exemplifies the effects of chopping and cutting on the tool.

Comparison: No similar specimens were found in other publications.

Type 2: (1 specimen, Fig. 25z) Thin, pinnate blade with long, gradually tapering haft element.

Blade outline: Biconvex.

Haft: Slightly narrower and thicker than the blade, the edges of the haft are straight and taper gradually to a convex base. There are no abrupt shoulders between the blade and haft element. The haft comprises approximately one-half the total length of the tool.

Flaking: Broad, regular thinning flakes on the blade, with a transition to narrower, less regular flakes on the haft element. The blade edges show irregular bifacial retouch while the edges of the haft have unifacial retouch on opposing sides, giving the haft a slight bevel.

Use/Wear: Slight bilateral, bifacial attrition on blade edges. The tip is broken in a hinge fracture.

Comment: This tool was found in association with Figure 25x and several bone tools (Fig. 75) and may have been part of a tool kit. The fine, regular flaking and thin cross-section of the knife place it among the better examples of lithic craftsmanship recovered at 5LP110 and 5LP111.

Comparison: No directly comparative specimens were found in other publications, however this tool could be classed among what some authors (Carlson 1963:76, Plate 20d; Kidder 1932:17, Fig. 2) call "large projectile points and knives."

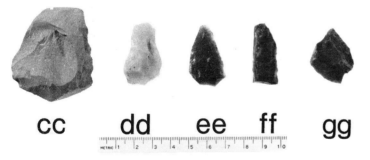

Figure 25. Projectile Points - Type 1: a-e; Type 2: f-g, Type 3: h; Type 4: i; Type 5: j; Type 6: k; Type 7:l. Drills - Types 1-5: m, n, o, p, q. Biface Blades - Type 1: r-s; Type 2: t-u; Type 3: cc-gg. Knives - Type 1: x-y; Type 2: z; Type 3: aa; Type 4: bb; Type 5: v-w.

Type 3: (1 specimen, Fig. 25aa) Narrow, parallel sided blade with long, rectangular haft element and asymmetrical shoulders.

Blade outline: Straight with blade edges terminating in a blunt, reworked tip.

Haft: Slightly narrower than the blade, with parallel edges and a squared base. The haft meets the blade in asymmetrical, slightly angular shoulders. The haft comprises approximately one-half the total length of the tool.

Flaking: Unifacial thinning flakes are combined with large bifacial retouch flakes to give the tool its shape. The central portions of both surfaces have cortex remaining. The lateral edges of the haft have been ground. The lack of thinning flakes gives the tool a fairly thick, convexo-trapezoidal cross-section.

Use/Wear: The blade edges have some bifacial attrition flakes, but the majority of the wear appears on opposing, unifacial surfaces, as though the tool were used in a rotary motion. The tip has been reworked into a small protruding facet which exhibits two small longitudinal flakes on one surface, possibly the result of use as a graver.

Comment: The tool appears to have been a hafted, multi-purpose tool whose blade was used for cutting, piercing, and possibly incising.

Comparison: The rectangular base resembles illustrations of drills in Kidder 1932:26, Fig. 10; or gouges in Carlson 1963:78, Plate 22i.

Type 4: (1 specimen, Fig. 25bb) This specimen fits Kidder's (1932:18) description of knives with tapering stems: "This is a rare but uniform type. The specimens are slender and relatively thick, with rounded shoulders and gradually tapering stems that are nearly as long as the blades. Among the examples in the collection there are few if any that can be considered arrowheads; the majority were probably hafted for use as small knives, though there is a possibility that they were in reality double-purpose implements, the blades serving as knives, and the tapering stems (which are more or less round in cross-section) as drills."

Blade outline: Straight to convex.

Haft: Tapering, with round cross-section.

Flaking: Bifacial thinning with steep bifacial edge retouch on entire periphery.

Use/Wear: Bifacial step fractures, attrition, and edge crushing along one blade facet. Unifacial step fractures and attrition on opposite lateral edge. The tip shows unifacial attrition and may have been used as a graver. With the exception of some edge crushing on inter-flake protrusions the haft element does not exhibit signs of wear. On this specimen, it would seem that the blade was used as a double-purpose implement, but not the stem.

Comparison: Kidder 1932:18-19, Fig. 3s-v.

Type 5: (2 fragments, Fig. 25v-w) Pinnate or triangular biface blades.

Blade outline: Convex or straight.

Haft: No distinct haft element. Convex to straight base.

Flaking: Irregular bifacial thinning, with occasional edge retouch.

Use/Wear: Blade and base edges show bifacial attrition. The blade on both fragments is broken diagonally in a hinge fracture. The blade edges on one specimen show some polish in addition to the attrition.

Comment: It is possible that these specimens may have resembled Brew's (1946:Fig. 170) example "h": a hafted knife with an asymmetrical pinnate blade. The base fragment (Fig. 25w) has one rounded corner which leads into a convex blade edge, while the other corner is more angular and continues in a straight lateral blade edge. The complete tool appears to have had a small lateral shoulder beyond the straight edge which possibly served in bracing or hafting the tool and would suggest one possible reason for the diagonal hinge fracture occurring where it does. The differing attrition patterns on the blade edges lend further evidence: the small, regular attrition flakes on the straight edge facet could be the result of a haft or brace, while the irregular step fractures and attrition flakes on the convex edge may be attributed to the cutting motion of the blade.

The tip fragment (Fig. 25x) could be the remains of any pinnate bifacial blade, but the polish on the longer blade facet suggests that the two edges were used differentially.

Comparison: Brew 1946:Fig. 170 g, h, i; O'Bryan 1950:Plate 27d.

Bifacial Blades (N=19)

Type 1:   (2 specimens, Fig. 25r-s) Serrated bifacial blades.

Blade outline: Straight.

Flaking: Bifacial thinning. The serrations tend to be formed by the unifacial removal of one or more pressure flakes. The specimen shown in Fig. 25s had flakes removed from the dorsal surface, while Fig. 25r was flaked alternately from both surfaces. This latter tool had two opposing serrations which were slightly broader than the others and may have served as notches for a haft element. Such a possibility is substantiated by step fractures and edge crushing on the concave edge of the flake scars.

Use/Wear: Worn serrations and attrition.

Comments: These specimens appear to have served as small cutting or sawing tools. Fig. 25r may have been the midsection of a serrated projectile point similar to those illustrated in Woodbury (1954) and Kidder (1932).

Comparison: Brew 1946:Fig. 171; Kidder 1932:23, Fig. 8a-e; Woodbury 1954:Fig. 26k-l.

Type 2:   (10 specimens, Fig. 25t-u) Flakes with one or more bifacially retouched edge facets.

Blade outline: Straight to convex.

Haft: None.

Flaking: Bifacial edge retouch on one or more facets. The rest of the flake is unmodified.

Use/Wear: Attrition and step fractures, both unifacial and bifacial.

Comments: The flakes appear to have been selected for thin, straight naturally sharp edges, which were perhaps utilized and subsequently retouched to maintain the edge. The retouch on most specimens is quite shallow and the wear is minimal. The five specimens from 5LP111 are thinner and more finely flaked than those from 5LP110.

Comparison: Woodbury 1954:136; Carlson 1963:39, Plate 21e.

Type 3:   (7 specimens, Fig. 25cc-gg) Bifacially utilized flakes.

Blade outline: Straight - 2; convex - 5.

Use/Wear: Attrition - 7; step fracture - 1.

Comparison: Kidder 1932:40; Woodbury 1954:137.

Scrapers (N=79)

No systematically shaped scraping tools were recovered at either site. However, a small number of flakes had either distal (Type 1) or lateral (Type 2) edge facets which had been unifacially retouched to enhance a scraping edge. Other scraping functions appear to have been performed with the aid of unmodified flakes which exhibit principal unifacial wear on the distal (Type 3) or lateral (Type 4) edges.

Type 1: (7 specimens, Fig. 26a-d) Flakes with retouched distal end scraping facets.

Blade outline: Convex - 4; irregular - 3. The irregular blades had small projections which may have been used as gravers.

Flaking: Steep unifacial retouch on the distal end of the flake. All specimens were flaked on the dorsal surface.

Use/Wear: Light to moderate attrition, and step fractures on the distal edge with light attrition on some lateral edges. Some had wear on the ventral as well as the dorsal surface.

Comparison: Kidder 1932:35; Woodbury 1954:136.

Type 2: (5 specimens, Fig. 26e-g) Flakes with retouched lateral edge scraping facets.

Blade outline: Straight - 1; convex - 4.

Flaking: Steep unifacial retouch on one (3 specimens) or two (2 specimens) lateral edges. Four tools were dorsally retouched, one was flaked on the ventral surface.

Use/Wear: Light to moderate attrition, step fractures, and some polish. Most of the wear was localized on the retouched edge but two of the flakes showed some attrition on non-retouched facets.

Comment: These tools were made from flakes with naturally straight sharp edges, which were subsequently retouched to sharpen or rework the facet. Three of the flakes are sub-rectangular, with one or both of the long edges showing utilization. The other two are ovate, with one of the longer curves having been used as a cutting edge.

Comparison: Carlson 1963:39; Hayes and Lancaster 1975:147; Kidder 1932:39; Woodbury 1954:136.

Type 3: (18 specimens) Flakes utilized on the distal end.

Blade outline: Convex - 5; slightly convex to straight - 12; concave - 1.

Use/Wear: Attrition - 13; edge grinding - 4; step fractures - 1. Only two of the flakes had signs of having been heavily used, one as a chopper or plane, the other as an end scraper. Three other flakes had moderate use which had dulled the utilized facet. The other 14 had only minimal use as evidenced by slight attrition or polish on one facet.

Comparison: Kidder 1932:40; Woodbury 1954:137.

Type 4: (49 specimens) Flakes utilized on the lateral edge facets.

Blade outline: Convex - 15; straight - 14; concave - 17; irregular - 7.

Use/Wear: Attrition - 43; edge grinding - 5; step fractures - 8; polish - 1. Twenty-seven of the flakes had been used on only one edge facet while 22 were worn on two or more edges. None of the flakes had been extensively utilized but eight showed signs of moderate wear on one edge and 41 were only slightly used.

Comment: Although utilized flakes were much more numerous than any other type of artifact, they were not present in the large numbers Kidder observed, nor was

Figure 26.   Scrapers - Type 1: a-d; Type 2: e-g. Cores - Type 3: i-j;Type 4: h.

every debitage flake "large enough to be held in the hand" utilized. Only 11% of the non-retouched flakes could be classified as utilized.

Comparison: Kidder 1932:40; Woodbury 1954:137.

Cores (N=47)

Cores were defined as lithic chunks or cobbles faceted by the removal of one or more flakes. Flakes were removed from one or more surfaces on the majority (54%) of the cores, which were then discarded with no secondary use. These were classified as Type 1, non-utilized cores. Type 2, utilized cores, were used as cutting or scraping tools subsequent to the removal of primary flakes (29%). These cores were distinguished by small attrition scars along one or more edges. Type 3 includes cores which were used as chopping tools and have edges which exhibit crushing and step fractures. Eight per cent of the cores showed wear of this type. Type 4, 8%, were cores which had been used as hammerstones and had at least one edge or surface which showed concentrated battering.

Type 1: (28 specimens) Non-utilized cores (no secondary wear).

Type of core: Unifacial - 1; multifacial - 6; residual - 11; split cobble - 10.

Material: Chert - 12 (43%); petrified wood - 2 (7%); quartzite - 11 (39%); siltstone - 2 (7%); granite - 1 (4%).

Type 2: (10 specimens) Utilized cores (with attrition).

Type of core: Multifacial - 2; residual - 3; split cobble - 5.

Material: Chalcedony - 1 (10%); chert - 1 (10%); quartzite - 6 (60%); jasper - 1 (10%); siltstone - 1 (10%).

Type 3: (6 specimens, Fig. 26i-j) Core choppers (with crushing and step fractures).

Type of core: Multifacial - 1; split cobble - 5.

Material: Quartzite - 5 (83%); schist - 1 (17%).

Type 4: (3 specimens, Fig. 26h) Core hammerstones (with battering).

Type of core: Multifacial - 1; split cobble - 2.

Material: Chalcedony - 1 (33%); quartzite - 1 (33%); siltstone - 1 (33%).

Non-utilized flakes (N=428)

		5LP110	5LP111
Total number of flakes:		218	210
Type of flake:	Primary cortex	16%	9%
	Secondary cortex	49%	41%
	Interior flake	35%	50%
Type of platform:	Faceted	3%	2%
	Battered	9%	6%
	Ground	2%	6%
	Struck	55%	56%
	Cortex	18%	10%
	Absent	13%	20%

Material distribution of flakes as compared with tools is summarized in Table 3.

Comment: All lithic material, debitage as well as tools, was collected, with slightly larger quantities being found at 5LP110. Some variations in distribution of types of flakes, materials, striking platforms, and tool manufacture may be noted.

5LP110 appears to have had slightly more core reduction activity as evidenced by the number of cores (27 compared with 20 at 5LP111), the precentage of debitage with primary cortex (16% compared with 9%), and secondary cortex (49% compared with 41%). Only 14% of the flakes at both sites showed any type of platform preparation other than the creation of a flat, struck surface.

5LP110 had more tools and debitage made from chert, while 5LP111 had more than twice as much petrified wood and obsidian. A slightly wider range of material types was recorded at 5LP110, both in the tools and flakes.

Concretions (N=24, Fig. 27a-d)

Among the stone artifacts recovered were 24 claystone and limonitic sandstone concretions which ranged in shape from spherical to sub-cylindrical, in size from 14mm to 110mm, and in color from grayish tan to red. The concretions were found in both the upper and lower fill levels and appeared to have been formed by natural geologic processes. Such concretions are often found in sandstone or shale formations, many of which are exposed in the Animas valley around Durango (Kilgore 1955). No concretions were observed in the alluvial soils outside the pithouses and it appears that they may have been concentrated in the archaeological features by human activity. Only one had any indications of intentional modification (Fig. 27c), a limonitic sandstone hemisphere which appeared to have been ground on the flat surfaces and the interior concavity lined with a clay-like residue.

Comparison: Woodbury (1954:188-189) mentions that nodules are found at sites in the Jeddito district from Basketmaker III times to the 17th century, but they are only found in significant circumstances in Pueblo IV and Pueblo V times.

O'Bryan 1950:86, Plate XXXIVk; Morris and Burgh 1954:60; Kilgore 1955:118.

Miscellaneous stone artifacts

Stone Bead: (1 specimen, Fig. 27e)
One discoidal white quartz bead was recovered from the upper fill of Feature 1,5LP111. The circumference had been ground to shape the bead; the perforation, slightly off center, was accomplished by drilling from both surfaces, resulting in a biconical hole 3 mm in diameter.

Stone Ball: (1 specimen)

One small round ball was recovered from the lower fill of Feature 1, 5LP111. The ball was shaped by grinding, from a fine grained sandstone which contained enough azurite particles to give the artifact a blue color.

Pigment (?) Nodule: (1 specimen)

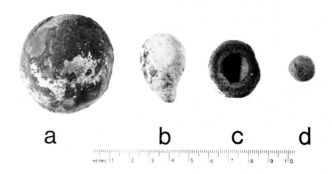

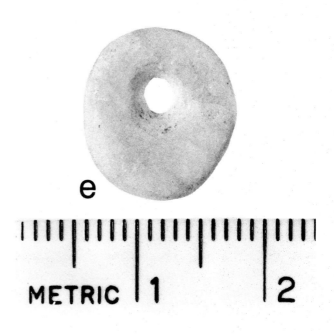

Figure 27. Concretions: a-d. Stone bead: e.

Table 3. Material Distribution: Flakes and Tools

Material	Flakes		Tools	
	5LP110	5LP111	5LP110	5LP111
Total number (100%)	218	210	107	61
Chalcedony	2%	6%	6%	3%
Chert	30%	18%	35%	15%
Petrified Wood	4%	20%	12%	30%
Quartzite	55%	49%	33%	34%
Jasper	1%	1%	3%	3%
Obsidian	--	2%	4%	8%
Basalt	2%	--	1%	--
Siltstone	4%	2%	4%	3%
Granite	2%	--	--	1%
Schist	--	2%	1%	--
Sandstone	2%	--	--	--
Rhyolite	--	--	1%	--

Ground Stone Tools
by
O D Hand

The ground stone tool assemblage at Durango South has been classified according to form and probable function. The tools can be divided into four classes: those used for grinding, those used for polishing, those used in construction, and those used for a variety of pounding, sharpening and digging purposes.

It is assumed that the first group, the grinding tools, were used principally in food preparation (metates, manos, mortars), in preparation of pigments (pigment grinders) and possibly for other grinding activities such as preparation of clay in the early stages of pottery making, although no direct evidence of other grinding activities was retrieved. With the exception of pigment grinders, both of which were recovered from the floor of the small pit structure at 5LP111, grinding tools were concentrated at 5LP110. This includes 93% of the metates (plus blanks), 60% of the manos, and 100% of the mortars.

The second group, the polishing tools, is comprised of floor polishers and polishing stones. This group was more evenly distributed between the two sites, with 61% at 5LP110 and 39% at 5LP111.

The third group, stone slabs, were used either as cist covers or in wall construction. There were six at 5LP110 and three at 5LP111.

The fourth group consists of axes, hoes, a grooved maul, choppers, hammerstones and a pecking stone. Tools in this group were often multifunctional. One axe and one hoe were retrieved from each site; the number of hammerstones is nearly equal in the two sites, with nine at 5LP110 and ten at 5LP111; 5LP111 yielded the grooved maul (Feature 1) and the pecking stone (Feature 2). The major difference in distribution within this tool group is in choppers, with 68% recovered at 5LP111.

Figures 28 and 29 illustrate ground stone artifact distribution at both sites.

Materials for the manufacture of ground stone implements were plentiful in the immediate vicinity of Durango South. Sandstone, quartzite and granite were most often used and represent respectively 42%, 37% and 14% of the total ground stone assemblage. Seventy-eight per cent of the grinding tools were made of sandstone, a common lithic material in the area. Polishing tools were predominantly quartzite (62%), as were choppers and hammerstones (65%). These last two types of tools were usually fashioned from river cobbles, abundant in the Animas River and in nearby stream beds.

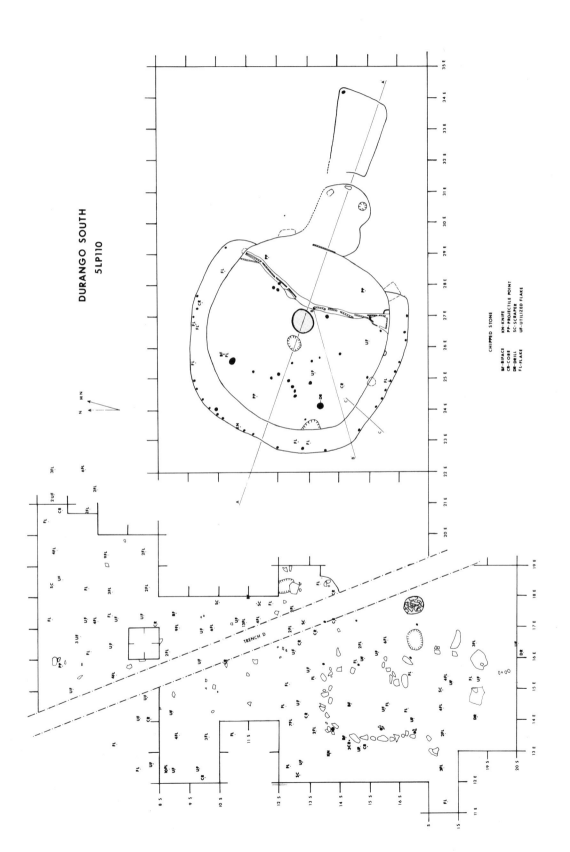

DURANGO SOUTH
5LP110

CHIPPED STONE

BF-BIFACE   KN-KNIFE
CR-CORE   PF-PROJECTILE POINT
DR-DRILL   SC-SCRAPER
FL-FLAKE   UF-UTILIZED FLAKE

Figure 28. Ground stone artifact distribution, 5LP110 Features 1 and 2, floor.

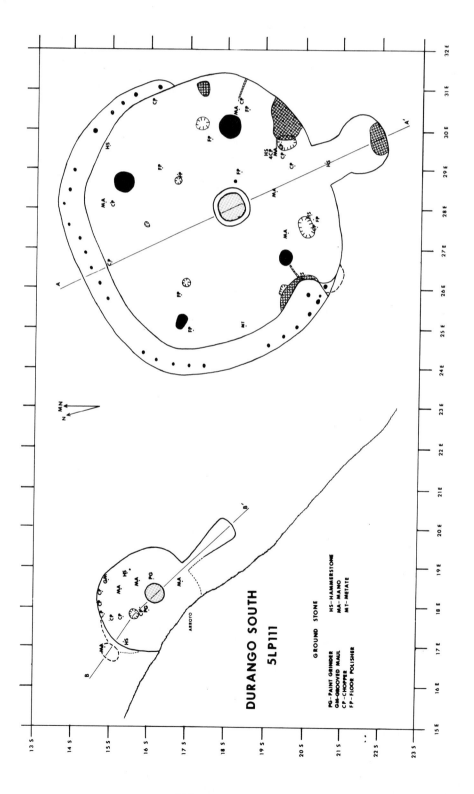

DURANGO SOUTH
5LP111

GROUND STONE

PG–PAINT GRINDER   HS–HAMMERSTONE
GM–GROOVED MAUL   MA–MANO
CP–CHOPPER   MT–METATE
FP–FLOOR POLISHER

Figure 29. Ground stone artifact distribution, 5LP111 Features 1 and 2, floor.

Table 4. Ground Stone Tool Summary

Tool Type/Site	Dist F1 L1	F1 L2	F1 L3	F1 L4	F2 L1	F2 L2	F2 L3	F2 L4	Totals	Sandstone	Quartzite	Siltstone	Granite	Schist	Chert	Basalt	Subrectangular	Rectangular	Natural Shape	Tabular	Pinnate	Palmate	Cobble	Round	Ovate	Fragmentary	Length Max/Min	Width Max/Min	Thickness Max/Min	M: Ground	Pecked	Flaked	Attrition	W: Striated	Ground	Polished	Pitted	Battered	Flaked	E: Ground	Pecked	Battered	Polished	Grooved
Trough Metates 5LP110	1	1	1	9			1	1	18	17			1				6			4	1				2	5	634/536	519/432	223/97	19	11	11		1	18		9			4				
5LP111								1	1	1							1	1									348	316	62	1	1	1			1		1							
Slab Metates 5LP110	3		2	1			1	1	8	5	1		2					1	1	1				1			613/488	468/407	87/62	8	4	5			6		4			2				
5LP111				1				1	1	1							1	1		1				1			284	236	47	1	1	1			1	1	1	1		1				
Metate Blanks 5LP110			1	1					2	2							1	1			1						601/543	445/305	41	1	1	1			1					1				
Convex-surfaced Manos 5LP110			1	8			1		9	8			1				3	1							3	2	213/169	142/79	63/35	9	4				10		1			3				1
5LP111				2				1	4	2	1		1				1	1		2						1	213/206	131/93	42/17	3	1	1			4	1	1	1		2				
Flat-surfaced Manos 5LP110	1		2	4	2		7	2	19	18			1				5			6					4	4	240/108	157/94	74/23	17	9	8			19		5	5		5				
5LP111	1		2	2			1	4	8	4			3	1				2		4					1	1	224/128	146/109	69/27	7	3				8	1		3		3				
Biscuit-shaped Manos 5LP110									1	1							1							1	1		107	83	53		1				1	1								
5LP111		1				1			1	1															1		80	73	63	1					1		1							
Mortars 5LP110		1		2				1	3	2			1				1			1			1		1		235/224	183/172	113/70	1	2				1		1			1		1		
Pigment Grinders 5LP111	2		2						2	2										1			1				174/92	146/80	56/29	1						1	1							
Floor Polishers 5LP110	2		2	4	1		2	1	13	4	6		3				1				2	2	2		3		346/91	283/217	116/40	2	5	1		2	4	6		5		2		2		
5LP111					1		8		9		6		3									2	6	2			386/100	84/88	116/54	1	1				1	9		1	2	1		1		
Polishing Stones 5LP110				1	1			1	3		3									1	1				2		34/30	32/20	19/22						2									
5LP111	1								1		1															1	53	39								1			1				
Stone Slabs 5LP110	1			5					6	6										5					1		635/167	520/124	35/24		1	1			1		1		5					
5LP111			1	1					3	2	1										1		1	1			564/250	388/221	99/18		1	1				1		1	2			1	1	
Axes 5LP110	1			1					1						1				1				1				117	84	25			1								1				
5LP111									1	1								1					1	1			108	87	30			1			1			1	1			1		
Hoes 5LP110				1					1	1											1						192	129	35				1		1				1	1				
5LP111						1			1		1			1			1										142	56	26				1		1			1	1			1		
Grooved Maul 5LP110				1				1	1		1								1						1		114	97	68		1	1				1		1						1
Choppers 5LP110	2	2	1	1	1		11	1	13	3	8		1		1						2		8		2	1	220/38	138/42	57/21	3	1	10	6		2	2	1	11	13	7				
5LP111		1		6		2	1	12	28	1	19		2	1	3	2	1	1	2		4	2	16		2	1	247/42	236/34	79/23	1	1	6	10	1	2	1	1	21	19	25				
Hammerstones 5LP110	1	1	1	1			6		9	1	5		2		1				1			1	5	3	2		163/132	94/90	82/37	1	1	4			1		3	9	3	8	1			
5LP111		1	1	2			1	5	10	1	7		1		1				1				4	3	3		—	53/50	79/33	1	1							10		10				
Pecking Stone 5LP111									1			1							1					3			42	39	24				1				1							2
Totals	5	13	11	54	6	7	40	42	178	80	63	1	23	3	6	2	19	8	3	25	12	5	45	9	31	21				77	48	53	19	2	86	22	28	66	49	28	2	55	1	2

Each ground stone tool type at Durango South is described below, and references to similar tools in other reports are included. Materials, morphology, measurements and wear characteristics are summarized in Table 4.

Trough Metates

Nineteen trough metates were recovered during the excavations. All the trough metates exhibit rectangular grinding surfaces, enclosed on three sides and open at one end (Fig. 30). Maximum and minimum measurements of the grinding surfaces are:

	Length	Width	Depth
maximum (in mm)	581	260	99
minimum (in mm)	364	204	8

The surfaces are marked by longitudinal striations, indicating a reciprocal grinding motion. Eleven specimens also retain evidence of pecking on the grinding surface, a method of maintaining the abrasiveness of the surface. The asymmetry in the concave trough shape indicates that the grinding process was more severe near the center of the metate. Here the trough is usually deepest and eventually wears through. One specimen (Fig. 30a) used in the construction of the partition wall of the pithouse at 5LP110 was worn through in this area.

The closed end of the grinding surface forms a small shelf, ranging from 20mm to 220 mm in width. Of the specimens collected at 5LP110 and 5LP111, only three have shelves less than 50mm wide. Most of the wider shelved specimens exhibit a lightly ground or polished area on this surface (Fig. 30b), suggesting possible utilization as a mano rest (Birkedal 1976 : 267-269).

The majority of the trough metates were made from naturally flat stone slabs; however, not all of the slabs were flat-bottomed (Fig. 30c) and Bartlett (1933) mentions that often smaller stones were placed beneath metates to lend support and to adjust the angle of the grinding stroke.

Two unusual metates came from the floor of the pithouse at 5LP110. Figure 30d shows two separate wear patterns. Originally the metate was used quite heavily, with a trough depth of 35mm. The second wear pattern started a new trough extending from the former open end and proceeding back through the shelf of the original grinding surface. The lower end of the original grinding surface then served as the second trough's shelf. The original shelf is no longer detectable.

Figure 31a is a relatively unused metate, with a trough depth of 8 mm. The original gray sandstone slab from which it was formed was fire scorched, resulting in a bright orange surface. The gray grinding surface of the trough is thus bordered in orange.

Comparison: Bartlett 1933:11; Birkedal 1976:267-269; Hayes and Lancaster 1975: 150-151; Woodbury 1954: 51-52.

Slab Metates

Nine metates with unifacial, irregular grinding surfaces were recovered. All the specimens were made from slabs whose natural shape conformed to the desired function with limited amounts of flaking or shaping. The grinding surface on each slab is irregular in outline and flat to slightly concave in cross-section. The striated wear patterns, generally parallel, are occasionally diagonal to the longitudinal axis of the slab. Heavy pecking on the grinding surfaces of some slabs probably served to maintain the abrasiveness of the surface. A majority of the slabs appear to have been used for only a limited time. On only one specimen (Fig. 31b) was the grinding surface used intensively. The surface was rectangular in shape, and may be an indication of a primary stage of trough manufacture.

"Grinding slabs" occur frequently in Basketmaker III sites. Also during late periods of Pueblo development, this type of metate is preferred over the trough style and is utilized within specialized grinding bins (Birkedal 1976).

Comparison: Birkedal 1976:274-276; Carlson 1963:41; Hayes and Lancaster 1975:151-152; Woodbury 1954:54.

Metate Blanks

Two sub-rectangular stone slabs were retrieved which had no utilized grinding surfaces but had unifacial pecking similar to that used to resharpen metates. One specimen had been shaped by bifacial percussion flaking and edge pecking; the other was an unmodified water-worn slab. Both had light, irregular pecking on one surface which resembles the pecked scars of a metate rather than the scars of an anvil. Since the areas in which these scars are

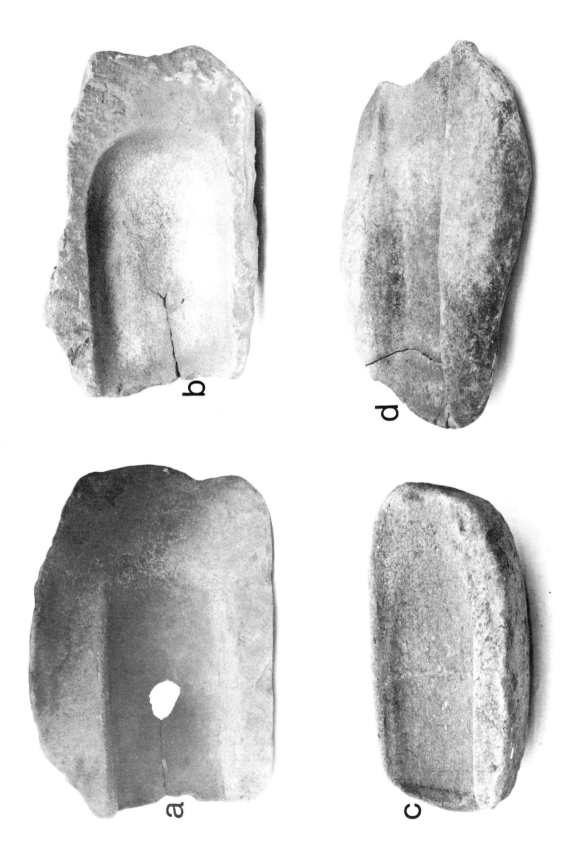

Figure 30. a - Trough metate with hole worn through the grinding surface; b - Trough metate illustrating ground or polished mano rest on the closed end of the grinding surface; c - Trough metate with irregular base, indicating the need for smaller stones to support or stabilize the stone during the grinding process; d - Trough metate in which the shelf of the initial trough has been worn away by a secondary trough.

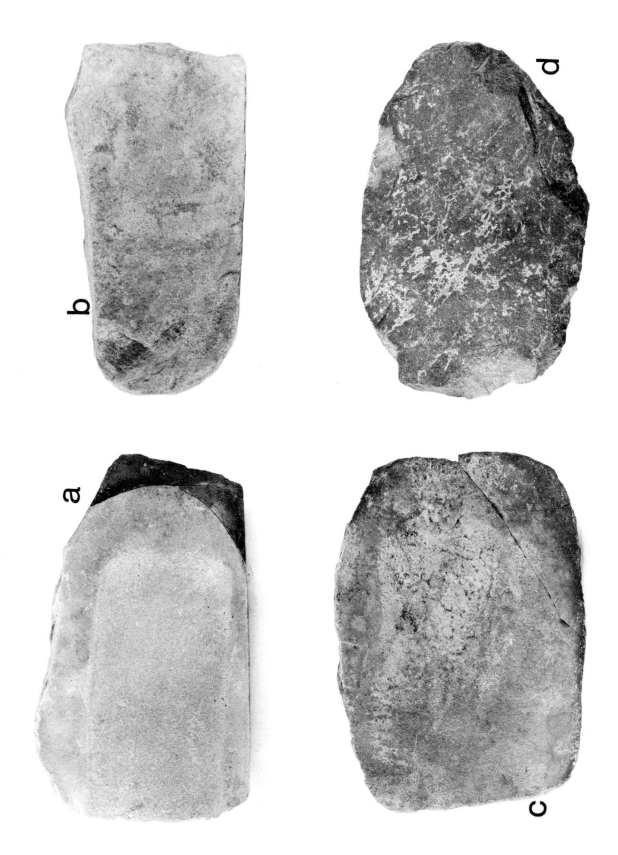

Figure 31. a - Trough metate with burned orange border around a light gray grinding surface; b - Slab metate; c - Shaped metate blank; d - Shaped stone slab.

located are flat and there was no need to level an uneven surface, it is unlikely that the pecked areas could have served any other function than that of sharpening the slab for grinding. The shaped specimen (Fig. 31c) conforms to Birkedal's definition of a "shaped slab" (1976:292-293). It is possible that it was utilized as a cover for a hatch or cist.

Comparison: Birkedal 1976:292-293.

Stone Slabs

Nine stone slabs were retrieved. Seven of these had bifacial percussion flaking around the edges, shaping the slabs into round or ovate forms (e.g. Fig. 31d). The remaining slabs are unmodified tabular river cobbles. Only one of the slabs was lightly ground on one surface; the others had no indications of use other than their having been peripherally shaped. This deliberate shaping and lack of wear suggests that the slabs were used in wall construction or as hatch or cist covers. All the specimens are too large to have served as vessel covers.

Utilization of stone slabs in the San Juan area is common throughout all periods of Anasazi occupation.

Comparison: Birkedal 1976:292-293; Hayes and Lancaster 1975:158-159.

Convex-surfaced Manos

Thirteen ovate to rectangular manos with distinctive convex grinding surfaces were recovered (Fig. 32a, b). The manos were roughly shaped by pecking, grinding, and occasional flaking along the edges. The grinding surface is markedly convex and terminates in polished upturned ends, formed by abrasion against the unsharpened sloping walls of a trough metate. Grinding striations are perpendicular to the longitudinal axis of the mano. The uniform orientation of the striations indicates a reciprocal grinding motion. Eight of the manos appear to have been used with consistent pressure applied to one side, resulting in a wedge-shaped cross-section (Fig. 32c). This suggests that manos were not reversed during use to balance the wear, but had pressure exerted on the lower or thinner side (Birkedal 1976:270-273). Six specimens were bifacially ground, and in each case the secondary surface was only lightly utilized.

Three specimens had a distinctive notch or indentation in the center of the proximal edge (Fig. 32d). The notches, which average 60mm in length and 7 mm in depth, were manufactured by flaking and pecking. Facets such as these are more likely to occur on manos used in trough metates (Hayes and Lancaster 1975:154). Their purpose is to provide a better grip on the mano for more control during the grinding process. The wedge-shaped cross-section of this type of mano limits the period of utilization of the indentation. One specimen was worn down to the notch. A second notch was then manufactured on the opposing edge, the mano was reversed, and grinding was resumed.

Only one mano (Fig. 32e) showed signs of secondary use as a large, two handed chopper or crusher. One end of this tool exhibited extensive battering scars.

Convex-surfaced manos are common during the Basketmaker III period.

Comparison: Birkedal 1976:270-273; Carlson 1963; Hayes and Lancaster 1975:152-154; Woodbury 1954:67-68.

Flat-surfaced Manos

Twenty-seven ovate to tabular manos with flat to slightly convex grinding surfaces were recovered (Fig. 33a). Seven stones were unmodified and the others were shaped by unifacial percussion flaking and pecking. The worked surface was generally evenly ground, with only three instances of uneven pressure resulting in a wedge-shaped cross-section. Most specimens exhibit only one grinding surface, but six specimens were lightly used on a second surface. Light striations perpendicular to the longitudinal axis indicate use in a reciprocal grinding motion. Occasional pecking scars suggest the tools were sometimes resharpened.

Within this classification, the size, shape, and material vary considerably (Table 4), with the unifying attribute being at least one flat ground surface. It is difficult to determine whether these manos were used solely with slab metates. Small specimens could have been used within a wide, flat trough with no different indication of wear.

Five specimens have at least one edge that appears to have been utilized in some type of chopping or crushing process. Four of these are the largest in this mano type and the fifth is a small wedge-shaped

Figure 32. Convex-surfaced manos; a - Longitudinal section; b - Plan view; c - Wedge-shaped cross-section; d - Notched manos; e - Mano used as a chopper or crusher.

Figure 33. a - Flat surfaced manos; b - Flat surfaced mano used as a chopper; c - Biscuit shaped manos.

tool (Fig. 33b). All specimens exhibit a bifacially percussion flaked edge dulled by subsequent battering. The wear on these manos is similar to that on the large, two-handed chopper/crushers found at both sites.

Comparison: Birkedal 1976:273-274; Carlson 1963; Hayes and Lancaster 1975:153-154; Woodbury 1954:68-69.

Biscuit-shaped Manos

Two ovate cobbles were used as manos (Fig. 33c). The stones were pecked around the edges and had two opposing grinding surfaces. The primary surface exhibits moderate to heavy wear while the second surface is only lightly used. Grinding striations are perpendicular to the longitudinal axis of the mano, indicating use in a reciprocal, rocking motion. This grinding motion produces a convex, elongated surface which extends onto the edges of the mano.

This type of mano resembles those utilized with basin metates by the Desert Culture and Basketmaker II peoples. However, the wear on the Durango South specimens is due to a reciprocal motion rather than to the rotary motion used in a basin metate (Hayes and Lancaster 1975:154). The wear is not as pronounced as that found on other manos associated with trough or slab metates. No pecked scars mar the grinding surfaces; pecking on these specimens is limited to modifying the edges of already well rounded cobbles.

Comparison: Hayes and Lancaster 1975:154; Woodbury 1954:78-79.

Mortars

Three mortars were recovered at 5LP110: one complete, one fragment, and one unmodified cobble. The complete specimen (Fig. 34a) is ovate with an ovate depression measuring 125mm by 97mm by 64mm. The edges are rounded by use and have flaked notches on opposing sides. This depression was probably manufactured by pecking and was enlarged in size and depth through utilization and subsequent resharpenings (Birkedal 1976). The interior surface still exhibits extensive pecking scars which obscure any wear patterns that might have been left by pounding and grinding.

The outer surface of the complete specimen has been blunted or flattened on both ends and on the base by flaking, pecking, and grinding. These modifications were probably essential for stabilization during the grinding process. The ground base helped to keep the mortar level, while the blunted ends could have been braced against the sides of the user's legs for support. No traces remain of the substance prepared in the mortar.

The fragment resembles the complete specimen described above. The depression is fractured, but the edges are rounded and the base is ground.

The third mortar (Fig. 34b) was an unmodified, irregularly shaped alluvial cobble. The cobble was evidently selected for the natural, angular indentation on the upper surface. The bottom of the indentation was smoothed through battering or grinding but the period of utilization was not long enough to alter the natural contours of the cobble. There are no pecking scars or other indications of modification or wear.

Comparison: Birkedal 1976:279.

Pigment Grinders

Two pigment grinders (Fig. 35) were recovered. One is ovate and the other tabular; neither appears to have been modified. The ovate specimen has an irregularly shaped grinding surface marked by the removal of a large flake. The lightly worn tabular grinder has a convex grinding surface with a small depression in one corner. The depression, probably a natural feature of the rock, measures 20mm in diameter and is 5mm deep. The sloping sides are smoothed from wear, but the bottom retains the irregular natural surface of the stone. The shape and size of the depression suggest that some type of pestle was used with the grinder, although the period of utilization was not long enough to alter the shape or to cause noticeable striations.

This depression and the grinding surface on the ovate specimen both contained remnants of a red pigment. The convex ground surface on the tabular specimen retained no pigment and may have been used in some other type of grinding or polishing process.

Grinding tools such as these are present in all stages of Pueblo development where mineral pigments are used.

Comparison: Birkedal 1976:276-278; Hayes and Lancaster 1975:160.

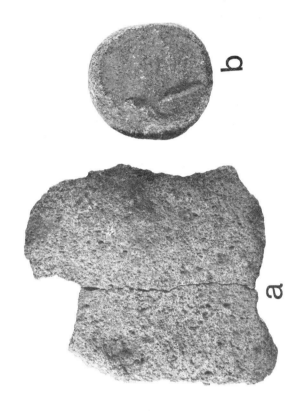

Figure 35.   Pigment grinders.

Floor Polishers

Twenty-two large unifacially polished alluvial cobbles were recovered (Fig. 36). The degree of polish on the utilized surface ranges from a slight sheen to an alteration in the shape of the stone. Only two of the specimens were altered by percussion flaking. In addition, five specimens have small pecking scars clustered in shallow, natural depressions in the center of the polished surface. The scars are much too small to be associated with a resharpening process, and they are recessed from the main polished surface. The wear seems similar to that found on anvils.

Similar stones are found in Basketmaker III as well as Pueblo III sites. Since they are too bulky to have served as pot polishers and too fine in texture to serve as abrading tools, these stones are often labeled floor polishers (Kidder 1932:64). The term "bluestone" also refers to such stones, especially to specimens exhibiting pecked areas similar to those found on anvils (Ives, personal communication).

Figure 34.   a - Shaped mortar, note flattened ends; b - Cobble mortar.

Comparison: Birkedal 1976:280-281; Hayes and Lancaster 1975:157; Kidder 1932:64.

Polishing Stones

Four small unmodified alluvial pebbles exhibit one or more highly polished flat to convex surfaces, suggesting use in smoothing pottery (Fig. 37). No striations are evident on the polished facets, and only the outline and velvety texture indicate utilization of certain surfaces. The polishing on the facets did little to alter the shape of the pebbles.

In modern Pueblos, pebbles such as these serve to smooth the surface of pottery before firing. Kidder (1932:63-64) noted that each potter at San Ildefonso owned from seven to sixteen stones. Older stones, often heirlooms, were preferred over newer ones.

Comparison: Birkedal 1976:290-291; Hayes and Lancaster 1975:157; Kidder 1932:63-64; Woodbury 1954:96-97.

Axes

Two axes with chipped, notched haft elements were found (Fig. 38). The axe from 5LP110 (Fig. 38a) is more extensively formed through bifacial percussion flaking. It is double-bitted with a convex blade outline and was hafted by means of two opposing, bilateral notches approximately 55mm wide. The second axe (Fig. 38b), from 5LP111, is only partially shaped with bifacial percussion flaking along its perimeter. The rest of the surface has been ground, which may indicate secondary use as a mano. This tool has a single blade, the original edge of which was fractured and slightly utilized after breakage. While the haft elements on both tools are similar, the notches on the second are only 20 mm wide. The notches and blade edges of both specimens bear evidence of use in step fractures and crushing.

Axes were probably multi-purpose tools serving for both cutting and digging. Early styles were nothing more than notched river cobbles with ground blades. Kidder (1932:53) mentions that after axes at Pecos were too dull to be used for chopping or digging, they were often put to use as hafted hammers.

Comparison: Carlson 1963; Hayes and Lancaster 1975: 148-149; Kidder 1932:45-54, 57-58.

Hoes

Two hoes were recovered (Fig. 39). One pinnate hoe (Fig. 39a) was roughly shaped by bifacial percussion flaking and has a convex blade or bit. The haft element consists of two opposing lateral notches 35mm to 40mm in length and 11mm deep. Both notches are marked with edge crushing along their interior surfaces. The base constricts sharply to a width of 55mm approximately 30mm from the end of the tool. While not indicated by wear, this constriction is also believed to be part of the haft element. The handle to which the tool was attached may have extended either perpendicularly from the dorsal side or vertically from the base, as a projectile point would be hafted. Flake scars on the ventral side of the blade have no striations but are rounded by a soft abrasion such as would be produced by digging or hoeing. The flake scars on the dorsal surface are shaped or worn as a result of unifacial percussion flaking or resharpening. The hoe appears to have been used after its last resharpening because there are step fractures along the blade edge.

The second hoe is rectangular, with flaked and ground lateral edges and ground ends (Fig. 39b).

It is often difficult to distinguish between hoes and axes; however, the difference between the two may be observed in the wear patterns. Polished and dulled flake scars, such as those found on these hoes, are due to the abrasive action of hoeing and contrast with the battered step fractures found on axes.

Comparison: Carlson 1963:Plate 23a; Kidder 1932:58.

Three-quarter Grooved Maul

One ovate maul was retrieved (Fig. 40). The maul was fashioned by peripheral pecking on an ovate river cobble. A grooved haft element extends around three-quarters of the circumference of the cobble and averages 20mm in width. The groove is lightly polished as a result of the haft. The two opposing ends of the maul exhibit battering scars from use. One end of the maul has been flattened from heavy use, with a battered area 35mm by 40 mm, while the opposing end is battered but the shape of the stone remains unaltered.

Figure 36.   Floor polishers.

Figure 37.   Polishing stones.

Three-quarter grooved mauls are more common in earlier Pueblo occupations (Hayes and Lancaster 1975:149). Kidder (1932:55) suggests that similar mauls at Pecos were utilized "for driving stakes into the ground or for pounding on wedges to split wood." He states that they seldom show signs of battering caused by striking other stones. However, this maul does exhibit battering and appears to have been used on a surface harder than wood.

Comparison: Birkedal 1976:281-282; Hayes and Lancaster 1975: 148-149; Kidder 1932:45-55.

Choppers

Forty-one choppers were recovered during excavation(Fig. 41).These tools, larger than the core choppers discussed in Chipped Stone Tools, this chapter, were generally formed from split cobbles, some of which had one or more facets retouched by percussion flaking while others had naturally sharp facets used without prior modification. A majority of the utilized facets have been rounded or have irregular fractures due to repeated utilization. Fifteen of the choppers were shaped into forms ranging from pinnate to ovate and rectangular; 24 retain the original shape of the cobble.

Seven of the specimens were so large that they could only have been used with two hands. The others were much smaller and were probably grasped in one hand. The cutting edges were used to cut with blows rather than with applied pressure

(Hayes and Lancaster 1975:148). Small cores, large flakes, and tool fragments were also often used as choppers. In turn, small worn choppers were often used as hammerstones.

Two of the larger choppers (Fig. 41e,f) appear to have been used in some type of grinding process. Each has a single grinding surface with striations running parallel on one, and perpendicular on the other, to the longitudinal axis. The specimen with the perpendicular striations (Fig. 41f) appears to have been used in a metate, as indicated by one upturned end similar to those found on convex-surfaced manos.

Figure 38.   a - Axe from 5LP110; b - Axe from 5LP111.

Figure 39. Hoes.

Figure 40. Three-quarter grooved maul.

Figure 41. Choppers.

The larger choppers might be compared with Hayes and Lancaster's (1975) classification of "crushers." The exact purpose of these stones is unknown, but Hayes and Lancaster suggest that they were used for cracking corn kernels.

Comparison: Birkedal 1976:253-255; Hayes and Lancaster 1975:148, 154-155.

Hammerstones

Nineteen hammerstones were found (Fig. 42) The specimens varied between unmodified cobbles, split cobbles, and intentionally shaped palmate, ovate and rounded forms. The size and the multifaceted wear patterns of most of the hammerstones indicate they were hand held. The number of utilized edges ranges from a single facet to entire peripheries with varying degrees of wear. The battered and crushed wear patterns occur on manufactured edges and on edges broken through utilization, but the majority are on natural ridges of the stones. These prominent areas increase the strength of the hammer as well as the efficiency of the tool.

Four of the tools had bifacial percussion flaking similar to that found on chopping tools (Fig. 42g). Since the processes of chopping and hammering are similar, it is reasonable to assume that these specimens were well-worn choppers utilized as hammerstones.

Two of the ovate hammers were marked by shallow indentations, approximately 30 mm in diameter, pecked in the center of opposing flat surfaces (Fig. 42i, j). It is suggested that the indentations functioned as finger grips during hammering, although they may be a result of using the stone as an anvil. The battered areas are confined to the ends of the oval. They cover the ends of the cobble, but do not alter the natural outline of the stone. One of these tools (Fig. 42i) seemed to have been used secondarily as a floor or wall polisher. One surface was so well polished that the indentations were almost obliterated. It is doubtful that such wear is a result of grinding, since there were no striations.

Comparison: Birkedal 1976:257-259; Hayes and Lancaster 1975:149-150, 156-157; Woodbury 1954:86-88, 89-91.

Pecking Stone

One pecking stone , a broken quartzite cobble, was recovered (Fig. 43). Pyramidal in shape, its tip exhibits chipping and small battering scars.

Morris (1939:128) describes the use of pecking stones in reducing stone without chipping or fracture. Such stones occur during Basketmaker III times and in all later periods.

Comparison: O'Bryan 1950:83, Plate XXVIIIb; Morris 1939:128.

Figure 42.   Hammerstones.

Figure 43.   Pecking stone.

Ceramics of Durango South

by
Priscilla B. Ellwood

Introduction

Nearly 2000 potsherds and 46 whole vessels were recovered from excavations at Durango South. Classification into type categories is based primarily on the descriptions, terminology, and criteria of Colton (1955) and Abel (1955), with further consideration given to other more recent modifications made by Carlson (1963), and Breternitz, Rohn and Morris (1974). Frequencies and distribution of the potsherds and vessels by feature and level are tabulated in Tables 5 and 6.

A general description of the ceramics by type will be followed by a comparison and contrast within the two sites, as well as within the Durango District. A brief review will then be made of some aspects of ceramics of this period from Alkali Ridge, Ackmen-Lowry and Yellow Jacket to the northwest; Chaco Canyon to the southwest; the Piedra District to the east; and the Mesa Verde and La Plata Districts to the immediate west.

Grayware

Anasazi pottery can be divided into two main categories: undecorated or plain grayware, thought to be used for culinary and storage purposes, and decorated ware, used for serving food. Early decorated ware is essentially Basketmaker III grayware with painted designs. There is no recognizable difference between the undecorated portions of these and plain gray vessels (Hayes and Lancaster 1975:98). Body sherds remain indistinguishable into Pueblo III times or until the advent of overall corrugation in the cooking ware and the use of sherd temper and surface slipping in the decorated ware. A sherd from a smoothed section of a corrugated cooking vessel cannot be distinguished from a sherd of a plain pot from Basketmaker III times (Hayes and Lancaster 1975:99). Researchers working with these basic utility pottery types have treated the problem of classification in different ways (Hayes and Lancaster 1975:103; Breternitz, Rohn and Morris 1974:viii; Lister 1964:45-56).

The present report will use the Wheat, Gifford, and Wasley Type-Variety system of classification (1958), a modification of Abel (1955), as exemplified in Carlson (1963). However, for purposes of expediency and clarity, sherds which lack criteria for specific typing such as the gray body sherds are placed in a Plain Gray category. As such they will be considered as a unit in the interpretation of Durango South ceramics.

Pottery Type Descriptions

The Basketmaker III pottery Lino Gray was first described by Kidder and Guernsey (1919:153), illustrated by Roberts (1929), and named by Hargrave (1932:11). Its decorated counterpart, Lino Black-on-gray, was described by Morris (1927), and named by Hargrave (1932:12), with Roberts' Shabik'eshchee Village as the type site. These are the common type names for Basketmaker III ware although geographically localized expressions include Chapin Gray and Chapin Black-on-white (Abel 1955), La Plata Smoothed (Hawley 1936:23), and Rosa Smoothed with Rosa Black-on-white (Hall 1944), which vary from Lino in attributes such as paint and temper. Carlson (1963:31) first recognized the Morris Hidden Valley material as another regional variety belonging to the Lino tradition and classified it as such according to the type-variety concept proposed by Wheat, Gifford and Wasley (1958) and modified by Phillips (1958).

This report employs Carlson's terminology for Basketmaker III ceramic material: Lino Gray, Durango Variety; Lino Black-on-gray, Durango Variety. It also includes two additional types, Twin Trees Plain, Durango Variety and Twin Trees Black-on-white, Durango Variety. Twin Trees Plain and Twin Trees Black-on-white are Abel's (1955) Ware 10A Type 2 and Ware 12A Type 2, and differ basically from Lino by the presence of polishing on the interiors of bowls and the exteriors of jars. Change in surface treatment is one of the important developments in Anasazi decorated pottery. The evolution in painted design is marked by increased control, complexity of design layout, and change in utilization of space. These developments were preceded first by smoother surfaces and later by slipped surfaces. Twin Trees is an indicator of one step in this improved surface treatment.

The above decorated types are not synonymous with Piedra Black-on-white. The designs of the latter type are executed with large strokes as if the whole composition was perceived as a unit rather than executed as small units built up or radiating from the vessel bottom. While Twin Trees is never slipped, Hayes and Lancaster (1975:114) report substantial percentages of Piedra Black-on-white with slipped surfaces. Piedra Black-on-white is considered to be a Pueblo I type and is affiliated with late Basketmaker types, as well as with Abajo Red-on-orange and other Pueblo I types, Bluff Black-on-red and Deadman's Black-on-red (Breternitz, Rohn and Morris 1974:30).

The preponderance of sand temper in Durango South Twin Trees ceramics differs from Abel's (1955) descriptions; a Durango variety of Twin Trees is based on this difference in temper.

Six groups of pottery occur at the Durango South Basketmaker III sites. The Durango variety of Lino Gray is the largest category and appears mainly in the form of jar sherds. The next most abundant type of pottery is the Durango variety of Lino Black-on-gray which occurs as vessels and bowl sherds with painted decorations on a gray to white surface. Also frequent in appearance is the polished version of Basketmaker decorated ware, Twin Trees Plain, Durango Variety and Twin Trees Black-on-white, Durango Variety, again most commonly in the form of bowls. Only one decorated jar sherd was uncovered (Fig. 52r). Categories of minor frequencies include Abajo Red-on-orange and a few sherds of mudware, possibly used to line a parching tray. One small jar exhibited the neck-

banding which is diagnostic of Moccasin Gray. Other artifacts of clay include a bead or disk in the shape of a miniature spindle whorl and a tubular pipe.

Lino Gray, Durango Variety and Lino Black-on-gray, Durango Variety are well described by Carlson (1963:31-33). Since the two Durango South Lino types fit that type description, it will not be repeated in detail.

Lino Gray, Durango Variety

Sample: Twenty-four whole or partial vessels and 226 sherds fit this type description. This is the most abundant type of pottery recovered from Durango South (Tables 5 and 6).

Forms: Twenty whole or partial jars and four bowls, all of which included portions of rims, were recovered. Rims are consistently tapered or rounded. Bowl forms are uniformly wide and shallow (e.g. Vessel 43, Fig. 45a). Included in the jar sample is one pitcher. Range of variation here is more in size than in shape. The most abundant jar form is the wide-mouthed jar in which rim diameter is almost equal to the greatest diameter of the vessel (Vessels 40 and 42, Fig. 44a,b). Two variations of this shape are present, the first (of medium size) has a moderately short neck with a fat, hemispherical body and a rounded base. The second wide-mouthed version is uniformly smaller in size, has a proportionately more elongated body, with a shorter neck and a slightly flattened base (Vessel 14, Fig. 48a). Seed jars (Vessel 9, Fig. 45b) tend to be squat and thick walled with thicknesses up to 10mm. Other wall thickness ranges from 6mm to 9mm with an average thickness of 7mm.

In the Durango South collection, there are two large ollas (Vessels 12 and 22, Fig. 46a,b), presumably used as storage jars since neither shows evidence of hearth contact. Vessel 12 has heavy, horizontal strap handles and an elongated neck. Vessel 22 has the same elongated neck but higher shoulders and no handles. The rim of Vessel 22 is tapered and the base is only slightly flattened; the rim of Vessel 12 is more rounded and the base has a more pronounced flattening.

The only small-mouthed jar recovered, Vessel 17 (Fig. 45d), is missing the rim. It displays the stub of a handle. The body is completely rounded except for a flattened base. A heavy layer of charcoal covers the entire vessel.

Table 5. Durango South Ceramic Types: Sherds

Provenience	Lino Gray, Durango var. #	%	Moccasin Gray #	%	Plain Gray #	%	Unfired #	%	Twin Trees Plain, Durango var. #	%	Lino B/g, Durango var. #	%	Twin Trees B/w, Durango var. #	%	Abajo R/o #	%	Unclassifiable Orange #	%	Total #	%
5LP110 **Feature 1**																				
Level 1																			0	0%
Level 2	16	9%			148	82%			5	3%	5	3%	4	2%	3	1%			181	100%
Level 3	31	15%			151	74%	2	1%	3	1%	13	6%	3	1%	1	1%			204	100%
Level 4	8	26%			10	32%	11	35%					1	3%	1	3%			31	100%
Feature 2																				
Level 1													1	100%					1	100%
Level 2					2	67%							1	33%					3	100%
Level 3	58	9%			510	81%	3	+	1	+	35	6%	18	3%	3	+			628	100%
Level 4					38	86%					5	11%			1	3%			44	100%
Site Total	115	10%	0	0%	859	79%	16	1%	9	1%	58	5%	28	3%	9	1%	0	0%	1092	100%
5LP111 **Feature 1**																				
Level 1	5	10%			41	85%					1	2%	1	2%					48	100%
Level 2	8	6%			84	62%			1	+	15	11%	25	18%	3	2%			136	100%
Level 3	27	12%			179	81%					7	3%	7	3%					220	100%
Feature 2																				
Level 1																			0	0%
Level 2	4	6%			53	81%					4	6%	2	3%			2	3%	65	100%
Level 3	25	8%			248	82%					16	5%	5	2%			8	3%	302	100%
Level 4	25	30%			52	63%					4	5%	1	1%			1	1%	83	100%
Site Total	111	13%	0	0%	657	75%	0	0%	1	+	48	5%	43	5%	3	+	11	1%	874	100%
Totals: Both sites	226	11%	0	0%	1516	77%	16	1%	10	1%	106	5%	71	3%	12	1%	11	1%	1966	100%

Table 6. Durango South Ceramic Types - Whole Vessels*

Provenience	Lino Gray, Durango var. bowls #	%	jars #	%	Moccasin Gray jars #	%	Plain Gray jars #	%	Twin Trees Plain, Durango var. bowls #	%	Lino B/g, Durango var. bowls #	%	Twin Trees B/w, Durango var. bowls #	%	Total bowls #	%	Total jars #	%	Total # Vessels
5LP110																			
Feature 1 Level 1																			0
Level 2			3	100%													2	100%	2
Level 3			3	60%					1	20%	1	20%			2	40%	3	60%	5
Level 4	1	6%	9	56%	1	6%	2	13%	2	13%			1	6%	4	25%	12	75%	16
Feature 2 Level 1																			0
Level 2																			0
Level 3			2	100%													2	100%	2
Level 4							2	100%									2	100%	2
Site Total	1	4%	16	59%	1	4%	4	15%	3	11%	1	4%	1	4%	6	22%	21	77%	27
Burial 1			1	33%							2	66%			2	66%	1	33%	3
Burials 2 and 3	1	50%	1	50%											1	50%	1	50%	2
Burials Total	1	20%	2	40%							2	40%			3	60%	2	40%	5
5LP111																			
Feature 1 Level 1																			0
Level 2																			0
Level 3																			0
Level 4	1	17%	1	17%							2	33%	2	33%	5	83%	1	17%	6
Feature 2 Level 1																			0
Level 2													2	100%	2	100%			2
Level 3			1	50%									1	50%	1	50%	1	50%	2
Level 4	1	25%	2	50%			1	25%							1	25%	3	75%	4
Site Total	2	14%	4	29%	0	0%	1	7%	0	0%	2	14%	5	36%	9	64%	5	36%	4
Totals: Both sites	4	9%	22	48%	1	2%	5	11%	3	7%	5	11%	6	13%	18	39%	28	61%	46

*No whole orange ware vessels were observed.

81

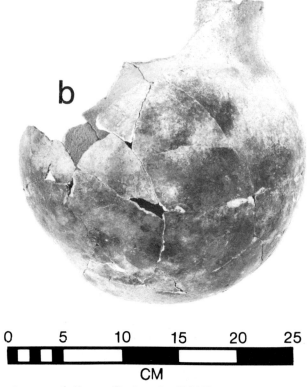

Figure 44.   Lino Gray wide mouthed jars: a - #40; b - #42.

Handles are not common. However, there are two examples of flat strap, horizontally placed handles on Vessels 12 and 33b (Figs. 46a and 45f). One flat strap, vertically placed handle is attached at the rim and again at the body below the rim on a pitcher, Vessel 20 (Fig. 48b). Another form is evidenced in Vessel 15 (Fig. 47a), which has a vertically coiled handle attached to the rim and to the body below the rim. The handle curves and diminishes slightly in diameter to assume the shape later displayed in the squash forms of the Pueblo I period. Partial Vessel 35b has a nubbin attached just below the neck that is too small to be a true handle but may have facilitated lifting.

Decoration: The one form of decoration displayed by this group of ceramics is the addition of a fine reddish brown powder to the exterior of Vessels 33, 36 and 37. This treatment has been recognized by other researchers and named fugitive red.

Twin Trees Plain, Durango Variety

The polished gray pottery recovered from Durango South fits Abel's (1955) description of Ware 10A Type 2, except for the predominant use of rounded and angular fragments of sand for temper. Establishment here of a Durango variety based on difference in temper follows Carlson's (1963) precedent for Lino types.

Sample: The sample includes five partial vessels and ten sherds.

Construction and firing: There is little direct evidence of the method of construction, since part of the manufacturing process is to obliterate the earliest steps. What evidence there is suggests vessels were started with continuous coils of clay built up in a basket container which was used as a base or mold. Twin Trees Plain, Durango Variety was fired in a reducing atmosphere, as inferred from its color.

Paste: Color varied from very light gray or grayish, white to a very dark gray with a graduation of grays and tans in between. Measurements were made with the use of Munsell Soil Color Charts (1954) and ranged from Munsell 4.5YR 8/0 to 3/0, and from 10YR 8/1 to 6/2.

Temper: Abundant quantities of rounded as well as angular fragments of quartz sand is the dominant form of temper. Crushed igneous rock, some light colored and fewer dark colored, is a secondary kind of temper added. In most cases a mixture of these is

Figure 45. Lino Gray vessels: a - #43, bowl; b - #9, seed jar; c - #30, miniature bowl; d - #17, small mouthed jar with the stub of a handle; e - #21, jar; f - #33b, horizontally placed handle.

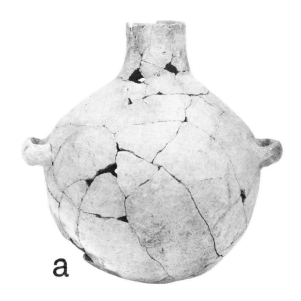

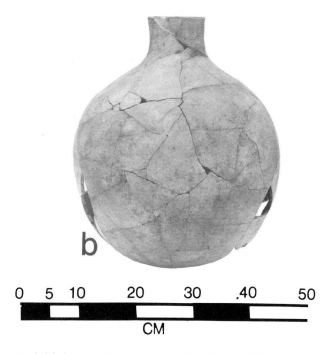

Figure 46.   Lino Gray ollas: a - #12; b - #22.

used with proportions of two-thirds sand to one-third crushed rock. No use of crushed sherd for tempering was observed in this material. The presence of micaceous sandstone, common in this part of the country, accounts for the sparkle visible on the vessel surface.

Carbon streak is not visible in the Twin Trees Plain, Durango Variety material from Durango South.

Texture of the paste observed in the sherds and partial vessels varies considerably and ranges from medium fine to coarse.

Hardness and fracture are variables of amounts of temper used. Throughout the sample, where temper occurs in abundance, pastes are friable and fractures are uneven. The denser pastes often break with a straight or right-angled fracture.

Fireclouds: Presence of this condition is difficult to determine, as the pithouse burned and pots were refired unevenly.

Surface finish: All surfaces are scraped and smoothed to obliterate evidence of coils and then polished before firing, especially bowl interiors and jar exteriors. Vessel 5 (Fig. 48c) is similar to other undecorated vessels in the collection but it demonstrates a distinct departure in surface finish

and thickness. The large shallow bowl with rounded rim varies between 5 mm and 11.5 mm   in wall thickness. Although the interior surface is slightly uneven, showing some dimpling and crazing, it is highly polished. Examination under a .binocular microscope did not reveal the addition of a separate finer clay (slip) to the surface. Shepard (1968:191) describes the technique of wet polishing used to achieve this degree of polish without slipping. When a surface is repeatedly wetted and lightly stroked, the platelets of a fine textured clay are redistributed and the fine particles tend to rise to the surface.

Form: There were two large shallow bowls of this type in the Durango South collection. Vessel 6 (Fig. 47d) is similar in paste color and texture to the Twin Trees decorated vessels; however, its diameter is almost double that of its decorated counterparts. The rim is rounded and the base is slightly flattened. Wall thickness is a fairly uniform 6mm, and the interior surface is smoothed and polished. The other large shallow bowl, Vessel 5, is described in detail above under surface treatment.

Lino Black-on-gray, Durango Variety

Sample: Four partial bowls (Figs. 49b and 50a) and 105 bowl sherds plus one decorated jar sherd (Fig. 52r) are classified in this category.

84

Construction: One example, Vessel 1 (Fig. 50a,b), clearly shows unobliterated coils used in manufacture.

Form: Bowls are shallow with tapered rims. Two separate rim sherds have small lugs placed in a position vertical to the rim. One of these is pierced vertically and the other is solid. Bases are rounded.

Decoration: Paints in this sample are glaze, mineral, and organic with comparative frequencies of 4:2:1. The glaze ranges in color from a clear greenish yellow (Munsell 5Y7/2) to a greenish-black (Munsell 5Y3/2). It is a lead glaze unevenly applied in a vegetal medium and is unevenly vitrified. Shepard's description (1939:258) of the Morris Hidden Valley and La Plata collections fits the Durango South material. The glaze is not always readily apparent because only part of the design is glazed and the remainder shows a negative pattern where the glaze did not adhere. The mineral paint is a dull gray black (Munsell 7.5YR 4/0 to 3/0). The organic paint appears to sink into the vessel surface and is a light flat gray (Munsell 5YR 8/1).

Twin Trees Black-on-white, Durango Variety

The polished decorated pottery recovered from Durango South fits Abel's description of Twin Trees Black-on-white, Ware 12A Type 2. Because of the predominance of rounded and angular fragments of quartz sand used for tempering, a Durango variety of Twin Trees Black-on-white is established here. Carlson's (1963) precedent for Lino types is again followed.

Breternitz, Rohn, and Morris state in their introduction:

> The basis for these descriptions of Mesa Verde ceramics rests on Abel (1955) and includes a consensus of present opinion and research, if one keeps two factors in mind: 1) descriptions of Mesa Verde Pottery are based on collections from within Mesa Verde National Park, and although local variations are elsewhere acknowledged, they are not well described; 2) descriptions of Mesa Verde pottery are presented specifically to facilitate field identification of sherds (1974:ix).

Their description of Basketmaker III pottery includes types named Chapin Gray and Chapin Black-on-white (1974:1,25). Both types are a part of the Northern San Juan tradition which specifies the use of crushed rock for temper, usually a dark-colored igneous rock such as andesite or diorite (1974:1, 25). The description of the polished version of the plain gray is incorporated within the description of Chapin Gray and is listed under "Synonyms" and again under "Varieties and Deviations"(1974:1). The description of the finish of Chapin Black-on-white reads, "Scraped, then rubbed, but usually not polished" (1974:25) and Twin Trees Black-on-white is listed as a synonym (1974:26).

These descriptions do not fit the Durango South pottery. Both the plain gray and the decorated ware from Durango South including polished and unpolished have predominantly glaze paint. The Lino designation can be appropriately used for the latter following Carlson's precedent (1963:31), but for the polished version another problem arises.The Durango South polished ceramic material is not the same as the original description of Obelisk Gray, which is the polished version of Lino Gray. The description of Obelisk Gray and the original sherds from the type collections at the Museum of Northern Arizona include a high polishing over a slightly wavy or dimpled surface. The pottery itself is fine grained, light mustard brown to pale light orange (Colton). The Durango South polished material consistently fits the description of Abel's (1955) Twin Trees Plain and Twin Trees Black-on-white (Ware 12A Type 2) with the exception of the use of sand temper in place of crushed rock, and the use of glaze paint instead of a mineral paint in the decorated pottery. For the above reasons, the polished Durango South Basketmaker material is called Twin Trees Plain, Durango Variety and Twin Trees Black-on-white, Durango Variety and is described in detail under those names.

It is proposed that collections of archaeological material including ceramics from little known areas or from areas not as throroughly documented as on the Mesa Verde, such as the Durango area, be meticulously described at every opportunity. The simplification of pottery types is understandable or acceptable particularly to facilitate field identification of the sherds. However, where there is archaeological meaning in the final analysis of a site, a type name is appropriate.

Sample: Five whole vessels and 71 sherds comprise this category.

Construction: It appears that this pottery was formed of coils of clay built up in a basket container and then scraped to obliterate the coil marks. No direct evidence of coil marks remains, but basket impressions are visible on the exteriors of some vessels.

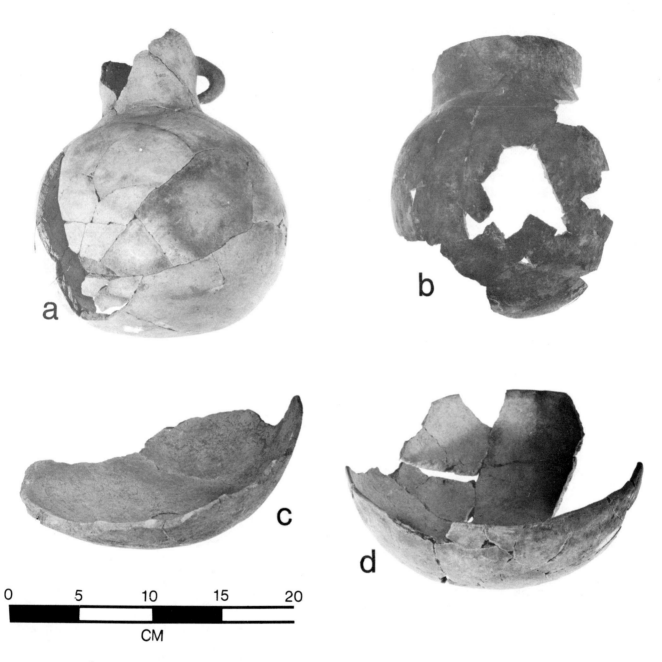

Figure 47.   Lino Gray vessels: a-#15, jar. Handle accentuates squash form. b-#34, wide-mouthed jar. Twin Trees Plain vessels: c-#37, platter; d-#6, bowl.

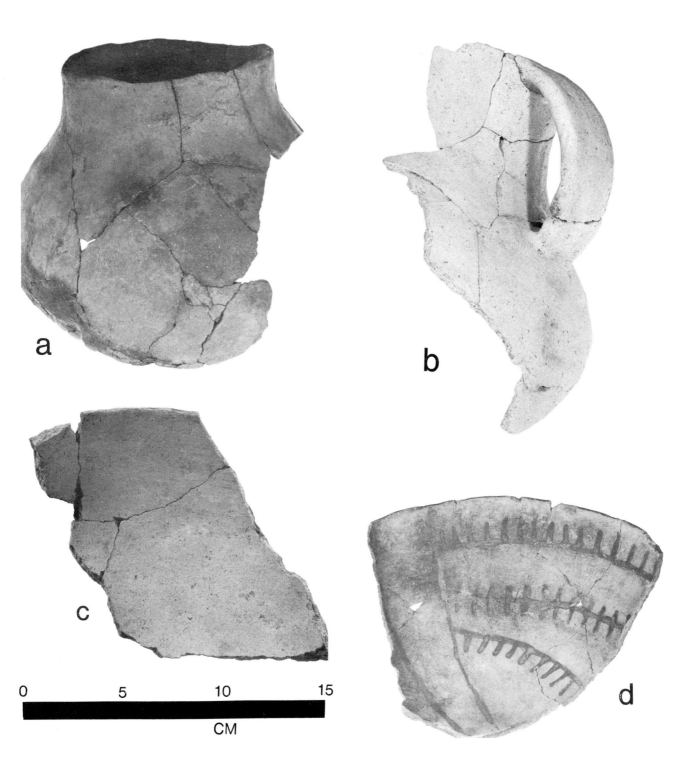

Figure 48.   Lino Gray vessels: a-#14, wide-mouthed jar; b-#20, pitcher handle. Twin Trees Plain bowl: c-#5. Twin Trees Black-on-white bowl: d-#35a.

Paste: Color variation ranges from a light buff color to a deep gray (7.5YR 8/0 to 3/0 and 7.5YR 8/2 to 4/2). This extreme variation can be explained by evidence that one bowl, Vessel 19 (Fig. 50c), was refired and partially fire-blackened when the pithouse burned and the roof collapsed.

Temper: Varying amounts of sand and crushed quartz, with lesser amounts of crushed light and dark igneous rock are present. Each of the partial vessels also displayed minor quantities of micaceous sandstone.

Carbon streak is not visible in any of the surface breaks.

Texture is medium fine to coarse although somewhat more dense than the clays observed in the Plain Gray sample.

Hardness and Fracture: Vessel walls are strong and fractures are somewhat straighter than in the Plain Grayware.

Surface finish and color: Bowl interiors in this category demonstrate surfaces that have been scraped and smoothed and then polished. The surface of Vessel 38 (Fig. 50d) is uneven, with only small sections of its interior highly polished while other sections including the exterior are unevenly smoothed. The exterior shows come crazing and has been dusted with fugitive red. Vessels 31 and 32 (Fig. 50e, f) are more evenly polished overall, particularly on the interior surface. Although Vessels 19 and 35a (Figs. 50c and 48d) display highly polished interiors, both of these reflect evidence of molding in basketry containers on the exterior. No slipped surfaces were observed.

Form: Wall thickness and contour vary from 4mm to 5mm at the rim and from 6mm to 8mm at the base with an average for the base of 7mm. Rim shapes vary from tapered to rounded. Four of the bowls were shallow with projected diameter almost double their height. Bases are uniformly rounded.

Decoration: Paints on vessels and sherds occur in proportions of one organic to two mineral to four glaze. Shepard's paint oxidation test (1968:387) was used to differentiate between iron and carbon paints on the whole and partial vessels. However this test is not conclusive with this material. All of the paints were unevenly applied to the vessel surfaces in varying densities. It is recommended that further technical or spectrographic analysis of paints be made as the usual visual criteria of identification are often misleading and inadequate.

Design

Although the sample of decorated ware is limited to eight restorable or partial bowls, some consistencies in design can be identified. The field of decoration encompasses the entire bowl interior, with design units sparsely distributed. Layouts for motifs are of three classes (Fig. 51): I) repeated individual motifs randomly spaced over the entire surface; II) radiating layout from a central circle in which the motif radiates up the bowl walls, sometimes dividing the surface area into three or four parts; III) isolated design units pendant from or emphasizing the rim. There are no banding lines, but a small circle sometimes appears in the center of the bottom of a bowl (Vessels 2 and 19, Figs. 49b and 50c).

Designs consist of widely spaced motifs repeated several times. No decorated jar sherds were large enough to describe. Design elements and units making up the motifs are dots, dots within lines, ticked lines, triangles embellished with ticks and flags, concentric circles, and zigzag lines (Fig. 52). The style of design is simple and direct, however lines lack control and the general impression is one of crudeness. In Twin Trees Black-on-white, there is a slight increase in design elaboration and stroke control due in part to a superior working surface.

The style exemplified by these Lino Black-on-gray and Twin Trees Black-on-white bowls illustrates Basketmaker design tradition, in contrast to the later Pueblo I style of increasing filling of space and a tendency for designs to be pendant from the rim.

Other Pottery Types

Moccasin Gray, described by Abel (1955: Ware 10A Type 3) and Breternitz, Rohn and Morris (1974:5) is represented by one small wide-mouthed jar with only a small portion of the neck and rim intact (Vessel 23, Fig. 49a). The paste color, texture, and temper fit the description of Lino Gray, Durango Variety. The neck of the jar starting above the shoulder displays evidence of three concentric rings applied one above the other. This vessel is poorly preserved. The paste is friable; fractures are uneven and occur in such a way as to minimize evidence of construction. The rim is rounded and

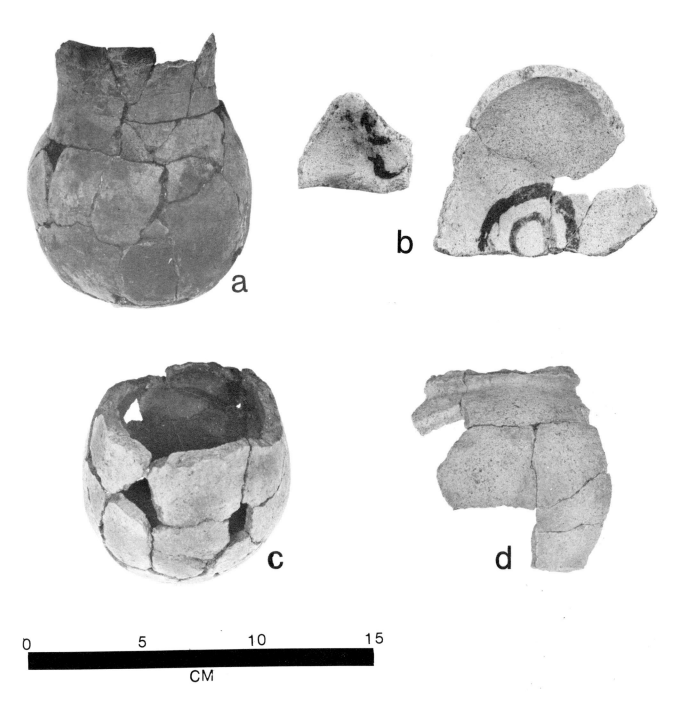

0   5   10   15

CM

Figure 49.   Moccasin Gray jar: a - #23. Lino Black-on-gray bowl: b - #2. Unclassifiable Grayware jars: c - #18; d - #26 (possibly double vessel).

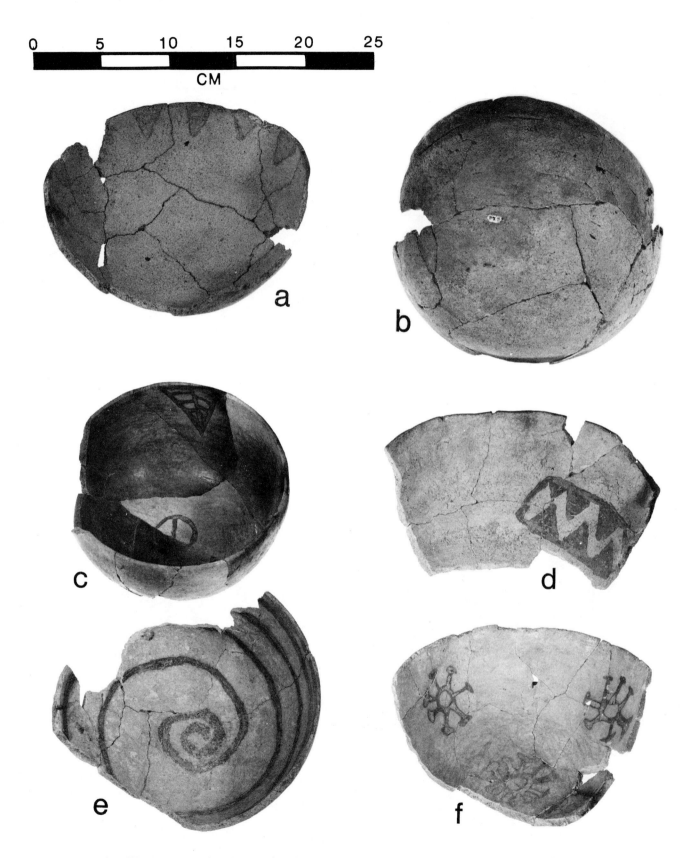

Figure 50. Lino Black-on-gray bowl: a - #1 interior; b - #1 exterior, note coil construction. Twin Trees Black-on-white bowls: c - #19, d - #38, e - #31, f - #32.

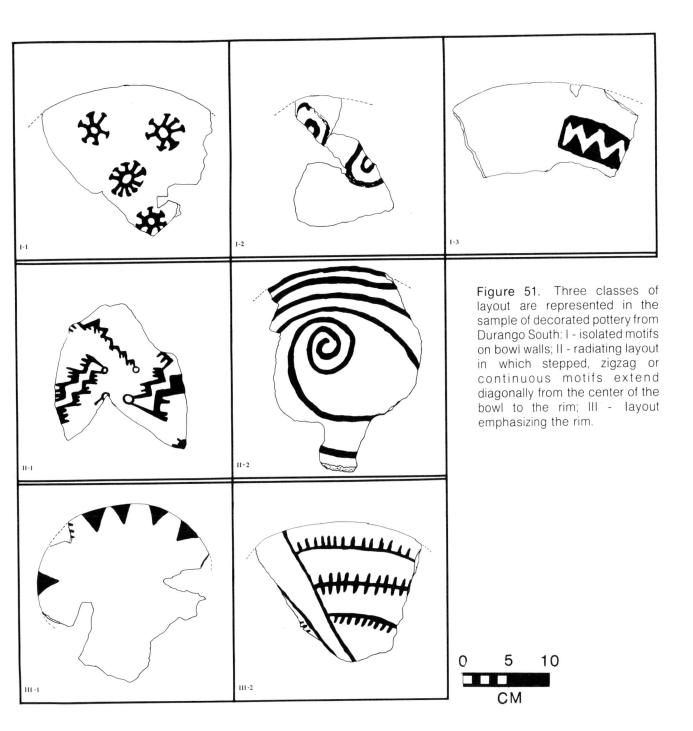

Figure 51. Three classes of layout are represented in the sample of decorated pottery from Durango South: I - isolated motifs on bowl walls; II - radiating layout in which stepped, zigzag or continuous motifs extend diagonally from the center of the bowl to the rim; III - layout emphasizing the rim.

0 5 10

CM

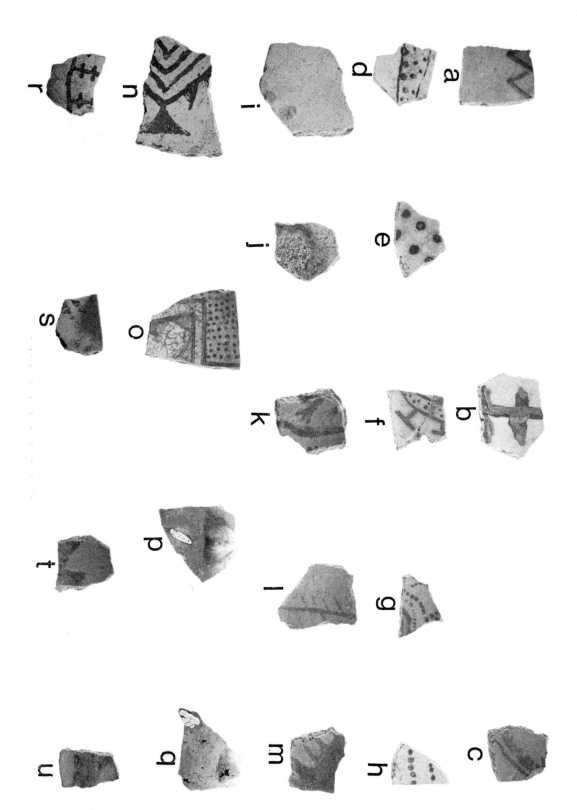

Figure 52. Sherds from Durango South: a-c,Lino Black-on-gray, Durango Variety; d-h, n, o, Twin Trees Black-on-white, Durango Variety; c-m, sherds with glaze paint, Lino Black-on-gray, Durango Variety; Durango Variety and Twin Trees Black-on-white, Durango Variety; p,q, Lino Gray sherds with small lug handles; r, Lino Black-on-gray jar sherd (the only decorated jar sherd recovered from either site); s-u, Abajo Red-on-orange.

wall thickness varies from 5mm at the rim to 11mm at the base, with projected rim diameter of 7cm compared to body diameter of 10cm. Definite shoulders are lacking and the vessel is taller than wide. The base is flattened and much of the body is fire-blackened. This vessel represents the only incidence of neck banding recovered from Durango South with the exception of one surface sherd.

Abajo Red-on-orange is fully described by Brew (1946:254), Abel (1955:Ware 5A Type 1), and Breternitz, Rohn and Morris (1974:49).

No whole vessels of this type were recovered at Durango South, but 12 bowl sherds including three rim sherds were found (Fig.52). The paste varies from orange to gray (Munsell 2.5YR 6/4 to 5/6). Temper includes variable amounts of quartz sand and crushed rock fragments. Surfaces range from smooth but unpolished to a polished-over decoration in three sherds from Durango South. Paint is red iron oxide with no glaze present in the sample. Paint color varies from Munsell 2.5YR 4/6 to 3/6. Sherds are too fragmentary to allow a complete description of design. Designs were pendant from the rim and consisted of broad parallel lines and solid triangle motifs.

Additional Clay Objects

Other fired clay objects uncovered during excavations at Durango South include a clay pipe or cloud blower and a clay disk or miniature spindle whorl(?).

The name "cloud blower" comes from contemporary Pueblo Indians who use similar pipes for ceremonial purposes. During a religious observance, small puffs of smoke, supposedly representing clouds, are blown to the cardinal directions by priests using pipes of this form (Roberts 1930:141). Eddy (1966:401) states that this practice is linked with rain-making ceremonies and purification with smoke.

These pipes have been reported in the Anasazi and Mogollon areas. Similar tubular pipes appear in such diverse materials as red clay called halloysite, brown clay, lava, basalt tuff, as well as fine-grained sandstone. They are also occasionally made of black-walnut wood (Joe Ben Wheat, personal communication). Carlson (1963:80) reports one pipe made of steatite.

The pipe from Durango South (Fig. 53a) is 7.2 cm in

length and has a maximum diameter of 2.7 cm. Short hollow reeds were reportedly placed in the small end to serve as a stem (Roberts 1929:124). This reed was not present in the Durango South specimen. The interior of the pipe is burned. A dottle of burned material was scraped from the pipe and treated with denatured alcohol to determine if nicotine was present (Joe Ben Wheat, personal communication); however, the results of the test were inconclusive.

The second object of clay was a circular gray-brown disk in the form of a miniature spindle whorl or bead (Fig. 53b). It measured 28mm in diameter and 14mm in thickness, with a 3mm collar around the perforation. The perforation itself was 2 mm wide and 1 mm thick. These objects are not uncommon in the Anasazi area and are reported in Basketmaker III sites near Durango (Carlson 1963:38). They have been called spindle whorls, but according to Joe Ben Wheat of the University of Colorado Museum, the object from Durango South is too small to be a true spindle whorl. Spindle whorls in this area are usually 3 to 4 cm in diameter with a center hole at least 1 to 1.5 cm in diameter, and are usually made of wood.

Ceramic Stratigraphy and Distribution

Percentages of pottery types from 5LP110 and 5LP111 indicate a terminal Basketmaker occupation (A.D. 750 or 775-800) with some Pueblo I influences evident.

Stratigraphy

The evidence for ceramic stratigraphy is recorded in Tables 5 and 6. The dominant type is Lino Gray, Durango Variety. It was manufactured over a time period of A.D. 575 to 875 (Breternitz 1963:83). Its decorated counterpart, Lino Black-on-gray, is the second most popular type, followed by Twin Trees Black-on-white, Durango Variety, and Twin Trees Plain, Durango Variety, also manufactured within a range of dates which fits the Basketmaker III - Pueblo I culture period (A.D. 675 - 898).

Evidence of either of the Pueblo I indicators, Abajo Red-on-orange or neck-banded Moccasin Gray, is minimal. The former type is limited to 12 sherds, or less than 1% of the total sherds. Moccasin Gray or any form of neck-banding is limited to one partial vessel (Vessel 23, Fig. 49a). Although Lino has been known to be associated with Pueblo I and even early Pueblo II wares such as the various indented

Figure 53. Clay objects: a - clay pipe from 5LP111 Feature 2, floor; b - clay disk from 5LP110 Feature 1.

corrugated wares (Martin and Rinaldo 1939: 271), at Durango South the positive evidence for any period later than Basketmaker III is exiguous. However, even this small amount of evidence indicates a pending transition.

Tree-ring dates do substantiate the ceramic evidence and indicate a construction date of A.D. 774-776 at 5LP110 Feature 1 (Table 1). The archaeomagnetic date processed from hearth material at 5LP111 Feature 2 also supports the ceramic classification.

Distribution

Sixteen whole or partial vessels were recovered from the floor or bench at 5LP110 Feature 1 (Fig. 54). On the bench, southwest quad, was a Lino Gray seed jar (Vessel 13a) and an unclassifiable jar base (Vessel 13b). Close by on the floor was a small unclassifiable gray jar with no neck or rim (Vessel 18, Fig. 49c) and a Lino Gray small-mouthed jar (Vessel 17, Fig. 45d). Vessel 22 (Fig. 46b), a large Lino Gray, Durango Variety olla, and Vessel 23 (Fig. 49a), a small Moccasin Gray jar, were recovered from the floor in the northwest quad near the bench. Another small group of pots in the northwest quad included an unclassifiable, unreconstructable jar (Vessel 10) with a large Twin Trees Plain shallow bowl (Vessel 6, Fig. 47d) and a Lino Gray shallow bowl (Vessel 24). The deep Twin Trees Black-on-white bowl (Vessel 19, Fig. 50c) was associated with several remnants of basketry. North of the partition wall was an unclassifiable jar base (Vessel 29). Near the firepit (southwest quad) was the large Lino Gray strap handled olla (Vessel 12, Fig. 46a). Found east of the partition wall was the Lino Gray jar (Vessel 14, Fig. 48a), the baseless Lino Gray jar (Vessel 11), the delicate pitcher (Vessel 15, Fig. 47a), and the unclassifiable gray base (Vessel 39). Figures 54 and 55 illustrate the association of these vessels and the vessels from 5LP111 with other material culture items.

Basically the material reflects Basketmaker pottery traditions, especially in paste and design. However certain vessel forms from this level do tend toward Pueblo I styles. The tendency to symmetrical and globular shaping of the bodies of the medium size jars (Vessel 14, Fig. 48a), the elongated body demonstrated in Vessel 18 (Fig. 49c) and the slight lowering of the shoulders in one of the ollas (Vessel 12, Fig. 46a) are all forerunners of the next period. The handle of the pitcher (Vessel 15, Fig. 47a) hints at the squash-shaped vessels of Pueblo I.

Whole or partial vessels recovered from the upper levels at 5LP110 Feature 1 include partial vessel 26 (Fig. 49d), unclassifiable because of no complete rim section, and a partial Lino Gray jar (Vessel 28). Vessel 26 has an unusual shape in that it appears to be a double vessel. Four of the Abajo Red-on-orange sherds present were from levels 2 and 3. The fifth Abajo sherd was recovered from the cist in the partition wall.

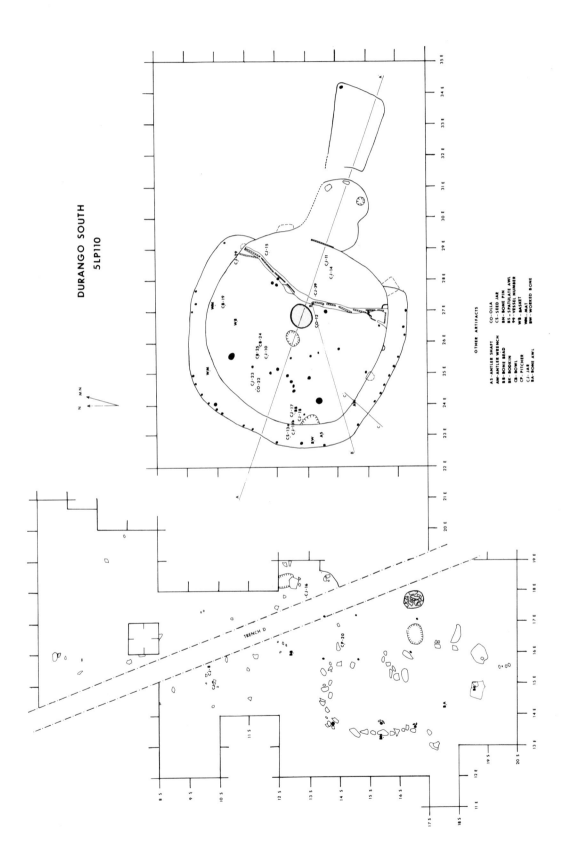

Figure 54.   Distribution of other artifacts (whole ceramic vessels, bone tools and weaving) at 5LP110 Features 1 and 2, floor.

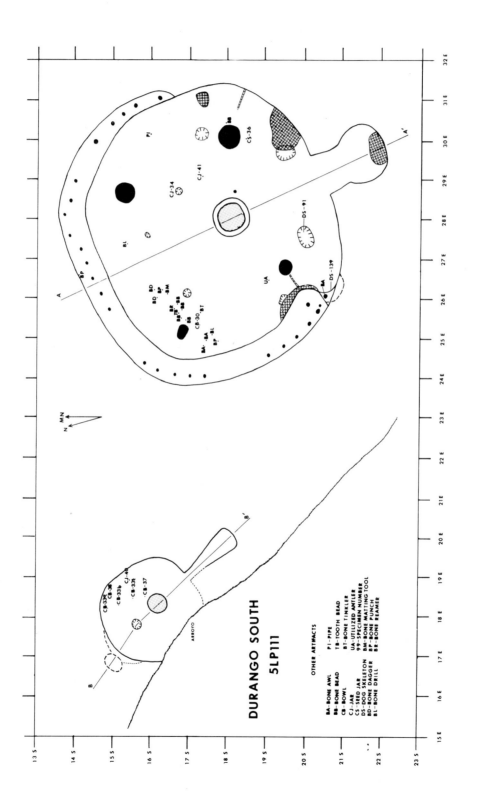

Figure 55.   Distribution of other artifacts (whole ceramic vessels and bone tools) at 5LP111 Features 1 and 2, floor.

Whole or partial vessels recovered from the floor of 5LP110 Feature 2 include a Lino Gray pitcher with strap handle (Vessel 20, Fig. 48b) and a Lino Gray jar fragment (Vessel 16) as well as two unclassifiable jar bases (Vessels 7 and 8).

Sherd and whole vessel distribution from 5LP111 Feature 1 (Tables 5 and 6) again show Lino Gray, Durango Variety as a dominant type. Of the decorated wares, Twin Trees Black-on-white, Durango Variety comprises 8% of the total for this feature while Lino Black-on-gray is less plentiful at 6%. However, the total sherd count at 5LP111 from both features reveals that Lino Black-on-gray totals slightly more than 5% and Twin Trees Black-on-white is slightly less plentiful. (At 5LP110 the comparative percentages are 5% to 3%). No neck-banded sherds were recovered from either feature of 5LP111. Three Abajo Red-on-orange sherds were recovered from Level 2 of 5LP111 Feature 1, the small pithouse. Partial bowls classified as Twin Trees Black-on-white (Vessel 33a and Vessel 38, Fig. 50d) and Lino Black-on-gray (Vessel 33c) were the decorated vessels from 5LP111 Feature 1. Vessel 33b (Fig. 45f); Vessel 37 (Fig. 47c), a Lino Gray platter; and Vessel 40, a Lino Gray jar (Fig. 44a) were also recovered from the floor.

The three Twin Trees Black-on-white partial bowls, Vessel 31 (Fig. 50e), Vessel 32 (Fig. 50f), and Vessel 35a (Fig. 48d) were recovered from the upper levels of the large pithouse, 5LP111 Feature 2. The floor contact material from this component was Lino Gray including a partial jar (Vessel 36), a jar (Vessel 34, Fig. 47b), a miniature bowl (Vessel 30, Fig. 45c), and an unclassifiable jar base (Vessel 41).

Comparative Studies and Interpretations

Durango South ceramics are compared below with ceramics from eight areas: the Chaco area, the Navajo Reservoir District, the Piedra District, the La Plata District, Alkali Ridge, the Ackmen-Lowry area, the Yellow Jacket District and the Mesa Verde District (Fig. 4).

The Chaco Area

Shabik'eschee Village in Chaco Canyon (Roberts 1929), the type site for Lino Black-on-gray, is important because it is an isolated example of a single culture stage. Similarities between Durango South ceramics and those of Shabik'eshchee Village can be seen in shared forms such as the shallow plain undecorated bowls which appeared in noticeable quantities at both sites. Also almost identical in shape were the large jars or ollas, presumably water vessels. Many sherds of these vessels were found at Shabik'eshchee Village and the projected shapes were drawn in outline form. Noticeable for its absence at both sites is the gourd-shaped pitcher of the next cultural period.

Seed jars differed at the two locations: the spherical jar with constricted and slightly incurving orifice which appears frequently at Shabik'eshchee Village contrasts with the thicker, shorter vessel from Durango South. Lacking at Durango South and present at the Chaco village were lateral spouted vessels as well as ladles. No ware with a shiny, intentionally blackened interior occurred at Durango South, while there were large fragments of 12 such bowls at Shabik'eshchee Village.

The Navajo Reservoir District

Sambrito phase sites on the San Juan River just below its junction with the Piedra and along the Pine River in the Navajo Reservoir District (Eddy 1972:24) are equivalent in time to Basketmaker III in the Pecos Classification. They are, however, distinct from the San Juan Basketmaker phases in architecture and ceramics. Locally made brown pottery, Mesa Verde imported grayware vessels with both rough and polished surfaces, and decorated black-on-gray types define the ceramic group, dated A.D. 500-600 (1972:27).

The Piedra District

Roberts' (1930:140) Pueblo I ceramic material exhibited banded instead of smooth necks on the culinary vessels and increased variation in vessel shape. Elaboration of painted designs from other than basketry sources was characteristic. Ornamentation was also present on large jars, pitchers, seed jars, bowls and ladles, and other vessels. The jar forms include full-bodied jars with long tapering necks and constricted orifices; globular jars with short necks and wide orifices; full-bodied vessels of an ovoid or elongated spherical shape with short necks and wide orifices; and double-lobed jars, plus cylindrical vases, effigy forms and other eccentric shapes. Forty-six per cent of the containers were slipped (1930:140). The one noticeable likeness between Roberts' Piedra collection and the Durango South pottery is the form of the globular-bodied jars with short necks and wide orifices.

The La Plata District

The strength of Earl Morris' La Plata report (1939) lies in its treatment of the ceramic history of the La Plata District. He reports that the squash pot, either globular or elongated with relatively wide incurving orifice, was the most common shape used by the La Plata people (1939:31). It may be stated that these La Plata Basketmaker III wares constitute a thoroughly typical exemplification of the ceramics of the period for the entire area over which Basketmaker III culture extended. Slight local differences could be pointed out. For instance, along the La Plata there was less range of form in culinary vessels than Roberts (1929) reports from Shabik'eshchee Village in the Chaco. In the basic features of structure, surface finish, and decoration, however, there is surprising uniformity wherever Basketmaker III wares have been found.

Anna Shepard's outstanding technological study of La Plata pottery emphasizes the potter's fundamental techniques such as the selection of clay temper, and pigment; whether or not there were distinct local variations in materials and practice; and the extent to which methods changed with general cultural development (1939:249). Basic technical analysis forces the researcher to consider how the pottery was made and to visualize the potter's environment and limitations (1939:286).

Shepard describes the glaze paint of Basketmaker III vessels from the La Plata area as glossy and free from opaque inclusions. A sample tested from the Durango area reveals that it is a lead glaze containing a small amount of silver usually found in western lead ores. Sodium is also a constituent of the glaze with some copper present (Shepard 1939:258). Shepard feels the potters must have been experimenting with lead ores. The powdered ore must have been applied with an organic vehicle, for many of the vessels, especially those on which the glaze is thin and patchy, show the stain of the plant extract. These glazes also reveal a high silica content which makes them harder and more impervious to acid attack (1939:259).

Although the ceramics of the La Plata District (Shepard 1939) demonstrate a more limited range of form than those of Shabik'eshchee Village (Roberts 1929), the Durango South material is even more conservative. However, jar body shapes from the La Plata District and Durango South fluctuate around a globular norm, with rounded bases and mouths wide in proportion to maximum diameter. No examples of slip were found on the sherds examined from either area. Glaze paints occur in both the La Plata and Durango Districts.

Alkali Ridge

At Alkali Ridge Brew found it nearly impossible to differentiate unpainted Basketmaker III pottery from that of Pueblo I (1946:291). The form he speaks of as diagnostic of Basketmaker pottery is the globular jar without a neck. The percentage of the black-on-white or gray decorated ware that could be considered as Basketmaker III (Lino Black-on-gray and La Plata Black-on-white) is small compared to the quantity of Pueblo I Abajo Red-on-orange (for which Alkali Ridge is the type site). Neck-banded sherds were rare.

The evidence presented by the ceramics and the associated architecture, the gradual shifting of domiciliary functions from below ground to the surface, and the increasing specialization of the subterranean chamber led Brew to date Abajo Red-on-orange pottery at Alkali Ridge as early Pueblo I rather than as Basketmaker III - Pueblo I, his previous field appellation (1946:248). He postulates that the manufacture of Abajo Red-on-orange could have begun as early as the Basketmaker III period at Alkali Ridge and diffused slowly southward to the Mesa Verde area as a demarcation of Pueblo I (1946:292). Percentages of Abajo Red-on-orange and black-on-white sherds are reversed at Durango South. Abajo Red-on-orange comprises less than one per cent here.

The Ackmen-Lowry Area

The comparison of ceramics from the Ackmen-Lowry area (Martin and Rinaldo 1939) is difficult because although some of the tree-ring dates given in that report are close to those from Durango South, the Lino Gray pottery from the Ackmen Site was unmistakably associated with indented corrugated pottery at all levels (1939:271), and with Mancos Black-on-white and Abajo Red-on-orange (1939:273). The associated architecture at Ackmen, Site 2 consisted of three long surface buildings which were two rooms in width. Site 1 was of masonry construction. Morris (1941:378) describes these sites as Pueblo I.

The Yellow Jacket District

The Stevenson Site, 5MT1, at Yellow Jacket is a Basketmaker III occupation. Pottery classifications (Ellwood 1973) included the traditional early types Chapin and Lino Gray, and Chapin and La Plata Black-on-white. Vessel forms included globular jars with short outcurving necks, spherical and elongated seed jars, one grayware jar with a recurving rim, and small grayware bowls with lateral spouts. No neck-banded jars or sherds were obtained and no orange or red ware occurred. The black-on-white decorated ware consisted of deep, hemispherical bowl forms with traditional Basketmaker designs. Motifs sparcely cover vessel walls either radiating upward from a small circle in the bottom of the bowl or appearing in opposing pairs. Design elements include dots between lines, flags, parallel zigzag lines, repeated Z's as in basketry stitching, ticked lines, and several solid triangles. A range˜ of tree-ring dates clustering largely between A.D. 376 and 676 as well as associated architectural features confirm the Basketmaker III horizon.

In comparison, the Durango South collections exhibit consistently later forms. The Durango South seed jars are short and thick, the medium sized jars have short straight necks and rounder bodies with relatively high shoulders, and the bowls, both plain and decorated, are shallow. The presence of one small Moccasin Gray neck banded and three Abajo Orange Ware sherds on the floor suggest a terminal Basketmaker III occupation at Durango South rather than the earlier Basketmaker III occupation at Yellow Jacket. Again the six tree-ring dates at Durango South, clustered between A.D. 774 and 776, support the ceramic evidence.

The Mesa Verde District

Mesa Verde: O'Bryan (1950) recognized as distinctive the pottery first found but not named by Morris in Obelisk, Broken Flute and other caves in the Red Rock Valley, northeastern Arizona (Morris 1936:35-6). Some pottery from O'Bryan's Mesa Verde Site 145 and from Step House exhibited the same characteristics (O'Bryan 1950:91). He gave it a local name, Twin Trees Plain and Twin Trees Black-on-white, until positive identification could be made and its proper relationship to other types determined. Abel (1955) revised the description of this type. He compares it to, and positively identifies it as a polished counterpart of Chapin Black-on-white, La Plata Black-on-white, and Lino Black-on-gray (Abel 1955, Ware 12A Type 2 and Ware 10A Type 2).

Vessel forms from O'Bryan's Mesa Verde Four Corners phase of Basketmaker III Grayware include spherical seed jars of various sizes and short necked jars with slightly outcurving rims. These forms occur in both Lino Gray and Twin Trees Plain. The Durango South collection did not include a polished. form of the Basketmaker seed jar although it did produce jars with slightly outcurving rims (Vessels 14 and 21, Figs. 48a and 45e).

Badger House: All locally made pottery types are represented from excavations in the three Badger House Community sites, providing a look at the entire spectrum of the Mesa Verde ceramic industry (Hayes and Lancaster 1975:98).

Hayes and Lancaster suggest that the artistic imagination of the potter is expressed in the wide range of forms found in Chapin Gray, the culinary pottery of Basketmaker III and Pueblo I periods. Because of the large amount of material from the continuous series of dated dwellings, minor changes and tendencies from early to late become particularly significant (1975:99). This affords contrasts and comparisons with other sites.

Polished Chapin Gray diminishes in popularity as the frequency of painted vessels increases (1975:100). However Hayes and Lancaster do not correlate surface polishing with the use of slip in the decorated ware. These are both evolutionary developments.

Neckless squash pots are the most popular Chapin Gray form in Basketmaker III, and as their numbers diminished other jar forms increased. Three Basketmaker III jar shapes are reported: large ollas with narrow mouth and high neck; squat wide-mouthed jars with short necks and rims that flare slightly outward; and subspherical, neckless squash pots with incurved rims and rounded lips. These jars from the pithouse were all slightly greater in diameter than in height and rim diameter was a little over half as wide as the maximum diameter of the pot (1975:101). Only one squash pot was found in an early Pueblo I house and it is a miniature.

The wide-mouthed jars from the early Pueblo I houses at Badger House are slightly larger than the Basketmaker jars, and all have a short straight neck and straight unflared rim. By late Pueblo I, jars are higher than wide with high necks and are identical in shape to the contemporary Moccasin Gray jars

(1975:100). Hayes and Lancaster report that the narrow-necked ollas were apparently equally important early and late. Those of Basketmaker provenience run slightly larger than later ones and tend to be globular with straight neck and unflared rim. The later jars tend to have a rounded well-defined shoulder near the midpoint of the body, most often with a pair of horizontally placed handles. The neck tends to be higher and is often tapered toward the mouth (1975:100). No pitchers were found in the pithouses and only one was recovered from the early Pueblo I houses.

Hayes and Lancaster state that stylized eccentricities, especially bird forms, appeared in the early Anasazi phases with the highest frequencies of both sherds and pots occurring in late Pueblo I (1975:102). Lateral spouted bowls were also reported.

Bowl shapes range from nearly perfect hemispheres to steep sided and flat bottomed shapes with some light polishing on one or both surfaces. Chapin Gray ladles were not numerous at either location; however broken ladle handles show a diversity not repeated in any other pottery type (1975:102). Both in total numbers and in the numbers of styles exhibited, handles are scarce in the earliest components and become increasingly common and varied through late Pueblo I. This range of variation also holds true for lug handles from Badger House Community.

Isolation of Moccasin Gray as a type depends on the surface treatment of leaving the fillets of the vessel neck unobliterated. Whole or restorable Moccasin Gray jars were found in Pueblo I houses at Badger House Community. Aside from one narrow-necked olla, all Moccasin Gray vessels from Badger House were wide-mouthed jars with short neck and straight unflared rim. By late Pueblo I these jars are higher than wide with high necks. Eighty per cent of the jars have from four to six neck fillets, most frequently six. These fillets or coils usually remain just as they are applied to the vessel as it was built up with each roll of clay (1975:103).

The decorated Basketmaker III - Pueblo I pottery from Badger House Community is of two types with Chapin Black-on-white earlier, and Piedra Black-on-white later (1975:111). Both types consist of Chapin Gray pottery with painted decoration. The two types are primarily distinguished by their styles of design with an increased refinement in the later type. Although the earliest and the latest representatives of these two types are clearly definable, many sherds could only be classified as Basketmaker III - Pueblo I black-on-white. According to Hayes and Lancaster, unusually high polish on both surfaces is a quality of Piedra Black-on-white (1975:112). They also state:

> Piedra Black-on-white differs from the earlier Chapin Black-on white notably in the gradual change in the placement of design from one that radiates from the center of the bowl to one dependant from the rim. Layout is frequently from a band or pattern below the rim but often employs the same simple elements (1975:114).

Only Chapin Black-on-white sherds were associated with the floors at Sites 1644 and 1676, both Basketmaker pithouse sites of the 7th century. Piedra Black-on-white first appears on the surface at House 3, Site 1676, and probably began to develop between A.D. 700 and 750 at Badger House.

The greatest difference between the grayware ceramics at Durango South and at Badger House Community is in the frequency of Moccasin Gray. Fifty-eight whole or restorable vessels of this type came from the houses at Badger House Community whereas there was a single specimen from Durango South. This jar had only three rings around the neck, while the Badger House jars had five or six.

The most popular form found at Badger House Basketmaker pithouses was a variety of neckless squash pot. These diminished in number as other jar forms increased. In contrast, squash pots from Durango South were squat and heavy and represented only 7% of forms observed.

Bowl shapes from both sites range from shallow to steep sided with flat bottoms although there is a tendency to shallowness in the Durango South collection. Both display light surface polishing but the Durango South bowls show more interior than exterior polish. Designs on the Durango South material radiate from the center of the bowl. Only one layout emphasizes elements pendant from the rim. None of the Durango South bowl design layouts are in the form of bands below the rim, although many of the same design elements are used. There is a definite foreshadowing of Pueblo I in the polishing and in the slightly more elaborate design on vessels from the upper levels of 5LP111 Feature 2 at Durango South (Vessels 31, 32 and 35a, Figs. 50e, 50f and 48d).

Wetherill Mesa Basketmaker Salvage Sites: Eighty-five per cent of the total yield of 3,273 potsherds from the Wetherill Mesa Basketmaker salvage sites as discussed by Birkedal (1976) were Chapin Gray. Seed jars and wide-mouthed jars with short necks as well as small spouted jars are the most common forms. Chapin Black-on-white is the most common decorated type represented in the various collections.

Although all of the Chapin Black-on-white bowls are decorated with mineral paint, 15 potsherds or 17% of the total collection show vitrified or glaze paint. All of these came from the fill of MV1940. Birkedal reports that cubes of galena were recovered from Bin 1 at the same site (1976:217). According to Shepard (1968:46), galena commonly served as a source of the lead sulfide which was used in the production of the Basketmaker III glaze paint.

Birkedal also states that the use of lead glaze paint in the decoration of Chapin Black-on-white is probably of temporal significance (1976:225). He continues:

The high incidence of lead glaze paint in the pottery collection from the late pithouse (MV1940) fits well with Shepard's observation that the use of intentional glaze paint was a short-lived phenomenon associated with late Basketmaker III occupations (Shepard 1968:46). Like their contemporaries in the Durango District, some of the late Basketmaker III groups of the Mesa Verde also must have been experimenting with this unique decorative technique (1976:226).

Except for variation in temper, there are similarities between Wetherill Mesa Salvage Project ceramics and Durango South ceramics. The forms of the pitchers and bowls from the two areas are alike. Pitchers have handles attached at rim and body, and bowls tend to be shallow. Of the ten photographed vessels in Birkedal's report, the greatest variations are in the seed jar form. Those from Durango South are short and thick; whereas the illustrated vessels from the Wetherill Mesa Salvage Project are larger, more hemispherical, and with consistently thinner walls (1976:231-232).

The Durango District

Within the Durango District, Carlson's (1963) report on Earl Morris' Basketmaker III sites is the only published report. The Durango South and the Hidden Valley ceramics are basically similar with predominantly sand temper and a quantity of glaze paints used on the decorated ware. Limited numbers

of vessel forms and the presence of polished surfaces on the majority of the Durango South decorated bowls are the major differences between the two collections. Exuberance of forms is a hallmark of Pueblo I pottery. The conservatism of the Durango South potter regarding form contrasts with the concern for improved decorative surface, a factor that indicates a transition between Basketmaker and Pueblo I culture periods.

Conclusions

Comparison of the Durango South material with ceramic collections from other site reports in this study emphasizes physical and morphological characteristics plus design motifs and layouts. These criteria allow the interpretation of changes on a temporal and developmental scale. Since the Lino tradition is continuous through Basketmaker III and Pueblo I cultural periods, making a clear distinction difficult, a review of tendencies from both periods follows:

Basketmaker III emphasis can be observed in the narrow range of forms. At Durango South no ladles or ladle handles, and no eccentricities such as bird-shaped, submarine, or double necked vessels were recovered. Neither were elbow-shaped pipes or vessels with lateral handles observed. The form most representative of Pueblo I ceramics, the gourd-shaped pitcher, was also absent, as were decorated jar sherds. One form characteristic of Basketmaker III was the large olla. The two specimens from the floor of 5LP110 Feature 1 had medium length necks and higher shoulders and the strap handles were placed relatively higher on the body than in the later Pueblo I counterpart, Moccasin Gray. Although there was some interior polishing of bowls, polishing was not noticeable on the exteriors.

Pueblo I sites have yielded few spherical seed jars, a shape that is the hallmark of the earlier Basketmaker III period and that is present at Durango South. The bowls in the Durango South collection are shallow and in several instances the design covers a greater percentage of the interior surface area. For jars, the short straight neck and globular body shape are Pueblo I attributes. The medium sized jar with curved handle from 5LP110 (Vessel 15, Fig. 47a) can be counted as a forerunner of the gourd-shaped jar, a characteristic of the later period.

101

The majority of the pottery from Durango South is derived from very near the Basketmaker III-Pueblo I transition. The large percentages of Basketmaker types (Lino and Twin Trees) as opposed to very small percentages of Pueblo I types (Moccasin Gray and Abajo Red-on-orange) indicate a late Basketmaker occupation. The one neck-banded jar of the entire collection plus the total absence of red ware and the minimal presence of orangeware suggests a terminal date for the occupation of about A.D. 800. Since construction based on tree-ring dates centered around A.D. 775, the span of occupation at Durango South was from A.D. 775 to around A.D. 800.

Recognition of the degree of overlap of attributes within the types increases the flexibility of the typology. Terminal or near-transitional periods, or those denoting change are the most interesting but often the most challenging to analyze. The intention of this paper in part has been to define and clarify the sequence of change between Basketmaker III and Pueblo I periods in the Durango District.

Carlson's description summarizes the development of Basketmaker ceramics in this part of the Southwest.

In general, the spread is from west to east with Lino Gray and Lino Black-on-gray or their varieties appearing earlier in northeastern Arizona and later in Colorado and northern New Mexico on a gently sloping temporal horizon. Varieties of both types seem to last later in the latter area also, and may have been diffusing eastward even as they were being superseded by later types in the west (1963:50-51).

Acknowledgments

The knowledgeable comments and critical advice of Joe Ben Wheat of the University of Colorado Museum and the use of comparative material from that museum was greatly appreciated. Acknowledgement is also made to A.J. Lindsay and Marsha Gallagher of the Museum of Northern Arizona, Flagstaff; to Thomas Windes and Marcia Truell of the Chaco Research Center, Albuquerque; to Betty Toulouse of the Laboratory of Anthropology, Santa Fe; and to Sarah Nelson and Paul Nickens of the University of Denver for access to comparative ceramic collections.

Perishables

by Signa Larralde

Perishable materials at Durango South include a small fragment of cordage, a knot, plaited sandal or matting fragments, and the charred base of a coiled basket. All were recovered near the northeast wall of the pithouse, 5LP110 (Fig. 54). No rims or selvages were present on any of the fragments. Materials from the cordage, fragment, the knot and the sandal or matting fragments cannot be identified as to animal or bast origin due to charring. Small bits of charcoal are present throughout the sample.

The one ply S-twist black cordage fragment is 10mm long and 1mm in diameter. The knot appears to be a half hitch tied with 2 ply Z-twist cordage; each ply shows a slight S-twist. Dimensions of the knot are 22mm by 8mm by 8mm.

Sandal or matting fragments are all coated with mud on one side and charred on the other, one large fragment measures 15.2 cm by 7.9 cm. Six fragments which may have all been part of the same object range in size from 5.6 cm by 4.2 cm to 3.1 cm by 2.0 cm with smaller pieces. The construction technique for all sandal or matting fragments is over-2-under-2 twill plaiting (Fig. 56), with each member 3 to 4 mm wide. The hairlike fibers in the members are unspun. A "twilled tule sandal" from a Basketmaker II site near Durango (Morris and Burgh 1954:Fig. 33) exhibits the same construction technique; since there are selvages on this sandal, the technique can be identified as flat braiding.

The basketry fragment is comprised of a circular starting knot 10mm in diameter, with 11 coils from the center knot to the edge at the widest point and two coils at the narrowest point. Greatest width of the fragment is 7.2 cm; greatest length is 8.6 cm. The slightly convex fragment is encrusted with mud and is badly charred. Width of each coil is 3 to 5mm; width of each splint is 1.5 to 2.4 mm. Splints are missing over most of the basket surface; in the one small area where they are present, there are five splints per centimeter. Stitches are interlocked and slant slightly to the right, indicating direction of work from left to right. The basket appears to have been very finely woven. Although both rods and grass-like materials seem to be present, charring and absence of splints prevents determination of foundation construction.

Morris and Burgh (1941:12-13) describe the technique of close coiling with uninterlocked stitches and two-rod-and-bundle bunched foundation as typical of Basketmaker III sites. Carlson (1963:43) suggests this construction technique for basketry from Basketmaker III sites near Durango on the basis of basketry impressions on ceramics. On the strength of these reports, one could postulate that the Durango South basket was similarly constructed.

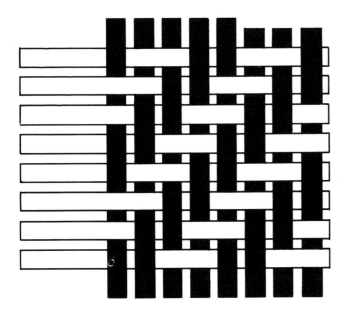

Figure 56. Over-2-under-2 twill plaiting used in construction of sandal or matting fragments at 5LP110.

Shell Beads

by
Barbara Love-dePeyer

A total of 49 shell beads was recovered from the two sites. Twenty beads were found scattered throughout the cist containing Burials 2 and 3, north of the pithouse at 5LP110. These shells may have been part of either or both burials. Encircling the wrist of the skeleton in Burial 3 was a bracelet composed of 27 shells (Fig. 57a), although no cordage remained to link them. Two well preserved, isolated shells (Fig. 57b) were recovered from the lower fill near the western bench of the pithouse, 5LP111 Feature 2.

All of the shells were identified as *Olivella* by S.K. Wu of the University of Colorado Museum. Further species identification was not possible, since species distinctions within the *Olivella* genus are based largely on color and these shells had been whitened by weathering. The shells from 5LP111 showed only superficial erosional action, which removed the color but left a hard glossy surface. The shells found at 5LP110, however, had been more severely eroded, as Tower describes (1945:4),

where loss of color and surface detail leaves a chalky, friable shell. Wu suggested that the shells probably came from the southern California or Baja coasts.This determination is supported by studies of shell trade routes in the Southwest (Tower 1945:22-23).

All of the shells were of similar size (ranging from 11-14mm in length and from 6-9mm in width) and had been modified to permit stringing. The closed spire on each shell had been carefully cut or ground off to leave a circular opening (Fig. 57c). Some of the shells were polished on both ends as a result of wear. Morris and Burgh (1954:71) indicate that long strings of olivellas were worn as necklaces, while shorter strands, such as those found at 5LP110, were used as bracelets.

Modification Attributes of Bone Tools From Durango South

by
John D. Gooding

The sample of 51 bone tools recorded and analyzed from the excavations at Durango South includes 19 specimens from 5LP110 and 32 from 5LP111 (Table 8). The total number of worked bone artifacts, which represents 12% of the nonceramic tools, also includes antler and modified bone discarded as waste in the tool manufacturing process. A great majority of the bone tools were located in lower fill or on the floor of the large pit structures.

The scope of this study is limited to classification of tool types and ornamental bone on the basis of wear patterns observed through microscopic inspection. Since the assemblage of bone tools from Durango South is a comparatively large Basketmaker III collection from the Northern San Juan Region (Lancaster and Pinkley 1954:53; Lancaster and Watson 1954:14; Hayes and Lancaster 1975:6-65; Hayes and Lancaster 1968:68; Hallisey 1972:13; Nordby and Breternitz 1972:27; Hibbets 1976:99-100; Carlson 1963:42; Birkedal 1976:294-303), it provides a relatively complete picture of preferred species, skeletal elements and bone portions (Tables 7 and 8) as well as manufacturing

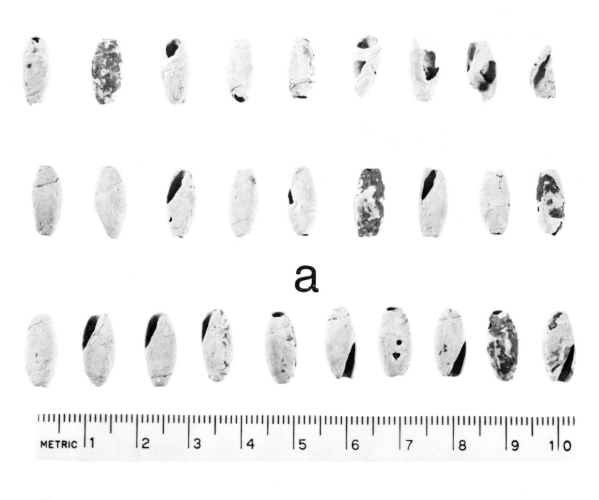

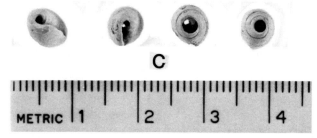

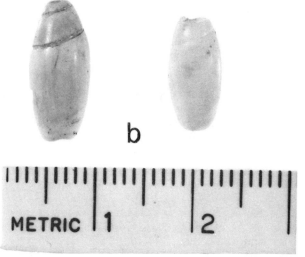

Figure 57.   a - Shells from bracelet found with Burial 3, 5LP110; b - Shells from 5LP111 Feature 1; c - Modifications on ends of shells.

Table 7. Species Represented in the Bone Tool Assemblage

Species	Common name	#	%
Odocoileus hemionus	mule deer	29	58%
Canis familaris/ latrans	dog or coyote	8	16%
Meleagris gallopavo	wild turkey	3	6%
Cervis canadensis	wapiti	2	4%
Canis lupus	gray wolf	2	4%
Sylvilagus audubonii/ nuttallii	cottontail	1	2%
Lepus townsendii	jackrabbit	2	4%
Ursus americanus	black bear	1	2%
unidentifiable		2	4%
Total Assemblage			100%

techniques and functional attributes. The collection contrasts with those from later Anasazi occupations in the region.

Awls are the most common bone tools at Durango South. The descriptive techniques for bone awls have been as diverse as the number of publications in which they have been discussed. However, this discussion will concentrate on differences and similarities between awls from 5LP110 and 5LP111 and other assemblages.

The tool category "bone awl" was first established by Kidder (1932:203) and is still extremely useful since the classes within the category are based on gross morphological attributes. However, the selection of specific skeletal elements as materials for tools does not necessarily result in predictable wear patterns; nor do some frequently described general morphological attributes, e.g. grinding of the articular head, bear a relationship to the function of the tool. Common definitions for awls concentrate on their use as "general" piercing tools (Kidder 1932:203; Morris 1939:119; Di Peso 1956:412; Kluckhohn et al 1971:304; Reed 1975:60). The implication is that awls are multifunctional tools and therefore each tool should display a wide range of wear patterns. Microscopic wear analysis of the bone awls from Durango **South** does not support this definition. On the contrary, the pointed bone tools commonly classified as awls can be divided into eight functional tool classes, seven of which display only occasional secondary wear. The true awls in this sample do not display all or even most of

the 16 attributes of wear one would expect to find on a "general" multipurpose piercing tool.

Ahler (1971:53) has discussed an extremely important point in reference to chipped stone tool classes at Rogers Shelter: the disparity between formal and functional artifact classes. This same point probably applies to the artifact class of bone awls. Creation of the wear patterns discussed here must be verified through experimental studies on bone tools. However, distinct types of wear can be identified and should be recognized as the result of specific functional activities.

Analytical Techniques

The bone and antler tools in the assemblage were divided into the gross categories of ornamental bone, antler tools, miscellaneous bone tools and bone awls or pointed bone tools. Each gross category was then subdivided into specific functional categories on the basis of microscopic inspection at powers 6.3x, 10x, 16x and 25x. The gross category that seemed to have the widest functional diversity was the bone awls. Surfaces where wear was likely to occur were inspected. These include: tip, shaft interior, shaft margins, shaft exterior, and the articular head. The *tip* (Fig. 58a) is the worked point of the tool and is usually the most intensively modified. The portion of each tool that was classified as the tip was considered to be 10% of the overall tool length. The *shaft interior* (Fig. 58b) is the surface that was the original interior of the bone. After splitting the bone for tool manufacture and after the marrow and soft tissue are scraped from the center, the exposed interior of the bone forms a concave surface. Because of its shape, this surface is least prone to wear and exhibits few attributes of wear. The *shaft margin* (Fig. 58c) is the exposed edge of the cancellous tissue in the midsection of the bone. This exposed surface is the result of the splitting or fracturing of the bone. The margin usually displays the incision lines from the splitting process. The *shaft exterior* (Fig. 58d) is the original exterior surface of the bone. The *articular head* (Fig. 58e) is the point of articulation of either the proximal or distal end of the bone.

Table 9 presents the range of wear patterns observed on the awls. Wear was recorded on the basis of presence or absence. Predominance of a specific type of wear, or two or more complementary wear attributes, were deemed sufficient for a tool to be placed into one of the eight

Table 8. Bone Artifact Inventory*

Genus	Provenience	Element	Artifact	Portion	Comments**
5LP110 Feature 1					
Odocoileus	No. 24 NE L3	metatarsal	punch	D	Ad, ½ saggital cut, many faint scratch marks,Lt 76.2, B across epiphysis 23.6
Odocoileus	No. 30 FS 67 SW L3		drill	D	Ad, highly polished, many scratch marks, Lt 59
cf Odocoileus	No. 63 FS 117 SE L3	cf metapodial	drill	Ms	scratch marks around edges, burned, Lt 60.3
cf Odocoileus	No. 64 FS 120 SE L3	cf metapodial	drill	Ms	tip absent, burned, Lt 79.5
Odocoileus	No. 69 SE L3 No. 80 SW L2	metapodial, 2 parts	awl	D	Juv, distal epiphysis lost, tip absent, burned, GLt 136.3
Odocoileus	No. 102 FS 153 SW L4	antler 14+ small frags	wrench	frag	GLt 97.6, GB 79.5
cf Cervus	No. 103 FS 17 SW L4	antler	shaft		burned, GLt 330
Canis	No. 194 FS 64 SE L4	MT III	bead refuse	LP	Ad, scratch marks, scorched, end beveled, Lt 48.6, B 11.6
cf Odocoileus	No. 106 SE L3	cf metapodial	awl frag	Ms	burned, Lt 19.6
Meleagris	No. 107 SE L3	tibiotarsus	punctured shaft	Ms	hole at one end, Lt 124.6
Odocoileus	No. 108 FS 109 SW L3	antler	handle	frag	burned, GLt 150,GB 34
cf Odocoileus	No. 109 SW L2		awl frag		burned, Lt 22.6
Lepus	No. 110 FS 22 SF 1 NW L4	tibia	worked?	RP	Ad, proximal end hollowed out, fibula broken off, Lt 81.4, PB 16.2
cf Lepus	No. 111 Test Trench A	long bone	bead frag	Ms	polished, end is incised. Lt 19.3, GB 7.1
5LP110 Feature 2					
Odocoileus	No. 1 FS 26 6S-15E	long bone	spatulate awl	Ms	Lt, 181
Meleagris	No. 1 FS 33 12S-15E	long bone	bead frag	Ms	deeply incised Lt 28
cf Odocoileus	No. 1 FS 6 15S-13E	cf tibia	pin	Ms	cut from shaft, Lt 70.7
Indet	No.1 FS 76 17S-14E		awl frag		
cf Odocoileus	No. 1 FS 80 18S-14E	cf tibia	bodkin	Ms	same curvature as tibia, Lt 140.4

*Measurements are in millimeters   **List of abbreviations in appendix.

Table 8, cont'd. Bone Artifact Inventory

Genus	Provenience	Element	Artifact	Portion	Comments
5LP111 Feature 1					
Meleagris	No. 46 L3	cf tibiotarsus	bead	Ms	shaft slightly curved, Lt 63
Odocoileus	No. 48 L2	antler	flaker	frag	end rounded, Lt 104
cf *Canis*	No. 49 L2	long bone	bead frag	Ms	scratch marks, end beveled, Lt 24
5LP111 Feature 2					
Odocoileus	No.3 FS 3 16S-26E L4	metatarsal	dagger	D	Juv, epiphysis distinct, Lt 162
Odocoileus	No. 4 FS 4 16S-26E L4	metatarsal	matting tool	D	Juv, epiphysis distinct, Lt 154
Odocoileus	No. 5 FS 5 16S-26E L4	metapodial	punch	P	Lt 142.8
Odocoileus	No. 6 FS 7 16S-30E L4	metapodial	dagger	Ms	Lt 111
Odocoileus	No. 8 FS 8 14S-26E L4	tibia	punch	D	Ad, Lt 98.2
Odocoileus	No. 10 FS 19 14S-26E L3	metapodial	awl	D	Ad, Lt 209
Odocoileus	No. 11 W L3	long bone	drill	Ms	Lt 81
Odocoileus	No. 12 FS 22 17S-24E L4	metapodial	drill	Ms	Lt 112.7
Odocoileus	No. 13 FS 23 17S-25E L4	metapodial	punch	Ms	Lt 114.5
Odocoileus	No. 20 FS 26 S L2	antler	rubbing tool	basal	basal ring eliminated close to skull, Lt 88.2
Odocoileus	No. 25 FS 27 17S-24E L4	metapodial	awl	P	Juv, epiphysis lost Lt, 102.5
Odocoileus	No. 26 FS 28 17S-24E L4	tibia	awl	D	Ad, many scratch marks, Lt 169
Odocoileus	No. 27 FS 31 16S-25E L4	tibia	reamer	D	Ad, Lt 157
cf *Canis*	No. 28 FS 33 16S-25E L4	long bone	bead	Ms	Lt 33, GB 15.4
Ursus	No. 29 FS 34 16S-25E L4	lower canine	bead pendant	W	worn GLt 52, alveolar Lt 13.6, alveolar B 9.0
cf*Canis*	No. 31 FS 32 16S-25E L4	long bone	bead	Ms	GLt 46, GB 12.1
cf *Canis*	No. 35 FS 39 16S-25E L4	long bone	bead	Ms	Lt 28.6, GB 13

Table 8, cont'd. Bone Artifact Inventory

Genus	Provenience	Element	Artifact	Portion	Comments
	**5LP111 Feature 2, cont'd.**
cf *Canis*	No. 36 FS 40 16S-25E L4		bead	Ms	Lt 28.4, GB 13.6
Canis	No. 37 FS 45 17S-25E L4	tibia	tinkler	LD	Ad, awl with hole on interior surface, Lt 86.8
cf *Canis*	No. 41 N L4	long bone	drill	Ms	Lt 48
cf *Canis*	No. 51 N L3	fibula	utilized	Ms	Lt 132
cf *Cervus*	No. 113 E L2	antler	rubbing tool		Rounded end shows wear. GLt 91.2
cf *Odocoileus*	No. 114 E L2	tibia	flaker	Ms	worked from inside, Lt 200
Odocoileus	No. 115 S L4	antler	rubbing tool	Ms	spike, Lt 78
Indet	No. 117 20S-26E L4		awl frags	Ms	5 + small frags (1 scorched), Lt 42.8
cf *Odocoileus*	No. 118 L3	long bone	awl	Ms	spongy, Lt 81.3
cf *Canis*	FS 88 E L4	cf radius	bead frag	Ms	end beveled, Lt 36.7
cf *Sylvilagus*	No. 119 Test Pit B	long bone	bead	Ms	Lt 15.5, B 5.3

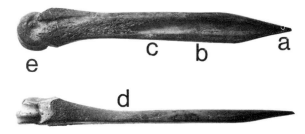

Figure 58. Two views of split deer metatarsal tool. Note articular head (a), shaft exterior (b), shaft margin (c), location of shaft interior (d), and anterior-posterior trimming of the tip (e).

Figure 59. Incising grooves in the cancellous tissue, the first step in the splitting process.

Figure 60. Tibia displays the spiral fracture type of breakage. Polish and attrition flakes along edge suggest that this tool functioned as a reamer.

Table 9. Wear Attributes Of Polished Bone Tools

Specimen Number	General Features				Tip							Tip Striations						Shaft Interior Striations								Shaft Margins Striations										Shaft Exterior Striations									Articular Head					
	splinter	split	whole	burned	spiral fracture	anterior-posterior trim	ground	tip	attrition	polish	impact fracture	rotation	counter rotation	diagonal	cross-hatch	longitudinal	transverse	polish	attrition	rotation	counter rotation	diagonal	cross-hatch	longitudinal	transverse	incised	ground	polish	attrition	rotation	counter rotation	diagonal	cross-hatch	longitudinal	transverse	ground	polish	attrition	rotation	counter rotation	diagonal	cross-hatch	longitudinal	transverse	absent	split	ground	battered	unmodified	polish
5LP110 Feature 1																																																		
No. 24		x				x	x	x	x		x		x													x	x	x	x			x		x	x		x				x		x			x				x
No. 30	x	x		x		x	x	x	x	x	x	x						x		x	x				x			x	x	x	x						x	x	x		x		x			x				
No. 63	x	x		x	x	x	x	x			x							x		x		x		x	x	x	x	x				x					x								x					
No. 64	x	x		x		x	x	x	x		x							x		x		x			x	x	x	x				x					x						x		x					
Nos. 69 and 80		x		x		x																						x																		x				
No. 106		x		x														x										x									x								x	x				
No. 109		x		x																							x	x	x			x					x	x			x		x		x					
5LP110 Feature 2																																																		
No. 1 FS 26	x	x			x				x											x		x		x		x		x									x	x			x				x					
No. 1 FS 76		x							x											x		x						x	x								x				x				x					
No. 1 FS 80	x	x			x				x	x								x								x	x	x								x	x	x			x		x			x				
No. 1 FS 6	x	x							x									x										x								x	x	x								x				
5LP111 Feature 2																																																		
No. 3 FS 3		x			x	x	x	x	x	x				x	x						x					x	x	x				x		x	x		x	x			x		x	x		x				x
No. 4 FS 4		x			x	x	x	x	x	x				x							x					x	x	x		x		x		x	x		x	x			x		x			x				
No. 5 FS 5		x			x	x	x	x	x	x		x									x					x	x	x				x		x			x	x					x			x				
No. 6 FS 7		x			x	x	x	x	x	x		x			x							x				x	x	x				x			x		x	x					x			x				
No. 8 FS 8		x			x	x	x	x	x	x								x								x	x	x				x					x				x		x			x				
No. 10 FS 19		x			x	x	x	x	x				x	x		x				x		x				x	x	x						x			x	x	x			x		x		x				x
No. 11	x	x			x	x	x	x	x			x								x					x	x	x					x					x	x					x							
No. 12 FS 22		x				x	x	x	x											x						x	x	x	x			x				x	x	x			x		x		x				
No. 13 FS 23		x				x	x		x	x		x		x						x						x	x	x				x				x	x				x		x		x				
No. 25 FS 27		x				x		x	x	x								x								x	x	x								x	x				x		x		x				
No. 26 FS 28		x				x			x	x	x									x						x	x	x	x				x			x	x	x			x	x			x				
No. 27 FS 31	x	x					x	x	x	x	x	x						x		x						x	x	x	x							x	x	x			x	x			x				
No. 41	x						x	x	x		x	x		x	x					x	x					x	x	x	x		x					x	x	x		x		x								
No. 117		x				x	x	x	x																		x	x	x					x			x							x		x				
No. 118		x				x	x	x	x		x	x		x	x					x						x	x	x	x					x	x		x					x		x	x		x				

x = presence

subgroups of pointed bone tools. Some of the specimens were more heavily worn than others and were thus easier to define. Certain types of wear that are commonly associated with pointed bone tools were not observed in this collection. Transverse grooves on the shaft of awls, attributed to the weaving process in other published reports (Rohn 1971:226) are not a characteristic of the tools here. This may be a result of the limited size of the sample but it does correlate with the hypothesis that weaving tools do not appear in the Northern San Juan Region until Pueblo II times (Hayes and Lancaster 1975:169).

Because of the small sample size, statistical tests were not attempted. A total of 16 attributes resulting from either the manufacture or function of the tool are tabulated in Table 9 and described below.

Manufacturing Attributes

Manufacturing attributes must be discussed separately from functional attributes because the manufacturing process for various tools is largely determined by the morphological characteristics of the bone. Specific manufacturing processes for pointed bone tools leave distinctive wear patterns that could be confused with functional attributes.

Splitting: The splitting process is the most common production technique by which deer metatarsals are made into tools (Fig. 58). Wear from this process most often appears on metapodials. The technique is economical, since as many as four tools can be produced from a single bone. To produce a pointed bone tool, the anterior and posterior surfaces of the metatarsal are deeply incised (see next category) so that the bone can be split and quartered. The tip is then fashioned at the midsection end of the quartered remains. The product is a pointed bone tool of variable length that is concavo-convex in cross-section. This technique is common in the Northern San Juan Region: numerous tools of this type have been recorded along with "tool blanks" or whole metapodials that display deep incising lines but were never split (Swannack 1969:155; Kidder 1932:204).

Incising striations (Fig. 59): The first step in the splitting process leaves longitudinal grooves in the cancellous tissue on the anterior and posterior surfaces of the bone, which are easily seen on the margins of the completed tool. These grooves are distinguished from longitudinal wear striations by

ridge and groove patterns that extend from the articular head to the tip.

Spiral fracture (Fig. 60): Spiral fractures were the most common type of bone breakage in the prehistoric butchering process. Such fractures are common on fresh bone broken for the extraction of marrow (Bonnischen 1973). Spiral fractures can be produced by hammering on the bone with a chopper or hitting the bone over an anvil. This production technique does not require that the bone be split as part of the process. The fracture usually results in a tip that is round in cross section, descending into a blade edge along the fracture line. This technique has consequently been associated with the production of reamers (Rohn 1971:224).

Splintering (Fig. 61): Pointed bone tools manufactured from splinters have been defined by Kidder (1932:213) as "class C awls." Splintering is produced through the same technique as spiral fracture. If the hammer or anvil blow is very hard, the bone shatters, leaving a fragment pointed at one or both ends and requiring little further modification. This technique does not result in the incising lines indicative of splitting; the tool formed is usually in such fragmentary condition that the exact element is not identifiable. Previous classifications of splinter tools (Kidder 1932:213; Swannack 1969:151; Rohn 1971:224) distinguish between the presence or absence of the articular head. All discussions follow Kidder's lead in the interpretation that "such awls were evidently used only once or twice and then thrown aside" (1932:213). Analysis of the wear patterns on the splinters found at Durango South, however, suggests that they were not expediency tools. The absence of the articular head allowed the splinter to be hafted, probably to a long wooden shaft, and utilized as a drill. Note Figure 61 for haft and drill tip wear.

Burning (Fig. 62): Most of the bone awls recovered from 5LP110 Feature 1 were burned. This was first thought to be the result of the burning of the structure at abandonment. However, wear striations and polish on the tools suggest that the bone had been burned prior to use. It is difficult to assess how this would improve the quality of the tool. Burning may simply be a technique occasionally used in the manufacturing process to soften the bone and make it more workable, as suggested by Semenov (1964:145).

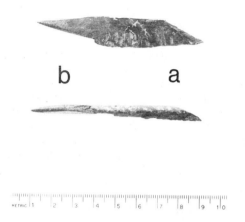

Figure 61. Pointed tool manufactured from bone splinter. Note haft scars (a) and rotation striations (b) on this hafted drill.

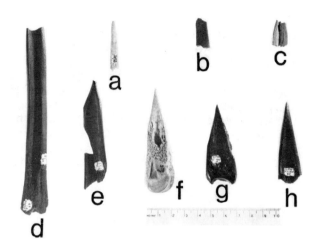

Figure 62. Pointed bone tools recovered from 5LP110 Feature 1. All but a and f were burned.

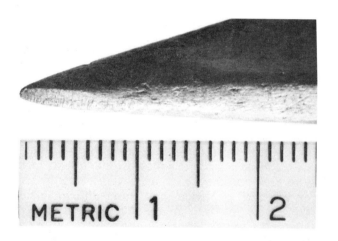

Figure 63. Tip of pointed bone tool displaying ground facet.

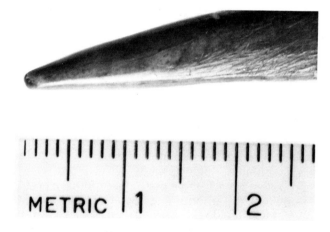

Figure 64. Tip of pointed bone tool displaying high polish. Note contrast to striations at right.

Anterior-posterior trimming (Fig. 58): This process is a technique of tip development that is unique to the split shaft variety of pointed bone tools. It is achieved through grinding the shaft margins from the anterior and posterior surfaces exposed at the split. This results in a flattened or oval tip (in cross-section) on the lateral or medial exterior surface of the midsection of the bone.

Grinding (Fig. 63): Aside from its use in anterior-posterior trimming, this technique is used in thinning of tips by abrading the interior surface. This may be a rejuvenation process as well as a

manufacturing process. The technique is evidenced by unidirectional striations on the interior side of the tip, probably achieved by a back and forth motion at a 45° angle to the long axis of the bone.

Functional Attributes

Functional attributes are those attributes that are the result of tool use and are the distinguishing characteristics in the determination of the function of the tool.

Polish (Fig. 64): This attribute is found on almost all the tools but is most distinct on pins, bodkins and punches. Polish is probably the result of use on soft material with low abrasive qualities. In some cases the surface is smoothed to a finish that can best be described as a sheen or luster.

Figure 65.   Tip displaying flake scar from impact fracture.

Impact fracture (Fig. 65): This attribute is a negative flake scar at the tip of the tool that is the result of the removal of a flake through sudden impact.

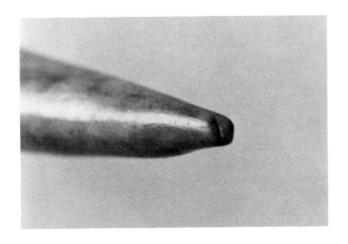

Figure 66.   Tip displaying flake scar from attrition.

Tip attrition (Fig. 66): This attribute is a negative flake scar at the tip of the tool resulting from the removal of a flake through regular wear or steady pressure.

Microscopic scratches on the surface of a bone tool are typically the result of abrasion against the surface on which the tool is being used. These include:

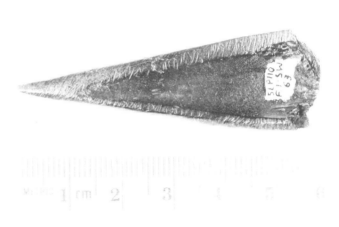

Figure 67.   Rotation striations from drill wear. Note spiral configuration of striations on first 15 mm of tip, suggesting unidirectional motion.

Rotation striations (Fig. 67): Striations are spirals approximately perpendicular (90° - 65°) to the long axis of the tool. This wear indicates a rotary motion rather than a piercing motion and suggests that the tool functioned as a drill.

Figure 68.   Counter-rotation striations from drill wear. Note bidirectional configuration separated by central ridge.

Counter-rotation striations (Fig. 68): Striations differ from rotation striations in that the spirals occur in both clockwise and counter-clockwise directions from the tip. They result from a reciprocal sideways motion of the tool.

Figure 71.   Longitudinal striations indicative of a direct thrust motion.

Longitudinal striations (Fig. 71): Longitudinal striations are approximately parallel to the long axis of the tool (15° to 0°) and are discontinuous. Striations would be caused by a direct thrust and are thus associated with punches and daggers.

Figure 69.   Diagonal striations typical of awl wear.

Diagonal striations (Fig. 69): Striations are generally diagonal (65° to 15°) to the long axis of the tool. They indicate a twisting and piercing motion that is commonly associated with the function of an awl.

Figure 72.   Transverse striations indicative of a reciprocal sideways motion.

Transverse striations (Fig. 72): Striations are generally perpendicular to the long axis of the tool but differ from rotation striations in reflecting a reciprocal sideways motion rather than a rotary motion.

Bone Tools

The bone tools have been placed in the categories described below; the first eight are functional categories of pointed bone tools.

Bone pin (Fig. 73c), one specimen. This tool was

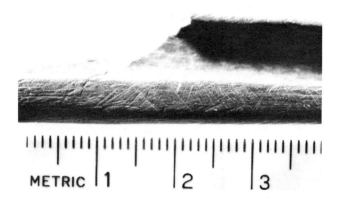

Figure 70.   Cross-hatch striations on shaft margin of awl.

Cross-hatch striations (Fig. 70): Cross-hatch striations occur when diagonal thrusting and rotation are both clockwise and counter-clockwise from the tip.

manufactured from a deer tibia ground into a cylinder. It is distinguished from a needle by the absence of the eye. A hinge fracture on the butt indicates that a portion of the original tool is absent. The surface wear is a uniform high polish.

Comparisons: Kidder 1932: Fig. 188b; Hayes and Lancaster 1975:Fig. 219c, d, e.

Bodkin (Fig. 73d), one specimen. This tool, also manufactured from a deer tibia, was shaped through a great deal of grinding. The eye was biconically drilled. Bodkins differ from those tools commonly classified as needles: bodkins are longer, more massive and have larger eyes. The surface wear is a uniform high polish. The lack of wear striations and the high polish on bodkins suggest that they were sewing implements for soft material.

Comparisons: Hayes and Lancaster 1975:Fig. 219a; Rohn 1971:Fig. 261 extreme left and extreme right; Swannack 1969:Fig. 149d, 151d, e.

Punches (Fig. 75f), four specimens. All specimens were manufactured from tibias and metapodials. They are characterized by tip attrition, high polish at the tip, and longitudinal striations on the shaft exterior and margins. There is occasional evidence of diagonal striations. These tools probably functioned to pierce holes in soft material with a direct thrust.

Comparisons: None published.

Daggers (Figs. 74 and 75d), two specimens. These tools can be distinguished from punches by wear patterns that reflect a greater force during use. Both specimens were manufactured from split metapodials with tips modified by anterior-posterior trimming. The characteristics of wear include negative flake scars from impact fractures, high polish on the margins and interior surfaces but little or no polish on the exterior surfaces. Longitudinal striations are the predominant wear on all surfaces at the midsection of the tools.

Comparison: Hayes and Lancaster 1975:168.

Drills (Fig. 61), six specimens. This tool category has often been grouped with the multipurpose category of awls but displays uniquely different wear patterns at the tip (Figs. 61, 67, 68), where the wear striations are perpendicular to the long axis of the tool. Under microscopic inspection, the striations are comparatively deep and close

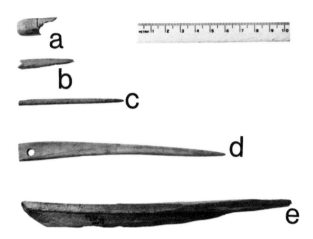

Figure 73. Bone artifacts from 5LP110 Feature 2: a - Bead fragment; b - Awl fragment; c - Pin; d - Bodkin; e - Spatulate awl.

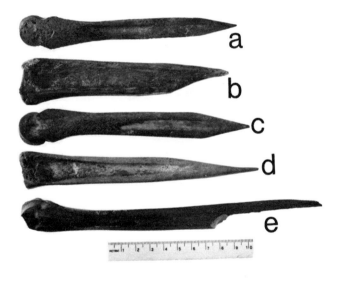

Figure 74. Pointed bone tools from 5LP111: a - Matting tool; b - Reamer; c - Dagger; d - Awl; e - Awl.

115

Figure 75. Pointed bone tools from 5LP111: a - Punch; b - Punch; c - Drill; d - Dagger; e - Awl; f - Punch; g - Tinkler-awl; h - Awl; i - Drill; j - Drill.

together, in contrast to awls (see below). Drills are generally manufactured from splinters and would have been only marginally useful as hand held tools. It is obvious from the hafting scars on the exterior surfaces (Fig. 61a), that at least some if not all of the specimens were hafted on stick shafts and were probably used as bow drills or stick drills. One tool shows rotation striations; the other shows counter-rotation striations. This would suggest that the specimen in Figure 67 was used in a different kind of drilling action than the specimen in Figure 68. It is impossible to test whether these wear patterns are the result of the method of drilling or of the material being drilled.

Comparisons: None published.

Reamer (Fig. 60), one specimen. Until recently (Rohn 1971:224) this tool category was classed with the general category of awls. However, manufacturing technique and wear patterns suggest that the category represents a specific-function tool, perhaps used for enlarging holes. The specimen in Figure 60 was manufactured incorporating the spiral fracture of a deer tibia and displays a great deal of wear along the fracture line. The wear patterns suggest a rotation motion quite different from that of drills. This tool is presumed to have been hand held, because of its size. The tip exhibits a high polish over two impact fractures. Obviously a great deal of force has been applied to the tool at some time, but the polish suggests that it was used predominantly on soft materials. The polish extends from the tip back for the entire length

of the fracture. The fracture margin behind the tip displays attrition flakes and striations, suggesting that at various times this tool may have been used on hard or abrasive materials.

Comparisons: Rohn 1971:Fig. 260.

Matting Tool (Fig. 72), one specimen. The manufacturing technique resembles that of many awls and daggers. This tool is unique in exhibiting uniform transverse striations. At the tip there is an attrition flake scar and high polish. All other wear on the tool is comprised of transverse striations on the interior and exterior surfaces of the shaft. This wear is extremely heavy, resulting in a tool that is flatter in cross-section than other tools manufactured in the same way.

Comparisons: Reed 1975:68.

Awls (Fig. 58), ten specimens. After the seven other functional tool types were sorted out, the remaining ten pointed bone tools could justifiably be classed as awls. The awls therefore comprise 38% of the pointed bone tools. They display characteristics of the whole range of wear patterns. In the Durango South collection, awls are usually made from deer but two exceptions were manufactured from canid long bones: a tip fragment, and a tibia tinkler utilized briefly as an awl. Tip manufacture was most commonly anterior-posterior trimming. In terms of wear, polish at the tip is the most common attribute. Shaft margins are most often characterized by diagonal striations, and longitudinal striations are frequent on shaft exteriors. Presence or absence of the articular head was not a critical factor in the distinction of this tool class. It is possible that in previous classifications (Kidder 1932:202; Swannack 1969:150) which used this characteristic to distinguish awl types, the lack of epiphysial fusion and the resultant lack of an articular head was confused with the possibility of the head being ground off. None of the specimens at Durango South exhibited grinding of the articular head. Nor did any of the specimens exhibit any wear on the articular head beyond occasional high polish. Consequently the presence or absence of the articular head on any pointed bone tool is most likely a function of the manufacturing technique and the age of the animal from which it is taken rather than of wear associated with the awls. The only pointed bone tool class where the absence of the articular head may be a critical functional factor is the drills. Only one specimen in six from that class had retained an articular head.

Comparisons: There are undoubtedly true awls in the collections represented by all references cited in this discussion; however, as with all other functional categories, the tools would have to be examined for wear patterns before these could be identified.

Previous excavations in the Northern San Juan Region have recorded "kits" of bone awls, i.e. tightly clustered groups of four or more such tools found *in situ.* Examples of such clusters are:

Rohn 1971:Fig. 259. This group of seven tools was found with the burial of a man, M31, at Mug House. Its principal function was hypothesized to have been stitching and basketmaking.

Hayes and Lancaster 1975:Fig. 216. A group of nine pointed bone tools was found with burial 4 at Site 1676. A second group of four assorted bone tools was associated with burial 3 at Badger House.

Swannack 1969:Fig. 149. This kit of nine tools was located in Kiva B at Big Juniper House. Swannack hypothesized that the tools were all awls and divided them into two groups on the basis of length.

It seems unlikely that a group of pointed bone tools located in a single provenience would all have the same function. The kit recorded on the floor of 5LP111 Feature 2 (Figs. 74 and 75) is an assemblage of what ostensibly may be called awls. However, the analysis of wear patterns suggests that this kit was comprised of: two daggers, one matting tool, three punches, two drills, one reamer, and three awls. Such a large kit would very likely be composed of an array of tools rather than of 12 copies of the same tool.

Worked tibia (tinkler), Fig. 75g, one specimen. This specimen is the distal end of a left canid tibia. the tool category is unusually homogeneous in its principal features. The element in all described cases is the tibia of a cervid, canid, felid, or leporid, or the tibiotarsus of a turkey. Manufacturing techniques are also extremely homogeneous (Hayes and Lancaster 1975:170). The discussion of these tools in the Badger House report points out a distribution that is predominantly associated with kivas. This distribution is consistent with that described in various other reports (Swannack 1969:155; Gillespie 1976:151; Rohn 1971:249; Lancaster and Pinkley 1954:66). The specimen from the Durango South collection displays a fracture which presumably happened after the bone had been made into a tinkler and had dried. The fracture

was modified to a tip that displays wear patterns which include polish, rotation striations and diagonal striations. These patterns indicate that the tool was used briefly as an awl. It is difficult to determine whether or not this specimen was part of the kit described above.

Comparisons: Hayes and Lancaster 1975:170; Swannack 1969:155; Gillespie 1976: 151; Rohn 1971:249; Lancaster and Pinkley 1954:66.

Tibia flaker (Figs. 76 and 77), one specimen. This unique tool recovered from 5LP111 was manufactured from a split deer tibia. One end has a screwdriver tip with rounded edges. The wear patterns at the tip include attrition and short longitudinal striations (Fig. 77). This may suggest that the tool was a flaker hafted to a long stick so the craftsman could apply his full weight to the tool (Joe Ben Wheat, personal communication).

Miscellaneous worked bone (Fig. 78), one specimen. This specimen is possibly the midsection of a canid fibula, with one end flattened and no points of articulation present. The cause of this type of modification is open to speculation. Several possibilities are offered: 1) the specimen could be a genetic deformity; 2) flattening could be the result of some type of pathology; 3) the flattening could be the result of human activity. There are wear striations on the edge of the flattened surface. The function of the tool cannot be discerned.

Ornamental Bone

The small collection of ornamental bone consisted of nine specimens, including fragments. The collection suggests that domestic as well as wild species were exploited for ornamentation and that intensive ornamental decoration of the bone itself, such as incising, was not common.

Pendant (Fig. 79), one specimen. A pendant was fashioned from the lower canine of a black bear. The string hole was biconically drilled through the uppermost end of the root.

Canid beads (Fig. 79b-e), four specimens. These beads, fashioned from the midsections of canid long bones, were found in association with the pendant. The beads were cut, then ground and polished, resulting in slightly rounded ends.

Turkey bead (Fig. 80), one specimen. A tubular bone bead was fashioned from the midsection of a

Figure 76.   Tibia flaker.

Figure 77.   Wear striations on tibia flaker.

Figure 78.   Flattened canid fibula.

turkey tibiotarsus. The turkey bone was cut and ground, with polish and smoothing on the ends.

Cottontail bead (Fig. 81), one specimen. One bead was shaped from the long bone of a cottontail. The manufacturing process for this specimen appears to be the same as for the turkey and canid beads discussed above.

Bead fragments, three specimens. Two fragments of canid long bones and one fragment of a *Lepus* long bone were recovered.

Bead refuse. Waste from the bead manufacturing process was present in the pithouse and surface rooms at 5LP110. On the floor of the pithouse was the proximal end of a left canid metatarsus. Toward the proximal end of the midsection was a deeply incised groove extending around the circumference of the bone and almost entirely through the cancellous tissue, which apparently caused the bone to snap apart (Fig. 82). From the surface room a bead fragment was recovered which proved to be the midsection of a turkey tibiotarsus (Fig. 83). The bead appears to have broken in the manufacturing process. Here again the bone is deeply incised, but fracture lines suggest that the snap split the bone longitudinally instead of following the incision.

Antler Implements

Antler tools comprise approximately 8.5% of the bone tool collection from Durango South. Two of the specimens are elk and four are mule deer. It is interesting to note the paucity of antler artifacts recorded from the La Plata District (three specimens, Morris 1939:121) and from Alkali Ridge (four specimens, Brew 1946:245). Although only seven antler tools were recovered from Durango South, they represent a substantially larger percentage of the total number of bone and antler tools than was recorded in the above two studies.

Antler shaft (Fig. 84), one specimen. This fragmented and burned elk antler specimen was located on the bench in the southwest quadrant of the pithouse at 5LP110. Reconstruction of the antler revealed that it was partially cut below the burr before it was broken from the cranium. Both tines of the antler were also partially cut, then broken very near the first bifurcation, leaving a shaft over 26cm in length. Although this tool would have served as an excellent baton for flint knapping, no characteristic wear patterns were observed. The tines that had been removed from the antler were not found in the pithouse.

Comparisons: None published.

Antler wrench (Fig. 85), one specimen. This tool was embedded in the bench in the southwest quadrant of the pithouse at 5LP110. The broken tool was incorporated into the bench wall as a hook or

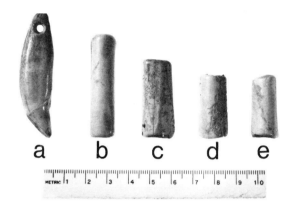

Figure 79.   Pendant and beads from 5LP111.

Figure 80.   Turkey bead.

Figure 81.   Cottontail bead.

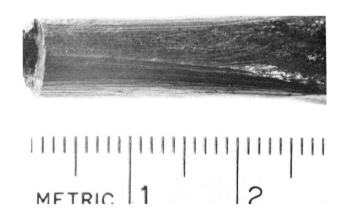

Figure 82.   Refuse from bead manufacture. Note saw striations and snap fracture.

Figure 83.   Bead refuse from turkey bone. Note incision groove.

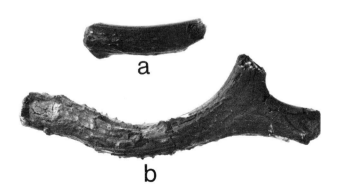

Figure 84.   a - Antler handle; b - Antler shaft.

Figure 85. Reconstructed antler wrench from bench face.

Comparisons: Wrenches have occasionally been located in the Northern San Juan Region, but only two are known in the published literature (Brew 1946:245; Hayes and Lancaster 1975:171). The manufacturing technique for this specimen resulted in a tool morphologically similar to that described and illustrated by Brew (1946:Fig. 189a). Three bone wrenches were recorded by Kidder (1932:240).

Rubbing tools (Fig. 86), three specimens. One of the tools was fashioned from an elk antler tine; the others are of deer antler. The tools are relatively short , approximately 9cm long, and are characterized by polish and striations on the tips.

Comparisons: The attrition, denting, striations and polish on Figure 86 resemble those in Kidder (1932:Fig. 236a-i, 276-277). Other comparisons include Brew (1946:245) and Reed (1975:76).

Antler flaker (Fig. 87), one specimen. Presence on this tool of a conical butt and wedge-like tip place it in Kidder's classification (1932:282) of antler flakers. In cross-section, the tool is rectangular with rounded corners. The wear at the tip is predominantly battering and denting, with a slight amount of polish. The tool surface appears to have suffered erosion through natural causes.
Comparison: Kidder 1932:282.

a   b   c

Figure 86. Antler rubbing tools.

Figure 87. Antler flaker.

IV. Economy and Subsistence

Fauna

by
Elaine Anderson

Introduction

One species of bird and 19 species of mammals were identified at Durango South (Table 10). All except the wolf, *Canis lupus,* are found in the area today. A minimum of 1758 bones was recovered (Table 11); of these, 1524 mammal bones and 15 bird bones were identified, 166 fragments were indeterminable and there were 53 bone tools (Table 8). Of the 20 species, five were found only in 5LP110 (*Cynomys gunnisonii*, sciurid sp., *Perognathus apache*, *Microtus* sp., and *Canis lupus*), four species were found only in 5LP111 (*Neotoma cf mexicana, Canis latrans, Urocyon cinereoargenteus* and *Ursus americanus*); the remainder were found in both sites. Canids are well represented--wolf, coyote, Indian dog and gray fox were identified, and a minimum of 14 individuals was recovered. Scavenging by dogs was an important factor limiting the preservation of bones. Deer, rabbit, turkey, and perhaps dog were utilized for food; and the bones of deer, wapiti, dog, bear, jackrabbit, cottontail, and wild turkey were used in making artifacts.

A number of factors govern bone recovery and identification. Among these are 1) utilization of bones by the occupants of the site, i.e. tool making, cracking bones to obtain marrow, scavenging by dogs; 2) differential preservation (small bones, fragile elements, juveniles, and bird bones are less likely to be preserved); 3) mechanical damage (by weathering, plowing); 4) the ease of identification (ribs, vertebrae, phalanges are often unidentifiable); and 5) the availability of comparative osteological material.

Bias of the collector, i.e. screening the fill to recover microfauna, is an additional determining factor in faunal analysis. Small mammals, especially mice and shrews, that have limited habitat requirements are better indicators of local climate than are larger animals that live in a variety of habitats from deserts to high mountains. Thus every attempt should be made to recover the microfauna. There is always the possibility that rodent bones are intrusive, but if the preservation is similar to the other osteological material, it is quite likely that mice, gophers and ground squirrels inhabited the site during the main occupation.

At Durango South, the species that give indications of the environment include *Perognathus apache* which lives in arid and semi-arid regions from 1524 m to 2134m in areas of sparse brush and scattered pines and junipers, and *Neotoma mexicana* which dwells in pinon-juniper forests. *Sylvilagus audubonii* prefers open areas with grass, sagebrush, and pinon-juniper while *Sylvilagus nuttallii* inhabits thickets and forest edges. Presence of these species indicates that the habitat around Durango South was probably semi-arid with stands of pinon-juniper, brushy areas, some grass, and nearby forests extending up the canyons to the high country. The absence of aquatic species such as beaver and muskrat may indicate a scarcity of permanent water. Several species found at Durango South range from the foothills to timberline and were thus common throughout the region.

Discussion

Birds

Family Meleagrididae
Wild turkey, *Meleagris gallopavo*

Minimum number of individuals: 5 Number of specimens: 18 (3 artifacts)

Remains of wild turkeys are common in archaeological sites in the Southwest. Indians of the Four Corners area commonly captured turkeys and kept them in pens as early as Pueblo I times (Schorger 1966). Besides use of the birds as a food item, turkey bones and feathers were utilized in making tools and decoration.

Largest of the upland game birds, wild turkeys inhabit mountain forests and broken woodlands in the eastern, southern and southwestern United States southward to Central America. *Meleagris gallopavo* was extirpated over much of its northeastern range during the last century, but in the west its range has expanded (due to introductions). It is a resident species in south-central Colorado. The diet of turkeys includes acorns, nuts, seeds, berries and insects.

At Durango South, 18 turkey bones were identified including three that were fashioned into artifacts. The remains are mostly fragmentary; none are burned or show butchering marks. A fragment of a metatarsus with the spur belonged to a tom turkey, since the spur is absent in females.

123

Table 10. Faunal Lists

Fauna		Min. No. of Individuals	No. of Items
5LP110 Feature 1			
Aves	**Birds**		
Meleagris gallopavo	wild turkey	1	6
Indeterminate birds		---	6
Mammalia	**Mammals**		
Thomomys cf *talpoides*	northern pocket gopher	1	2
Perognathus apache	Apache pocket gopher	1	1
Reithrodontomys megalotis	western harvest mouse	1	1
Peromyscus sp	white-footed mouse	2	7
Microtus sp	vole		
Indeterminate mice			75
Lepus cf *townsendii*	white-tailed jackrabbit	3	12
Sylvilagus audubonii/ nuttallii	cottontail	3	66
leporids			8
Canis lupus	gray wolf	2	110+
Canis sp	dog/wolf/coyote	3	420+
Odocoileus hemionus	mule deer	1	12
Cervus canadensis	wapiti	1	9
Indeterminate mammals		---	37
5LP110 Feature 2			
Aves	**Birds**		
Meleagris gallopavo	wild turkey	1	2
Indeterminate birds		---	4
Mammalia	**Mammals**		
Marmota flaviventris	yellow-bellied marmot	1	2
Cynomys cf *gunnisonii*	Gunnison's prairie dog	1	1
Sciurid sp	squirrel/ground squirrel	1	1
Thomomys cf *talpoides*	northern pocket gopher	2	3
Microtus sp	vole	1	1
Sylvilagus sp	cottontail	1	1
Canis familaris	Indian dog	2	3
Odocoileus hemionus	mule deer	1	3
Indeterminate mammals		---	5
5LP110 Burial 1			
Aves	**Birds**		
Meleagris gallopavo	wild turkey	1	1

Table 10, cont'd. Faunal Lists

Fauna		Min. No. of Individuals	No. of Items
5LP111 Feature 1			
Aves	**Birds**		
Indeterminate birds		---	1
Mammalia	**Mammals**		
Marmota flaviventris	yellow-bellied marmot	1	4
Lepus cf *townsendii*	white-tailed jackrabbit	1	2
Sylvilagus sp	cottontail	2	3
Canis familiaris	Indian dog	1	5
Odocoileus hemionus	mule deer	1	8
Indeterminate mammals		---	18
5LP111 Feature 2			
Aves	**Birds**		
Meleagris gallopavo	wild turkey	1	1
Indeterminate birds		---	3
Mammalia	**Mammals**		
Marmota flaviventris	yellow-bellied marmot	2	4
Thomomys cf *talpoides*	northern pocket gopher	2	2
Reithrodontomys megalotis	western harvest mouse	1	2
Peromyscus sp	white-footed mouse	1	1
Neotoma cf *mexicana*	Mexican wood rat	3	5
Lepus cf *townsendii*	white-tailed jackrabbit	2	3
Sylvilagus audubonii	desert cottontail	2	2
Sylvilagus nuttallii	mountain cottontail	2	2
Sylvilagus audubonii/ nuttallii	cottontail	4	22
Canis latrans	coyote	1	1
Canis familiaris	Indian dog	3	550+
Urocyon cinereoargenteus	gray fox	1	2
Ursus americanus	black bear	1	2
Odocoileus hemionus	mule deer	1	10
Indeterminate mammals		---	89
5LP111 Burial 1			
Mammalia	**Mammals**		
Sylvilagus sp	cottontail	1	1
Indeterminate mammals		---	1
5LP111 Burial 2			
Aves	**Birds**		

Table 10, cont'd. Faunal Lists

Fauna		Min. No. of Individuals	No. of Items
Meleagris gallopavo	wild turkey	1	5
Mammalia	**Mammals**		
Canis cf *familiaris*	Indian dog	1	2
rodents		1	1
Indeterminate mammals		---	2

Table 11.   Inventory Of Faunal Remains·

Genus	Provenience	Element	R-L	Portion	Comments
		5LP110 Feature 1			
Sylvilagus	SE L3	innominate	R	W	Ad
		innominate	R	W	Ad
		femur	R	Ms	Ad
		ulna	L	P	Ad
		ulna	L	P	Ad
		radius	L	P	Ad
Lepus	SE L3	radius	-	D	Juv, epiphysis lost
Canis lupus	SE L3	cuboid	-	W	Ad, burned
cf *Odocoileus*	SE L3	femur	-	D	Juv, partial epiphysis, burned
Indet bird	SE L3				5 frags including 2 scapulae
Indet mammal	SE L3				9 frags (3 burned)
Lepus	SE L2	radius	R	P	Ad, rodent-gnawed
		radius	-	Ms	rodent-gnawed
		MT III	-	W	Ad
Canis lupus	SE L4 FS 152	femur	L	P	Juv, head lost
Lepus	SE L4 FS 116	ulna		Ms	
		radius	R	W	Ad, deformed: shaft curved, distal half expanded
cf *Meleagris*	NE L2	vertebra			frag
Indet mammal	NE L3				1 frag
	NW L2				7 splinters, 2 frags (2 burned)
Lepus	NW L3	ulna		Ms	Juv
Indet mammal	NW L3				3 frags
	NW L3 SF 1				1 frag, burned
	SW L2				2 frags

*List of abbreviations in appendix.

Genus	Provenience	Element	R-L	Portion	Comments
		5LP110, Feature 1, cont'd.			
Microtus	SW L2	incisor			
		4 molars			
		skull frag			assoc
		6 vertebrae		W	
Odocoileus	SW L3 FS 52	antler			4 frags, burned
Indet mammal	SW L3 FS 52				7 frags, burned
Odocoileus	SW L3 FS 53	antler			1 frag, burned
Sylvilagus	SW L2 FS 14	femur	L	Ms	
		long bone		Ms	
Odocoileus	SW L2 FS 14	middle phalanx	half sagittal section		weathered
Indet bird	SW L2 FS 14			Ms	1 frag
Indet mammal	SW L2 FS 14				2 frags
	SW L4 FS 42	tibia		P	Juv, deformed
Canis sp	SW L4 FS 25	frag skull:			Ad, burned, 200+ small skull frags
		L max w/alv of PM^3-M^1			
		frag R max w/alv M^1			
		frag L max w/alv PM^2			
		frag max w/alv PM$^{2-3}$			
		2 tooth frags			
		7 tooth root frags			
		frag parietal w/sagittal crest			
		3 frags zygomatic arch			
		frag squamosal			
		frag auditory bullae			
		frag occipital condyle			
Lepus	SW L4 FS 62	scapula		P	burned, assoc w/**Canis** metapodial, glenoid cavity
Indet mammal	SW L4 FS 64				1 frag, burned
Sylvilagus	SW L4 FS 121	long bone		Ms	
Lepus	SW L4 FS 121	tibia	L	Ms	Juv, both epiphyses lost, assoc w/ fecal material
Canis lupus	SW L3 FS 62	MT II, MT III	R	P	articulated, burned
		MT IV, MT V	R	P	burned
		calcaneum	R	D	burned
		cuboid	R	W	burned
		navicular	R	W	burned
		lateral cuneiform	R	W	burned
		MT III	L	P 3/4	burned
		calcaneum	L	W	burned
		cuboid	L	W	burned
		navicular	L	W	burned

Table 11, cont'd. Inventory of Faunal Remains

Genus	Provenience	Element	R-L	Portion	Comments
		5LP110 Feature 1, cont'd.			
Canis lupus	SW L3 FS 62, cont'd.	lateral cuneiform	L	W	burned
		scapholunar	L	W	burned
		2 cuneiforms	R-L	W	Left is burned.
		2 pisiforms	R-L	W	burned
		2 magnums	R-L	W	Left is burned.
		MC I	L	W	burned
		MC I	R	P	
		MC II	L	W	articulated, burned
		MC III	L	P	articulated, burned
		MC IV	L	P	burned
		MC V	L	P	burned
		MC II	R	P	scorched
		MC V	R	W	Distal end is burned.
		3 metapodials		D	burned
		6 proximal phalanges		W	burned
		2 proximal phalanges		P	burned
		1 proximal phalanx		D	burned
		3 middle phalanges		W	burned. Two have cut marks on distal end (Fig 90).
		4 caudal vertebrae		W	burned
		8 misc carpals and tarsals		W	5 burned
cf *Canis*	SW L3-4 assoc w/FS 62	59 small bone frags			45 burned
Canis sp	SW L3-4 assoc w/FS 62	2 frags calcanea			burned
		cuboid		W	burned
		pisiform		W	burned
		MC V		P	burned
Sylvilagus	SW L3 FS 54	17 teeth			Juv
		9 skull frags			
		humerus		D	
		radius		P	Ad
		radius		D	Ad
		calcaneum	R		
		2 patellae	R-L	W	
		3 claws		W	
		femur		head	
		femur		D	
		15 frags, metapodials			
Microtus	SW L3 FS 54	4 molars			assoc w/fecal material
		4 incisors	R-L		upper and lower
		frag mandible	L		w/alv of M_{1-2}
		thoracic vertebra		W	
		2 frags scapulae	R-L	P	
		metapodial			
		3 claws			

Table 11, cont'd. Inventory of Faunal Remains

Genus	Provenience	Element	R-L	Portion	Comments
5LP110 Feature 1, cont'd.					
Sylvilagus/ Microtus	SW L3 FS 54				small bone frag assoc w/fecal material
Microtus	SW L3	6 molars			
		incisors			
		mandible	L	Ms	
		tibia	L	W	Juv
		tibia	R	W	Juv
		innominate		Ms	
Perognathus	SW L3	mandible	L	W	w/I, PM$_4$-M$_1$, alv M$_{2-3}$
Reithrodontomys	SW L3	femur	R	W	Ad
Peromyscus	SW L3	femur	L	W	Ad
		humerus	L	W	Ad
		3 innominates		Ms	
		scapula	R	W	Ad
Indet mice (*Peromyscus, Reithrodontomys, Microtus*)	SW L3	5 upper incisors			
		2 lower incisors			
		2 ulnae	P		Ad
		2 humeri	D		Ad
		femur	D		Ad
		3 tibiae	Ms		Juv
		6 cervical vertebrae	W		
		14 thoracic/lumbar vertebrae	W		
		2 clavicles	W		
		9 ribs			
		29 frags			
Canis sp	SW L3	frag palate w/PM$^{1-2}$			skull "A," Ad, burned
		frag frontal			burned
		rim of orbit			burned
		frag occipital condyle			burned
		4 frags auditory bullae			burned
		frag palate w/alv of incisors			burned
		basisphenoid			burned
		frag parietal w/sagittal crest			burned
		frag max			burned
		2 frags of ramus			burned
		30+ small frags			burned
Canis sp	SW L3	frag condyle femur		D	burned, assoc w/ skull "A"
Canis sp	SW L3	top of skull w/R parietal and sagittal crest			burned, young Ad, skull "B"
		basioccipital w/L condyle			burned
		basisphenoid			burned
		frag squamosal			burned

Table 11, cont'd. Inventory of Faunal Remains

Genus	Provenience	Element	R-L	Portion	Comments
	**5LP110 Feature 1, cont'd.**				
		frag max w/alv of M^{1-2}	R		burned
		frag max w/alv of M^{1-2}	L		burned
		frag zygomatic arch			burned
		3 frags auditory bullae			burned
		50+ small frags			burned
Canis sp	SW L3-4	upper canine	R		burned
		upper canine	L		burned
		PM_1	R		burned
		87 tooth frags			burned
cf *Odocoileus*	L2	rib			
		vertebral border of scapula			
Sylvilagus	L2	ulna	L	P	Ad, rodent-gnawed
Indet mammal	L2				2 frags
Sylvilagus	NE L2 SF 5	femur	R	Ms	rodent-gnawed
		long bone		Ms	
cf *Odocoileus*	NE L2 SF 5	rib		Ms	
Meleagris	NE L2 SF 5	2 vertebrae		W	
		frag vertebra			
		ulna		D	
		metatarsus		D	
Sylvilagus	NE L4 SF 5	ulna			Ad, rodent-gnawed
		radius		P	Ad, rodent-gnawed
Lepus	L3 SF 1 FS 22	tibia			
Indet	Floor SE			W	
Cervus	FS 42, fill above cist depression	antler		frag	8+ frags, burned
Thomomys	SW lower fill	mandible	L		w/alv of PM_4-M_2
		molar			
Odocoileus	NW L3-4 assoc w/FS 62	long bone		frag	burned
Lepus	NW L3-4 assoc w/FS 62	tibia		D	Ad, burned
		radius		Ms	burned
leporid		MT III		P	burned
		proximal phalanx		W	burned
		2 proximal phalanges		P	burned
		proximal phalanx		D	burned
		middle phalanx		W	burned
		middle phalanx		P	burned
		middle phalanx		D	burned

Table 11, cont'd. Inventory of Faunal Remains

Genus	Provenience	Element	R-L	Portion	Comments
	**5LP110 Feature 2**				
Sylvilagus	14S-18E L3	radius		D	Ad
cf *Canis*	4S-20E L3	radius		Ms	
Odocoileus	5S-17E L3	middle phalanx		frag	
Microtus	6S-15E L3?	mandible	R		Ad w/I, alv M_{1-3}
Indet bird	6S-16E L4				2 frags
Thomomys	6S-17E	mandible	L		Ad, alv PM_4-M_2
		tibia		P	Juv, proximal epiphysis lost
Indet mammal	6S-18E L3				1 frag
Indet mammal	8S-14E L2				1 frag
Meleagris	8S-17E	metatarsus w/part of spur		Ms	
Thomomys	9S-17E	femur	L	W	Ad
Marmota	10S-14E L3 FS 2	upper incisor		frag	
Indet mammal	10S-16E L2				
Odocoileus	13S-18E L3	proximal phalanx		P	Ad
cf sciurid	16S-13E	femur			Juv
Cynomys	16S-14E L3	mandible	R	W	Ad w/I, PM_4-M_3, moderate wear
Odocoileus	16S-14E L3	antler		frag	surface weathered
Indet mammal	16S-14E L3				1 frag
Canis	17S-15E L3	M_1	R		broken, slightly worn
Marmota	17S-15E L3	ulna		P frag	
Meleagris	L3 FS 31 surface room	coracoid		W	
Canis	17S-14E L3 Trench B	mandible	R	frag	Juv w/alv $\frac{1}{2}M_1$, M_2
	**5LP110, Burials**				
Meleagris	5LP110 Burial 1	metatarsus		P	
	**5LP111 Feature 1**				
Indet mammal	L1			Ms frag	1 frag
Sylvilagus	L2	radius		Ms	
Odocoileus	L2	middle phalanx		D frag	Ad
Marmota	L2	upper incisor	L		
		ulna	L	P	Ad
Sylvilagus	L2	radius	R	P	Ad
Canis	L2	jaw symphysis			Ad w/R I_{1-3}, C, PM_2-M_2;

Genus	Provenience	Element	R-L	Portion	Comments
			**5LP111 Feature 1, cont'd.**		
					L I$_{1-3}$, C, PM$_1$-M$_1$ teeth moderately worn, jaws broken off behind M$_3$ alv of R PM$_1$ obliterated
Canis		MC V	R	W	Ad
Odocoileus	L2	distal phalanx		W	Ad
Indet mammal	L2				4 frags
Marmota	L3	femur	R	P	
Sylvilagus	L3	radius		Ms	
Odocoileus	L3	rib		Ms	
		proximal phalanx		D frag	Ad
		distal phalanx		D frag	Ad
		distal phalanx		D frag	Ad
		distal phalanx		D frag	Ad
cf *Canis*	L3	caudal vertebra		W	Ad
		rib		P	Ad
		lower border of jaw		Ms	
Indet bird	L3	metatarsus		Ms frag	1 frag
Indet mammal	L3				8 frags
Odocoileus	L3	proximal phalanx		P frag	Ad
Marmota	L3	premaxillary	R		frag w/alv of I
Indet mammal	L3				4 frags
Lepus		innominate	L	Ms	Ad
		radius		Ms	Ad
Indet mammal					2 frags
		**5LP111 Feature 2**			
Canis	L2 FS 26	innominate	R	Ms	Ad
Indet mammal	L2 FS 26				1 frag
Meleagris	L4 FS 47	long bone		Ms	spiral fracture, possible artifact
Odocoileus	L4 FS 62	antler			frag
Odocoileus	L4 FS 67	metapodial		Ms	Ad
Canis cf *latrans*	L3 No. 19	mandible	R	W	Ad w/M$_2$ slightly worn alv of I$_{1-3}$, C-M$_1$, M$_3$
Ursus	L4 FS 92	calcaneum	L	D half	Ad
Canis	L4 FS 91	skull, mandible, skeleton			224 items, young Ad, not burned, no nearly scratch marks; left forelimb

Table 11, cont'd. Inventory of Faunal Remains

Genus	Provenience	Element	R-L	Portion	Comments
5LP111 Feature 2, cont'd.					
				complete	shorter than right; teeth moderately worn
Indet mammal	E L2				8 frags
Marmota	L2	mandible	R		w/M_{1-3}, teeth slightly worn
Odocoileus	L2	rib		Ms	frag
Indet mammal	L2				1 frag
Sylvilagus	L4	tibia		D	Juv
Indet mammal	S L3 SF 3				5 frags (2 burned)
rodent	S L3 SF 16	incisor		frag	
Indet mammal	S L3 SF 16	ulna		Ms	
cf rodent	S L3 SF 16	metacarpal		W	
cf *Canis*	L3	caudal vertebra		W	Ad
		rib		P	Ad
		lower border of jaw		Ms	
Indet bird	L3	metatarsus		Ms frag	1 frag
Indet mammal	L3				8 frags
Odocoileus	L3	proximal phalanx		P frag	Ad
Marmota	L3	premaxillary	R		frag w/alv of I
Indet mammal	L3				4 frags
Lepus		innominate	L	Ms	Ad
		radius		Ms	Ad
Indet mammal					2 frags
Indet bird	S L3 SF 16				1 frag
Indet mammal	S L3 SF 16				13 frags
Sylvilagus	S L3 SF 28	ulna	L	Ms	Ad
Odocoileus	S L3 SF 28	middle phalanx		D frag	
Neotoma	S L3 SF 40	mandible	R		Ad w/I, M_{1-2}
Marmota	S L3 SF 40	lower incisor		frag	
rodent	S L3 SF 40	femur	R	Ms	
Odocoileus	S L3 SF 40	humerus		Ms frag	
Indet mammal	S L3 SF 40				11 frags, 1 Juv vertebra One bone is rodent-gnawed.
Sylvilagus	S L3 SF 44	premaxillary	L	W	W/I^1
		innominate	R	P 3/4	
Indet mammal	S L3 SF 44				5 frags
cf *Reithrodontomys*	N L3 cist fill	femur	R	P 3/4	Juv, distal epiphysis lost

Table 11, cont'd. Inventory of Faunal Remains

Genus	Provenience	Element	R-L	Portion	Comments
5LP111 Feature 2, cont'd.					
Peromyscus	N L3 cist fill	innominate	R	W	Ad
Indet mouse	N L3	lower incisor	L	W	
Sylvilagus nuttallii	N L3	mandible	L		Ad w/PM$_3$-M$_2$, I broken
Thomomys	N L3	palate		W	Ad, toothless
rodent	N L3	incisor		W	
rodent	N L3	incisor		W	
Indet mammal	N L3				8 frags, 1 of which is rib cartilage
Indet mammal	N				6 frags
Marmota	S L3	tibia		Ms	Juv, rodent-gnawed
Neotoma	S L3	tibia	L	D 3/4	Ad
		upper incisor	R	W	
Sylvilagus nuttallii	S L3	mandible	R		Ad w/PM$_3$-M$_3$ moderately/worn
Sylvilagus	S L3	tibia	L	D half	Ad
		thoracic vertebra		W	Juv, 1 epiphysis lost
		thoracic vertebra		W	Juv, 1 epiphysis lost
		MT II	R	W	Ad, rodent tooth marks on proximal end
cf *Odocoileus*	S L3	rib		Ms	
Canis	S L3	tibia	R	P	Ad. Top of bone has been cut off, cut marks visible.
		rib		W	
		rib		W	
		rib		W	
Indet bird	S L3	metatarsus		D	
Indet mammal	S L3				10 frags
Thomomys	N bench	femur	R	Ms	Juv, both epiphyses lost
Sylvilagus	N bench	tibia	R	D	Ad, rodent-gnawed
Canis	N bench	MC IV	R	P	Ad
		rib			
		middle phalanx		Ms	Juv, both epiphyses lost scratch marks on distal end
		metapodial		Ms	scratch marks on shaft
Indet mammal	S bench				1 frag
Sylvilagus audubonii	E L3	mandible	R		Ad w/I, PM$_3$-M$_3$ moderately worn

Genus	Provenience	Element	R-L	Portion	Comments
		5LP111, Feature 2, cont'd.			
Sylvilagus nuttallii	E L3	mandible	L		Ad w/M$_1$-M$_3$ slightly worn, I broken
Sylvilagus	E L3	maxillary	L	W	Ad w/PM^4
		3 isolated teeth			
		scapula	R	Ms	
		humerus		D	Ad. End is rodent-gnawed.
		femur	R	P frag	Ad
		tibia	L	D half	Ad
		tibia		Ms	
		tibia		Ms	
Lepus	E L3	ulna	L	P	Ad
		radius	*Thomomys*	Ms	
Canis	E L3	zygomatic arch	L		
		MT III	L	W	Juv, articulated, distal epiphysis lost
		MT IV	L	P	Juv, articulated
Odocoileus	E L3	astragalus	L	W	
rodent	E L3	cervical vertebra		W	
		occipital condyle			
		innominate	L	D	
		5 metapodials		W	
		middle phalanx		W	
		claw		W	
Indet bird	E L3	metatarsus		Ms	
Indet mammal	E L3				19 frags
Neotoma	W L3	radius	R	P3/4	Ad
		ulna	R	P 3/4	Ad
Sylvilagus audubonii	W L3	mandible	L		Ad w/I, PM$_3$-M$_3$ moderately worn
Sylvilagus		long bone		Ms	
Odocoileus	W L3	tibia	R	D 3/4	young Ad, distal epiphysis unfused
Indet mammal	NW L4				1 frag
Sylvilagus	N L4	tibia		Ms	
Indet mammal	NW L4				1 frag
Lepus	Trench D	ulna	L	P	Ad

Table 11, cont'd. Inventory of Faunal Remains

Genus	Provenience	Element	R-L	Portion	Comments
		5LP111 Feature 2			
Odocoileus	Lower fill, bench L3	rib		Ms	
Odocoileus	L4 FS 70	radius	L	W, sagittal section	Ad. Bone is split lengthwise, scratch marks visible.
Ursus	surface	femur	R	D 2/3	Ad. Condyle is weathered.
Urocyon	L2 No. 116	mandible	R	W	Ad w/C, PM$_2$-M$_2$ slightly worn
		mandible	L	W	Ad w/C, PM$_1$-M$_2$ slightly worn
Canis familiaris	SF 12 wall cist FS 139	anterior palate maxillary	L		young Ad w/L I^3, R C w/PM^4-M^2-M^1 heavily worn
		3 frags auditory bullae			
		frag parietal	L		
		mandible	L		w/C, PM$_2$-M$_2$ moderately worn
		mandible	R		w/C, PM$_1$-M$_3$ moderately worn
		100+ small skull frags			
		6 incisors			
		2 PM$_3$			
		P^4	R		
		M^1	R		
		scapulae	R-L	W	
		innominates	R-L	W	
		ulna	L	W	
		radius	R	W	
		femora	R-L	W	
		2 humeri	R-L	P	weathered
		2 humeri	R-L	D	
		radius	L	D	
		2 tibiae	R-L	Ms	
		tibia	L	D	
		4 frags fibulae			
		ulna		Ms	
		15 ribs			
		6 cervical vertebrae		W	
		9 thoracic vertebrae		W	
		12 lumbar vertebrae		W	
		sacrum		W	
		12 caudal vertebrae		W	
		clavicle			
		5 sternabrae			
		patellae	R-L	W	
		15 metapodials		W	
		19 carpals/tarsals		W	

136

Table 11, cont'd. Inventory of Faunal Remains

Genus	Provenience	Element	R-L	Portion	Comments
5LP110 Feature 2, cont'd.					
Canis familiaris	SF 12 wall cist	14 proximal phalanges		W	
	FS 139, cont'd.	15 middle phalanges		W	
		13 claws		W	
		9 sesamoids		W	
5LP111, Burials					
Sylvilagus	5LP111 Burial 1	humerus		D	Ad
Meleagris	5LP111 Burial 2	femur	L	P	
		tibia		P	
		tibia		Ms	
		carpometacarpus		D	
		radius		P	
Canis	5LP111 Burial 2	metapodial		D	Ad, pitted
		canine root	L		
rodent	5LP111 Burial 2	femur	L	P	Ad
Indet mammal	5LP111 Burial 2				2 frags
Indet mammal	5LP111 Burial 2	femur		Ms	Scratch marks on edge. Bone is whitish.

Mammals

Family Sciuridae
Yellow-bellied marmot, *Marmota flaviventris*

Minimum number of individuals: 4   Number of specimens: 9 (0 artifacts)

This heavy-bodied yellowish-brown terrestrial squirrel ranges from the foothills to timberline in a variety of habitats in the western United States and British Columbia. Diurnal in habits, marmots feed on grasses and forbs.

Marmot remains are not common at Durango South. The bones are fragmentary and none show butchering marks. Marmots constitute a possible food item.

White-tailed prairie dog, *Cynomys gunnisonii*

Minimum number of individuals: 1   Number of specimens: 1 (0 artifacts)

A single mandible belonging to *Cynomys* was recovered in 5LP110 Feature 2. The complete (I, PM$_4$ - M$_3$) dentition is moderately worn. White-tailed prairiedogs live in mountain parks and valleys up to 3658m. Colonial in habits, they form loosely organized towns sometimes composed of only a few individuals. They are strictly diurnal and feed primarily on forbs. Some workers also recognize *Cynomys leucurus* and *Cynomys parvidens* as valid species in the Rocky Mountains, but Armstrong (1972) recognizes only *Cynomys gunnisonii* in southwestern Colorado.

Indeterminate sciurid

A juvenile sciurid femur with both epiphyses missing was recovered in Feature 2, Level 3 of 5LP110. It may be referable to *Spermophilus variegatus,* the rock squirrel or *Sciurus aberti,* Abert's squirrel. Both species are presently found in the region in which the site is located.

Family Geomyidae

Northern pocket gopher, *Thomomys talpoides*

Minimum number of individuals: 5   Number of specimens: 7 (0 artifacts)

The pocket gopher remains are tentatively referred to *Thomomys talpoides*, a species found in the northern two-thirds of La Plata county. It differs from *Thomomys bottae,* the valley pocket gopher, by smaller size and in having a more northern distribution. In Colorado *Thomomys talpoides* has the widest geographical and altitudinal distribution of the pocket gophers and is found from 1524m to timberline.

Of the five individuals recovered from 5LP110 and 5LP111, two were juveniles. The remains may be intrusive.

Family Heteromydiae

Apache pocket mouse, *Perognathus apache*

Minimum number of individuals: 1 Number of specimens: 1 (0 artifacts)

Pocket mice are small slender rodents with fur-lined cheek pouches, and hind limbs slightly longer than forelimbs. The lower premolar is smaller than the last molar. They inhabit arid and semi-arid regions, feed primarily on seeds and seldom drink water. The Apache pocket mouse is found at elevations between 1542m and 2134m in areas of sparse brush and scattered pines and junipers where there is sandy soil for burrowing. A single mandible with I, $PM_4 - M_1$ and the alveoli of M_{2-3} was identified.

Family Cricetidae

cf. Western harvest mouse, *Reithrodontomys megalotis*

Minimum number of individuals: 2 Number of specimens: 3 (0 artifacts)

This widespread species ranges from the Great Lakes to the Pacific Coast in a variety of habitats including grasslands and open deserts. A distinctive character is the longitudinal groove on the upper incisor. Western harvest mice feed primarily on seeds but take some insects. Only postcranial material was recovered at Durango South.

White-footed mouse, *Peromyscus sp.*

Minimum number of individuals: 3 Number of specimens: 8 (0 artifacts)

Several species of *Peromyscus* are found in southwestern Colorado; all are medium-sized mice with white feet. They feed chiefly on seeds and nuts. Although the postcranial material from Durango South is not identifiable to species, the eight referred elements belonged to adult animals.

Vole, *Microtus* sp.

Minimum number of individuals: 4 Number of specimens: 39 (0 artifacts)

Both the montane vole, *Microtus montanus,* and the long-tailed vole, *Microtus longicaudus,* are found in the region today in moist grassy meadows from 1524m to timberline. The vole bones, all from 5LP110, are not identifiable to species. *Microtus* remains were found in association with those of *Sylvilagus* in a fragmentary, probably canid coprolite. Another accumulation of mouse bones representing *Microtus, Peromyscus,* and *Reithrodontomys* was recovered from Level 3, northwest quad of Feature 1; at least one adult and one juvenile are present in this assemblage. Although there is always the possibility that mice remains in an archaeological site may be intrusive, it is quite likely that mice inhabited the trash middens during the time of occupation.

Mexican wood rat, *Neotoma mexicana*

Minimum number of individuals: 3 Number of specimens: 5 (0 artifacts)

Woodrats are often found in archaeological sites both during and after occupation. Their burrowing and their habit of picking up an object and trading it for something else often results in a disruption of the stratigraphy. Three species of *Neotoma* are found in La Plata county today: *N. cinerea,* largest of the woodrats, has a squirrel-like bushy tail and lives in spruce-fir forests and rocky areas throughout western Colorado. *N. albigula,* a medium-sized species inhabiting deserts and mixed coniferous forests, is found in the southern half of the county up to an elevation of 2134m. *N. mexicana,* the smallest of the three species, is found in higher, more mesic conditions, especially in pinon-juniper forests from 1311m to 2530m.

The specimens, all from 5LP111 Feature 2, are tentatively referred to *Neotoma mexicana* because of their small size and because the habitat requirements of the species match the location of the site.

Family Leporidae

White-tailed jackrabbit, *Lepus townsendii*

Minimum number of individuals: 6 Number of specimens: 18 (2 artifacts)

Three species of *Lepus* are found in southwestern Colorado. *Lepus townsendii*, the white-tailed jackrabbit, inhabits open grassy plains and mountain valleys from 1524m to timberline. *Lepus californicus*, the black-tailed jackrabbit, lives in warm dry valleys up to an elevation of 2134m and has a range that only borders southwestern Colorado. *Lepus americanus, the snowshoe rabbit,* is found in coniferous forests from 2438m to 3353m. The jackrabbits from Durango South are tentatively referred to *Lepus townsendii*. A minimum of six individuals including both juveniles and adults is represented. Many of the bones are rodent-gnawed. Burned fragments of a scapula, radius and tibia were associated with the burned canid metapodial (FS 62). One specimen (FS 116), a right radius, is severely deformed; the shaft is curved and the distal half greatly expanded (Fig. 88). Jackrabbits were probably an important food item in the diet of the inhabitants of Durango South.

Figure 88. *Lepus townsendii.* Severely deformed right radius (FS 116) and a normal recent radius-ulna (UCM 5058), white-tailed jackrabbit.

Cottontail, *Sylvilagus audubonii/nuttallii*

Minimum number of individuals: 15   Number of specimens: 98 (1 artifact)

Both the desert cottontail, *Sylvilagus audubonii,* and the mountain cottontail, *Sylvilagus nuttallii,* are present at Durango South. In areas where the ranges of the two species overlap, *Sylvilagus audubonii* is found in more open areas with grass, sagebrush or scattered pinon-juniper usually at elevations below 1981m to 2134m while *Sylvilagus nuttallii* lives in thickets and forest edges at elevations from 1829m to 2505m. Distinguishing

one species from the other is often difficult. *Sylvilagus audubonii* is slightly larger and has larger ears than does *Sylvilagus nuttallii*. Osteoligically, the depth of the lower jaw at PM_4 relative to the length of the alveolar tooth row (PM_3-PM_3, Fig. 89) is a diagnostic characteristic; *Sylvilagus audubonii* has a deeper jaw and a shorter tooth row than does *Sylvilagus nuttallii*. The enamel pattern of PM_3 is also distinctive. In *Sylvilagus audubonii* the posterior external reentrant angle shows pronounced crinkling of the enamel; in *Sylvilagus nuttallii* the enamel is smooth or only slightly crinkled (Findley et al. 1975). On the basis of these two characteristics, the presence of both species in 5LP111 Feature 2 was determined. Of the five mandibles recovered, three are referred to *Sylvilagus nuttallii*, the other two belong to *Sylvilagus audubonii*. The postcranial material is indistinguishable as to species and is referred to *Sylvilagus audubonii/nuttallii.* A minimum of 15 individuals recovered at Durango South includes both adults and juveniles. None show butchering marks but several of the specimens are rodent-gnawed. One assemblage was found in a coprolite (probably canid) along with the bones of *Microtus*.

Cottontails were an important food item in the human diet at the site. Their remains are common in other archaeological sites. Besides falling prey to man, rabbits are hunted by many avian and mammalian predators, and although they are prolific breeders, few survive one year.

Family Canidae

Table 12 shows some cranial differences between dogs and coyotes. Since dogs, wolves and coyotes show many similarities and hybridization between them is fairly common, a combination of diagnostic characters is more reliable than a single character for identification. Generally wolves can be separated from dogs and coyotes by much larger size, massive teeth, rounded auditory bullae, widely spreading zygomatic arches, and a better developed, often overhanging sagittal crest (Table 13). Dogs tend to be more variable; dental anomalies and skeletal malformation seem to be more common.

Gray wolf, *Canis lupus*

Minimum number of individuals: 2   Number of specimens: 110+ (10 artifacts)

Largest of the American canids, the gray wolf

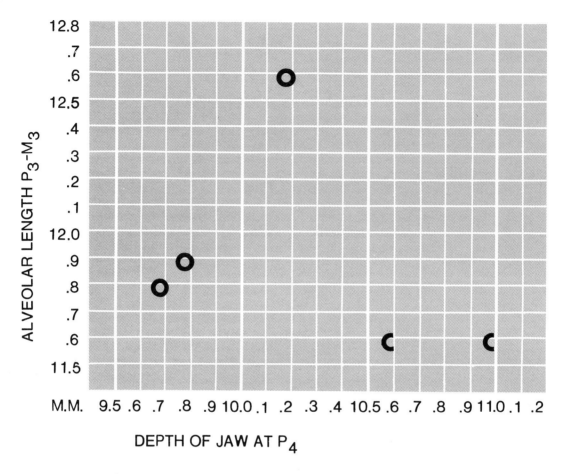

Figure 89. Relationship between alveolar length of P_3 - M_3 to depth of jaw at P_4 in *Sylvilagus nuttallii* (o) and *Sylvilagus audubonii* (c).

formerly ranged from Alaska and northern Canada to the Mexican Plateau and from the Atlantic to the Pacific coasts except in desert regions. Today *Canis lupus* is only found in Alaska, Canada, the northern Great Lakes region, and in a few widely scattered enclaves in the western mountains. Wolves were exterminated in Colorado between 1935 and 1941 through hunting, trapping, poisoning and den hunting. Before then, they inhabited much of western Colorado. An animal of tundra and mountain forests, the gray wolf preys on rodents and rabbits as well as big game. Hunting in packs, wolves run down large animals, but mainly take young, sick and crippled individuals.

Wolves are much larger than dogs and coyotes (Tables 13 and 14). The skull is characterized by a low braincase, a well developed sagittal crest, rounded auditory bullae, powerful jaws, and large carnassial teeth (PM^4 and M$_1$). Female wolves are about 20% smaller than males.

At Durango South, wolf bones were identified only in Feature 1 at 5LP110. The remains include a juvenile femur (FS 152) and burned metapodials (FS 62). All of the specimens are characterized by large size. Associated with the burned metapodials are a few foot bones of a smaller canid, possibly an adult dog. Three fragmentary, burned skulls (FS 25, skulls "A" and "B") are too crushed to make specific identification possible and are referred to *Canis* sp. Measurements of the alveoli of PM^4 and M^1 in partial maxillae of FS 25 and Skull "B" are smaller than measurements of adult male wolves in Young and Goldman (1944) but approximate measurements of extant coyotes, *Canis latrans*, given by Kurten (1974), Table 13. Therefore, three possibilities exist: 1) the specimens belonged to small wolves, either females or young adults, 2) the specimens are those of coyotes, or 3) adult dogs are represented by the burned fragments. Skull "A" appears to have belonged to a smaller animal than the other two skulls. Unfortunately, the fragments

Table 12. Cranial Differences between Dogs, *Canis familiaris* and Coyotes, *Canis latrans*

Character	Dog, *Canis familiaris*	Coyote, *Canis latrans*
skull profile	steep forehead, angled profile between rostrum and braincase	smoothly curved profile
rostrum	wider	narrower
frontal sinus	large	small
auditory bullae	small	large
length of palate	Bony palate extends beyond M^2.	Bony palate terminates in middle of M^2.
palatine foramen	Anterior palatine foramen is twice as long as wide.	Anterior palatine foramen is three to four times longer than wide.
upper canine	Tip of canine terminates above mental foramen in lower jaw when jaws are articulated. Canine is broader at base.	Tip of canine terminates below mental foramen. Canine is narrower at base.
premolars	broader	narrower
tooth row	Short, curved. Level of mandibular tooth row curved upward.	longer, straighter
crowding of teeth	often crowded or irregularly spaced	teeth more widely spaced
mandible	massive, deep dorso-ventrally, thick latero-medially, wider across molars	slimmer jaw, narrower across molars
PM_4	one cusp between main cusp and cingulum	two cusps between main cusp and cingulum

Table 13. Comparative Skull and Tooth Measurements (in mm): Canids from Durango South, Recent Coyotes (Kurten 1974), Recent Wolves from Colorado (Young and Goldman 1944) and Southwestern Basketmaker Dogs (Lawrence 1967)*

Element	Dog	Dog	Coyote	Dog	Gray Fox	Wolf, Recent	Coyote, Recent	Dog, Basketmaker
	5LP111 FS 91	5LP111 FS 139	5LP111 FS 19	5LP111 F1L2	5LP111 FS 116	N=6	N=6	N=5
condylobasal Lt	134.9	---	---	---	---	237.2	187.0	149.7
basal Lt	125.6	---	---	---	---	---	---	---
palatal Lt	69.8	---	---	---	---	---	---	79.7
rostrum B(C-C)	29.0	---	---	---	---	46.4	31.4	---
B across PM^4-PM^4	51.8	---	---	---	---	---	---	57.2
zygomatic B	78.3	---	---	---	---	137.9	---	89.6
mastoid B	52.0	---	---	---	---	---	---	---
Lt C-M^2	63.2	---	---	---	---	107.0	---	69.2
Lt PM^{1-4}	39.6	---	---	---	---	---	---	---
Lt M^{1-2}	16.7	---	---	---	---	---	---	---
Lt PM^4	15.8	14.6	---	---	---	25.2	20.0 (N=26)	17.5
max B PM^4 (protocone)	9.0	7.9	---	---	---	13.6	9.8 (N=26)	9.5
B M^1	14.4	13.1	---	---	---	23.3	17.6 (N=26)	---
Lt M^1	10.9	9.5	---	---	---	16.8	13.3 (N=26)	---
Lt mandible	105.5	101.5	ca 130.1	---	ca 86.4	182.3	144.4 (N=26)	---

*List of abbreviations in appendix.

Table 13, cont'd. Comparative Skull and Tooth Measurements

Element	Dog	Dog	Coyote	Dog	Gray Fox	Wolf, Recent	Coyote, Recent	Dog, Basket-maker
	5LP111 FS 91	5LP111 FS 139	5LP111 FS 19	5LP111 F1 L2	5LP111 FS 116	N=6	N=6	N=5
H mandible	43.6	40.4	45.3	---	38.0	76.8	---	---
De ramus at PM_{2-3}	15.7	15.3	15.4	17.0	9.2	---	---	---
De ramus at M_{1-2}	18.5	15.3	20.2	17.4	11.2	---	---	---
greatest thickness of ramus below M_1	10.1	8.8	9.3	9.8	5.8	---	---	10.6
Lt $C-M_3$	69.8	69.4	alv Lt ca 85.5	76.6	56.1	---	---	---
Lt PM_{1-4}	ca 31.2	29.8	alv Lt ca 38.7	32.2	ca 26.6	---	---	---
Lt M_{1-3}	28.4	27.1	alv Lt ca 35.3	ca 31.0	23.1	---	36.0	---
Lt PM_4	8.9	8.3	alv Lt 10.8	9.7	7.4	---	12.8	10.6
B PM_4	4.7	4.7	---	5.3	3.2	---	5.7	5.6
Lt M_1	17.7	17.3	alv Lt 20.5	9.7	7.4	---	12.8 (N=21)	10.6
B M_1 (talonid)	6.8	6.6	---	7.8	5.1	---	8.1 (N=21)	8.3
Lt M_2	7.2	6.5	9.9	7.4	6.8	---	10.1 (N=26)	8.4
B M_2	6.3	5.7	7.1	5.7	4.9	---	---	6.6
Lt M_3	4.1	3.7	---	---	---	---	---	---
B M_3	3.9	3.4	---	---	---	---	---	---

Table 14. Postcranial Measurements (in mm) of Dogs and Wolves from Durango South*

Element	Dog	Dog	Dog	Dog	Wolf	Wolf	Wolf
	5LP111 FS 91	5LP111 FS 139	5LP111 F2 S L3	5LP111 F1 L2	5LP110 F1 SW L3	5LP110 FS 62	5LP110 FS 152
GLt scapula	88.7	82.2	---	---	---	---	---
GLt glenoid fossa	21.5	20.9	---	---	---	---	---
GLt humerus	113.6	---	---	---	---	---	---
DB humerus	22.5	ca 21.2	---	---	---	---	---
LSB humerus	9.7	---	---	---	---	---	---
GLt radius	111.7	109.7	---	---	---	---	---
PB radius	13.2	11.3	---	---	---	---	---
DB radius	17.1	17.2	---	---	---	---	---
GLt ulna	132.2	---	---	---	---	---	---
B olecranon process	15.2	---	---	---	---	---	---
GLt innominate	104.0	101.0	---	---	---	---	---
GLt femus	121.4	114.6	---	---	---	---	---
PB femus	29.5	27.4	---	---	---	---	ca 44.2
DB femus	23.3	21.7	---	---	---	---	---
LSB femur	10.2	10.0	---	---	---	---	16.2
GLt tibia	123.9	---	---	---	---	---	---
PB tibia	25.7	---	22.8	---	---	---	---

*List of abbreviations in appendix.

Table 14, cont'd. Postcranial Measurements

Element	Dog 5LP111 FS 91	Dog 5LP111 FS 139	Dog 5LP111 F2 S L3	Dog 5LP111 F1 L2	Wolf 5LP110 F1 SW L3	Wolf 5LP110 FS 62	Wolf 5LP110 FS 152
GLt scapholunar	16.0	15.5	---	---	---	30.6	---
GLt astragalus	20.3	18.0	---	---	---	---	---
GLt calcaneum	32.1	29.8	---	---	---	ca 60.1	---
GB calcaneum	12.6	11.2	---	---	---	21.1	---
GLt cuboid	11.7	10.3	---	---	20.5	21.5	---
GLt MC II	38.0	39.7	---	---	---	86.3	---
shaft B MC II	4.9	4.8	---	---	---	8.9	---
GLt MC III	42.8	45.0	---	---	---	---	---
shaft B MC III	4.9	4.3	---	---	---	7.9	---
GLt MC IV	44.0	44.6	---	---	---	---	---
shaft B MC IV	4.4	4.3	---	---	---	7.6	---
GLt MC V	37.2	36.8	---	40.5	---	82.0	---
shaft B MC V	4.5	4.6	---	5.0	---	8.8	---
GLt MT II	42.0	---	---	---	---	---	---
shaft B MT II	4.8	---	---	---	---	7.1	---
GLt MT III	48.6	---	---	---	---	---	---
shaft B MT III	5.0	---	---	---	---	9.3	---
GLt MT IV	50.3	---	---	---	---	---	---
shaft B MT IV	4.7	---	---	---	---	7.7	---
GLt MT V	44.5	---	---	---	---	---	---
shaft B MT V	3.6	---	---	---	---	6.3	---

are too small for comparative study. Why only canid skulls and foot bones are burned remains a mystery. Two middle phalanges (FS 62) show butchering marks (Fig. 90), and terminal phalanges are absent indicating that they remained in the skin.

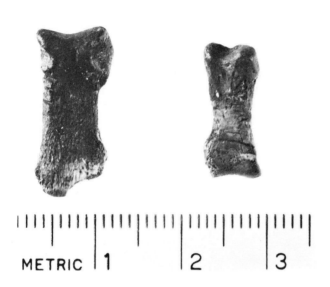

Figure 90. *Canis lupus.* Two burned middle phalanges (FS 62) showing butchering marks.

Coyote, *Canis latrans*

Minimum number of individuals: 1 Number of specimens: 1 (0 artifacts)

A single jaw (5LP111 Feature 2, No. 119) is tentatively referred to *Canis latrans.* The jaw is more slender, and the tooth row is longer and straighter than the specimens of Indian dog from Durango South. Only M_2 is present; it is slightly worn. Measurements of the jaw and alveoli of the teeth are close to those of recent coyotes in Kurten (1974), see Table 13.

Coyotes live in open woodlands, brushy areas and prairies from low desert valleys to timberline in western and central North America as far north as Alaska and as far south as Costa Rica. About the size of a border collie or half the size of a wolf, coyotes have a more slender build than wolves, with a long thin face and small feet. Coyotes eat everything that is edible and some things that are not; rodents and rabbits make up at least half of their diet, and carrion and at times fruit are also important. Although coyotes are relentlessly persecuted by man, these adaptable canids are expanding their range in some areas.

Indian Dog, *Canis familiaris*

Minimum number of individuals: 7 Number of specimens: 560+ (14 artifacts)

Dogs are descended from Old World wolves and apparently entered the New World in association with man. The earliest known occurrence of dogs in North America is from Jaguar Cave, Lemhi County, Idaho (dates 10,370 plus or minus 350 years BP) where two distinct size classes are recognized (Lawrence 1967). Indian dogs are common in many archaeological sites. Dog burials have frequently been found at Pueblo sites in the Southwest. Allen (1920) recognized three general types of Indian dogs: a large wolf-like Eskimo dog, an intermediate-sized animal and a much smaller terrier-sized canid. Each general type tended to form local, rather well defined breeds such as the Basketmaker dog and the Techichi, both of which belong to the terrier-sized group. Of course, all of them were mongrels and interbreeding was frequent. Dogs probably served many purposes prehistorically.

There was a minimum of seven dogs at Durango South. Of these, two are juveniles (epiphyses lost), three are young adults (permanent dentition in place, epiphyses nearly ossified) and two are adult animals (sutures not visible). There are no old animals (teeth heavily worn or lost, resorbtion of bone). In addition 14 artifacts including several beads were made from dog bones.

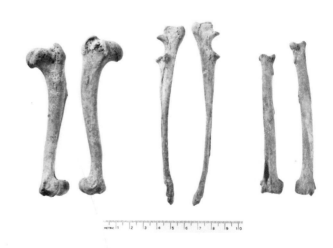

Figure 91. *Canis familiaris.* Left and right humeri, ulnae, and radii of Indian dog FS 91 showing the shorter left forelimb caused by a fetal deformity.

146

The most complete assemblage (FS 91, Fig. 21) is a skull, mandible, and nearly complete skeleton of an adolescent dog. The skull sutures are still visible and on the long bones, the epiphyses are fused, but the ephyseal lines are distinct. The teeth are moderately worn, probably reflecting a rough diet. There is a small depressed area on the left frontal, probably caused by a clubbing. The left forelimb is shorter than the right (Fig. 91, Table 15). The shaft of the left

Table 15. Measurements (in mm) of the Forelimb of FS 91, Indian Dog, *Canis familiaris.*

Element	Right Forelimb	Left Forelimb
humerus		
greatest length	113.6	110.0
depth proximal end	31.1	31.6
distal breadth	22.5	22.6
least shaft breadth	9.7	9.8
radius		
greatest length	111.7	100.6
proximal breadth	13.2	12.8
distal breadth	17.1	17.7
shaft breadth	8.6	8.9
ulna		
greatest length	132.2	129.2
breadth olecranon		
process	15.2	15.8
shaft breadth	7.0	7.4

ulna is slightly flattened and the styloid process is enlarged. The left radius has a deep (ca 6mm) groove that nearly penetrates the bone on the concave surface just above the distal epiphyses and extends about 16mm upward; the distal end is roughened with several protuberances. The right forelimb shows no abnormalities nor does either hind limb. There is a 15mm long cut on the shaft of the right humerus and a faint line on the shaft of the left humerus. Robert D. Strand of the Alpine Hospital for Animals, Boulder, Colorado suggested the shortened left forelimb must be a fetal deformity. The bones are not abnormally curved as they might be by a congenital deformity, and an injury which might have affected the development of one of the bones would not have shortened the others.

Another dog (FS 139) is represented by a fragmentary skull, mandible and partial skeleton. This dog is approximately the same age as dog FS 91. The cusps of M^1 are worn smooth as is the talonid of M_1; this is probably due to abrasive food. Most of the limb bones are broken, but there are no signs of butchering marks. A jaw symphysis belonged to an adult animal. The alveolus of right PM_1 has been resorbed and there is evidence of an abcess between the canine and PM_2. Another specimen, the proximal end of a right tibia, has been butchered--the medial and lateral condyles and the spine have been cut off. Two other foot bones have cut marks on them . None of the other dog material shows any signs of butchering.

Allen (1920) observed that the first premolar was usually absent in Indian dogs. Of the specimens from Durango South, PM_1 is either in place or the tooth has fallen out but the alveolus is open; on only one, the right mandible of No. 2, is the alveolus of PM_1 closed.

The Indian dogs from Durango South were long-nosed and stood about 33cm high at the shoulder. They belonged to Allen's (1920) third class of Indian dogs, small terrier-sized animals.

Gray fox, *Urocyon cinereoargenteus*

Minimum number of individuals: 1 Number of specimens : 2 (0 artifacts)

An inhabitant of brushy wooded areas, the gray fox is found from southern Canada to northern South America except in the Northwest and Great Plains. It is distinguished from other canids by its coloration--a black dorsal tail stripe, gray back and rusty sides. This fox is omnivorous, but small mammals, especially mice, make up a large proportion of its diet.

The only indication of the presence of the gray fox at Durango South is an associated right and left mandible belonging to the same individual. The dentition is slightly worn and is complete except for the incisors, M_3's and the right PM_1. The mandible of the gray fox is easily distinguished from that of the red fox, *Vulpes vulpes*, by the presence of a "step" between the condyle and the angle of the jaw (Fig. 92). There are no butchering marks on the specimens.

Family Ursidae
Black bear, *Ursus americanus*

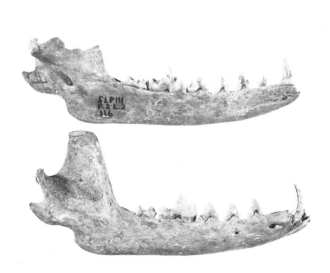

Figure 92. *Urocyon cinereoargenteus.* Left and right mandibles (FS 116) of a gray fox showing the "step" between the condyle and angle of jaw.

Minimum number of individuals: 1 Number of specimens: 3 (1 artifact)

The forest-dwelling black bear is found in montane regions of Canada, the United States and northern Mexico. Smallest of the American bears, it weighs from 90 to 214+kg, and is generally solitary except for females with cubs. Black bears are omnivorous and feed on berries, tubers, small mammals, eggs, and carrion.

Only three elements, the distal end of a right femur, a partial left calcaneum and a lower canine, probably from the same adult individual, were found in 5LP111 Feature 2. The canine had been drilled for use as a pendant (see Modification Attributes of Bone Tools, Chapter III, Fig. 79a). There is no trace of butchering marks on the other bones. Bear hunting was apparently not common in southwestern Colorado during late Basketmaker times; bears are not reported from Yellow Jacket (MT3) or Mesa Verde (sites 499, 866, and 876, Lister 1966).

Family Cervidae
Wapiti, *Cervus canadensis*

Minimum Number of individuals: 2 number of specimens: 11 (2 artifacts)

Compared to deer, remains of wapiti are never abundant in archaeological sites; their large size and formidable appearance probably deterred Indians from hunting them regularly, and they were only taken when an easy opportunity presented itself. Wapiti formerly ranged over the northern two-thirds of the continent, but today they are restricted to isolated areas in the west. Their habitat is semi-open forests and mountain meadows where they feed on grasses, herbs, twigs, and bark. Antler fragments were the only remains recovered; FS 17 (probably used as a baton) and FS 42 (not utilized) were burned. FS 113, an antler tip, is not burned and belonged to a smaller animal.

Mule deer, *Odocoileus hemionus*

Minimum number of individuals: 4 Number of specimens: 63 (30 artifacts)

Mule deer are widely distributed from high mountains to desert valleys in southwestern Canada and the western United States southward to the Tropic of Cancer in Mexico. In late fall, they drift downward from the mountains to sheltered valleys to escape heavy winter snows. Browsers, deer feed on shrubs and twigs. Mule deer are the most important big game animal in the west.

Deer are common in Southwestern archaeological sites, having been used for food, possibly clothing, and bone and antler tools. A minimum of four animals are represented at Durango South mainly by antler and rib fragments and foot bones. In addition, 30 artifacts made from deer bones were recovered. Many of the bones are burned, gnawed or weathered.

At most sites, including Durango South, distal ends of long bones of large mammals are more numerous than proximal ends. This can be attributed to preferences of scavengers for the spongy proximal ends. In tool manufacture distal ends of bones are more often used than proximal ends and metatarsals are favored over metacarpals since they are denser and straighter-walled.

Although the faunal sample from Durango South is not inclusive, it gives a good indication of the animals present in the area and how some of them were utilized by the local inhabitants. The fauna is similar to that found at other archaeological sites in southwestern Colorado (e.g. Mesa Verde, Yellow Jacket) except for the presence of *Perognathus, Reithrodontomys, Canis lupus, Urocyon cinereoargenteus,* and *Ursus americanus* at Durango South.

148

Acknowledgments

I would like to thank Joe Ben Wheat for help in identifying the bone tools. Judith Van Couvering permitted me to use comparative skeletal material at the University of Colorado Museum. Finally, thanks are due to the crew who collected and numbered the specimens from 5LP110 and 5LP111.

Pollen Analysis

by
Susan K. Short

Introduction

Palynology in the Southwest has been used: 1) to recover information about past physical environments; 2) to recover information about prehistoric diet; 3) to date sites relative to one another; 4) for intrasite dating (Hill and Hevly 1968); and 5) to isolate functionally distinct areas within and between sites (Hill and Hevly 1968). The purposes of this project were loosely defined at the time the samples were collected, but the main goal was to recover information about prehistoric diet and use of the environment.

Field and Laboratory Methods

Thirteen samples were collected by Joel Brisbin from 5LP110 and 5LP111 (Table 16). Samples were taken from specialized occupational features such as pots, cists, hearths, etc. and from occupational and postoccupational levels defined in the field.

Pollen was extracted from the sediments following a procedure adapted from Mehringer (1967) and Schoenwetter (personal communication), involving flotation and screening of the samples, solution of the inorganic fraction in HCl, HF, and HNO_3, and reduction of the organic fraction with caustic soda and Erdtman's acetolysis. For more detailed information on the chemical processing, see Table 20. Eleven of the samples yielded sufficient pollen for analysis.

Table 16. Pollen Samples from 5LP110 and 5LP111

Sample	Description
5LP110, FS 1	bowl fill, vessel 1
5LP110, FS 64	jar fill, vessel 17
5LP110, FS 73	jar fill, vessel 23
5LP110, FS 31	jar fill, vessel 21
5LP110, FS 46	olla fill, vessel 12
5LP110, SF 57	heating pit fill
5LP110, SF 43	hearth fill
5LP110, FS 83	mortar fill
5LP110, SF 47	floor, wing wall bin
5LP111, FS 26	bowl fill, vessel 32
5LP111, SF 3	firepit fill
5LP111, SF 1	hearth fill
5LP111, SF 7	cist fill

Counting and Analysis

Pollen preservation was generally poor and there was a large amount of debris consisting primarily of charcoal fragments on the slides. Counting was consequently slow and difficult. Two samples, 5LP110 SF 43 and 5LP111 SF 3, did not produce sufficient pollen for analysis. Because of the sparseness of the material, most of the slides were counted under low power (200x). Only one sample, 5LP110 FS 1, produced sufficient pollen to be counted under 500x magnification. A standard 200-count was achieved on all but one (5LP111 SF 1) of the samples. This sparseness of pollen is not uncommon in pollen samples from Southwestern archaeological sites. In a study of pollen analysis of soils, Dimbleby (1957) states that alkaline soils, especially those with a pH greater than 6, are virtually useless for pollen analysis because of the decomposition of the grains; differential destruction of smaller pollen grains is also likely. In addition, pollen content of soils is reduced by fire (Dimbleby 1957:27). "Dilution" of the pollen rain by the soil is a third factor to consider.

No attempt was made to duplicate Schoenwetter's research design based on the adjusted pollen sum and AP (arboreal pollen) percentages (Schoenwetter and Eddy 1964; Schoenwetter 1970). The total of 11 samples from these sites is too small to test either the validity of the adjusted pollen sum or the hypothesis that decreasing AP values represent decreased rainfall or changes in the rainfall pattern. Without modern pollen deposition data from the area, it is difficult to interpret archaeological AP values.

Researchers in the Southwest exclude various pollen types from the total pollen sum, depending on their research design. Most are interested in separating the effect of human activity from the effect of climatic change on the vegetation, and hence on the pollen rain. Southwestern palynologists are not unified, however, on what to exclude from the pollen sum or what constitutes an economic type. Although at least one "definite" economic type *(Zea)* was recovered and a number of others may have been present, the percentage data (Fig. 93) are represented without exclusions. Removing *Zea* from the 200-count totals did not change the percentage results for any other taxa by more than a few percentage points (Table 17).

Pinus edulis (pinyon pine) was not distinguished from *Pinus ponderosa* (ponderosa or yellow pine) in this study. The size of pine pollen is often used in the Southwest as an index to species (Hansen and Cushing 1973). Smaller grains are usually referred to *P.edulis* and larger grains to *P. ponderosa.* However, the reliability of size frequency identification of eastern pine species has been criticized by Whitehead (1964). Most of the grains in this study were small and in poor condition, although there was a range of variation that probably included *P. ponderosa* grains.

Schoenwetter (personal communication) has noted that in poorly preserved material, *Artemisia* (sage) pollen exhibits a great range of morphological variation. In this study poorly preserved grains resembling *Artemisia* are assigned to that taxa.

The Cheno-Am group combines the pollen of the *Chenopodiaceae* (goosefoot) family and *Amaranthus* (pigweed). It is almost impossible to distinguish the pollen types within this group with the use of the light microscope.

A relative (percentage) data diagram (Fig. 93) and an "absolute" data diagram were constructed from the pollen counts. However, only the former is included here. The absolute data diagram contributes little to the interpretations presented in this paper. Factors affecting the density of pollen grains in archaeological sites have been discussed above. Fire, especially, can reduce the pollen content of a sample and the majority of the analyzed samples contained abundant charcoal fragments. Thus, the "absolute" values do not necessarily reflect the prehistoric values.

Common names for all pollen types used in this

Table 17. Adjusted AP Values - Minus *Zea*

Sample	AP	Adjusted AP
5LP110, FS 1	33	33
5LP110, FS 64	37	38
5LP110, FS 73	25	27
5LP110, FS 31	18.5	19.5
5LP110, FS 46	27	29
5LP110, SF 57	33	35
5LP110, FS 83	25.5	27.5
5LP110, SF 47	20	20
5LP111, FS 26	22.5	23.5
5LP111, SF 1	34	38
5LP111, SF 7	57	59

paper or recorded on the diagrams can be found in Table 21.

Vegetation

The area immediately surrounding the sites can be characterized as semi-desert (see The Setting, Chapter I, for elevation and climate). An *Artemisia*-association dominates the alluvial fan on which the sites are located, with other shrubs and pinyon pines also common. A variety of plant communities are present on higher plateau areas in the immediate vicinity. A list of the modern flora, observed by J. Steven Meyer, is presented in Table 18.

Maher (1963) studied the modern pollen rain in the Animas River valley upstream from Durango. Because no modern surface pollen samples were collected from the Durango South sites, his results for the Durango City Reservoir will serve as a control for the archaeological pollen record. Table 19 lists values for 11 selected taxa at the Durango City Reservoir station (Maher 1963:Fig. 3).

Pollen Analyses

Although the reconstruction of the past vegetation is not a stated goal of the study, it would appear that most of the present vegetational taxa (Tables 18, 19) were present at the time the sites were occupied.

The pollen samples can be divided into two main groups: 1) vessel contents and 2) samples from other occupational features (cists, hearths, etc.). The diagram reflects this division. The six vessel samples will be considered first, five from 5LP110

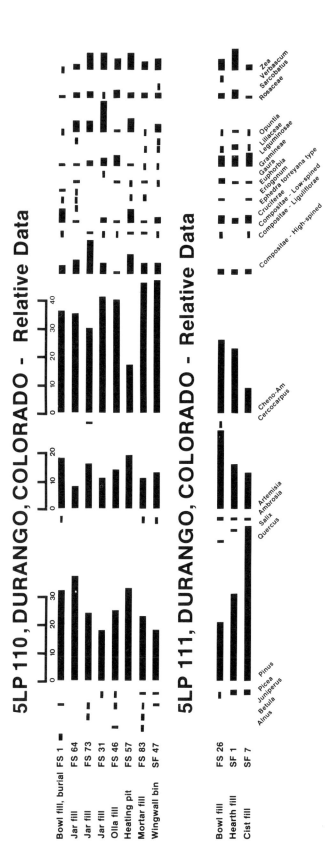

Figure 93. Relative pollen data from 5LP110 and 5LP111: percentage of pollen grains per type, with 100% = standard 200-count from each soil sample.

Table 18. Flora List, 5LP110 and 5LP111

Taxa	Family	Common Name
Pinus edulis	Pinaceae	pinyon pine
Quercus gambelii	Fagaceae	scrub oak
Artemisia tridentata	Compositae	big sagebrush
Artemisia ludoviciana	Compositae	prairie sage
Chrysothamnus parryi	Compositae	rabbitbrush
Gutierrezia sarothrae	Compositae	snakeweed
Helianthus tuberosus	Compositae	sunflower
Lactuca scariola	Compositae	prickly lettuce
Descurainia pinata	Cruciferae	tansy mustard
Salsola kali	Chenopodiaceae	tumbleweed/Russian thistle
Kochia scoparia	Chenopodiaceae	burning bush
Chenopodium album	Chenopodiaceae	lambsquarters
Opuntia davisii	Cactaceae	prickly pear
Oryzopsis hymenoides	Gramineae	Indian ricegrass
Bromus tectorum	Gramineae	cheat-grass
Sitanion hysterix	Gramineae	squirrel-tail
Lotus wrightii	Leguminosae	red-and-yellow deervetch
Euphorbia glyptosperma	Euphorbiaceae	spurge
Malva neglecta	Malvaceae	cheeseweed
Verbascum thapsus	Scrophulariaceae	great mullein
Verbena braceata	Verbenaceae	large-bracted vervain

Table 19. Surface Sample Spectrum, Durango City Reservoir, Station 25 (Elevation: 2095 m, 6870')

Taxa	# Grains	Percentage
Pinus	50	16%
Picea	4	1%
Abies	1	.3%
Pseudotsuga	1	.3%
Quercus	41	13%
Salix	4	1%
Artemisia	6	2%
Ambrosia-type	6	2%
Cheno-Am	104	33%
Gramineae	81	26%

and one from 5LP111. In the following discussion, percentage values are compared internally within the two Durango South sites.

5LP110 FS 1

This sample, bowl fill from a burial, is characterized by moderately high pine percentages (32%), moderate sage values (18%), and moderately high Cheno-Am percentages (36%). All three of the above taxa are large producers of pollen, and all three are reported to have ethnographic and archaeological significance. However, by comparison to the other spectra and by comparison with the modern Durango sample, economic usage cannot be definitely stated.

5LP110 FS 64

This sample, the contents of a jar, is characterized by high pine (37%), moderately high Cheno-Am (35%), and low sage (8%) percentages. The values recorded in this sample do not suggest any specific economic use.

5LP110 FS 73

This jar sample contains moderately low percentages of pine pollen (24%), moderate sage (16%) and Cheno-Am (30%) percentages, and large values of the high-spine compositae group (12%). Since high-spine compositae is insect-pollinated, such a large value would not be expected in the local pollen rain which is dominated by wind-pollinated species. In addition, members of this group produce seed clusters in the form of "heads" which are easily harvested and which will usually incorporate pollen with the seed collection. Thus, it is suggested that composite seeds, possibly *Helianthus* (sunflower, a long-spined Compositae), were stored in the jar.

Zea percentages are moderately low (6%) in this sample; percentages in this range or slightly lower characterize the majority of the samples in this study. Although wind-pollinated, *Zea* does not contribute heavily to the natural pollen rain. In one study of modern Indian corn fields (Martin and Byers 1965), values as low as .22% in one sample of 24,000 grains and .14% in another sample of 13,000 grains were reported. Also, it is unlikely that much corn pollen would adhere to shelled ground corn (Martin and Sharrock 1964). Either these values are an accurate representation of the quantity of corn pollen in the background pollen rain or most of the samples record the actual use of corn pollen-- storage in jars, cists, etc. It is tentatively suggested that these relatively larger corn percentages do not indicate economic use of corn in the specific vessels and that the background pollen rain at the sites contained generally 2-6% *Zea* pollen.

5LP110 FS 31

This sample, jar fill, is characterized by a rather different spectrum: low pine (18%), moderate sage (11%), moderately large Cheno-Am (41%), and large *Opuntia* (prickly pear, 11%) percentages. *Zea* percentages are moderately low (6%).

Opuntia pollen, a large, heavy, grain not suited to air travel, is rare in surface soil samples (Martin and Sharrock 1964); large values of this genus are generally interpreted to represent the use of the flowers. There is ample ethnographic and coprolite evidence for such use (Bryant 1975). Therefore, it is suggested that cactus flowers were being utilized at this site as a food and/or ceremonial item.

The large value for the Cheno-Am group is more difficult to interpret. This group is anemophilous (wind-pollinated), and is abundant in the local pollen rain throughout the Southwest. The Cheno-Am group contains many disturbance plants, that is, plants favored by construction activities and/or agriculture. Thus, larger percentages might be expected during the prehistoric occupation of the area. In addition, plants from this group are known to have been an important food source, both ethnographically and archaeologically (Elmore 1944; Whiting 1939; Bryant 1974). Amaranth and

chenopod seeds were found at 5LP111 (see Seed Remains, this chapter). Finally, unlike most economic types, high percentages of Cheno-Am pollen could result from utilizing the seeds, the leaves, or the flowers (Bryant 1975). Individual plants flower continuously over a period of weeks, even months, ensuring a relatively constant supply of pollen. A value of 41% cannot be interpreted as an "economic" value based on the other samples and the limited knowledge of the modern pollen rain in the area.

5LP110 FS 46

This sample, olla fill, is characterized by low to moderate pine (25%), moderate sage, and moderately high Cheno-Am (40%) percentages. Again, the large Cheno-Am value of this sample cannot be interpreted as evidence of the economic use of that group.

5LP111 FS 26

This bowl fill sample is characterized by moderately low pine (21%), high sage (28%), and moderate Cheno-Am (26%) values. The sage value is almost twice as large as that recorded in any other sample.

The range of variation in the natural pollen rain of this genus is quite large, but it is tentatively suggested that sage flowers, leaves or seeds were used at this site.

The remaining five samples are from specific occupational features that were sampled for their possible economic importance.

5LP110 SF 57

This sample represents the contents of a heating pit; it is characterized by moderately high pine (33%), moderate sage (19%), low Cheno-Am (17%), moderately high high-spined composites (7%), and moderate *Opuntia* (5%).

This spectrum probably does not differ significantly from the background pollen rain, but the high-spined composite and prickly pear values may indicate economic use of these taxa. It is difficult to interpret these two values without a better knowlege of the modern pollen fallout.

5LP110 FS 83

This sample, mortar fill, is characterized by very

high Cheno-Am values (46%) plus moderately low pine (23%) and sage (11%) percentages.

As discussed above, it is difficult to establish the range of variation for any specific taxa in the archaeological pollen rain without a suite of modern pollen samples from the same area. The large percentage of Cheno-Am pollen in this sample may suggest the use of Cheno-Am as a food item at the site; specifically, seeds may have been ground in the mortar. However, the observed value of 46% could occur as part of the natural variation in the pollen rain.

5LP110 SF 46

The spectrum recorded for this sample, the contents of a bin built into the partition wall of the structure, is roughly similar to the above sample with large Cheno-Am (47%), low pine (18%), and moderately low sage (13%) percentages. Again, it is possible that the observed 47% Cheno-Am value indicates storage of seeds in the bin, but further sampling would be necessary to definitely establish this hypothesis.

5LP111 SF 1

This was the only hearth sample that produced countable pollen. This sample is characterized by the largest *Zea* percentage, 11%. Pine (31%) and sage (16%) percentages are moderate, and Cheno-Am values are low (23%).

The large corn percentage here may indicate the presence of flowers, pollen or possibly green corn in the hearth area. Destruction of pollen by fire may explain the very low "absolute" values recorded. In this case, the corn pollen was probably deposited subsequent to the actual use of the hearth.

5LP111 SF 7

The cist sample contains a unique spectrum dominated by pine pollen (58%); all other taxa record very low values.

Rough size measurements were taken and the morphology of this sample was analyzed. The size studies alone are ambiguous. With a combined body and bladder length of about 60μ, most of the grains involved are either large *P. edulis* or small *P. ponderosa* grains (Hansen and Cushing 1973: Fig. 8). Morphological analysis of the bladders (Hansen and Cushing 1973:Fig. 6g) suggests that the majority of the pine grains in this sample are large *P. edulis*. However, an analysis of reference material of the two species suggests considerably more variation than the tables in Hansen and Cushing indicate. Also, the effects of different chemical preparations and the size differences between fresh (Hansen and Cushing) and fossil pine grains (this study) have not been evaluated. Thus, the species of pine pollen present in this cist sample cannot be definitely identified at this time.

Whichever species is represented, it is suggested that the large pine value indicates the actual presence of pine pollen--branches, needles, pine buds--in the cist.

Two samples did not produce sufficient pollen for counting. Partial counts, however, were completed. 5LP110 SF 43, hearth fill, is especially interesting because only composite pollen--four high-spined composites and four low-spine composites-- was recorded. 5LP111 SF 3, the contents of a firepit, produced pollen typical of the background pollen rain *(Pinus, Artemisia, and* Gramineae).

Summary

A stated goal of this project was to recover information about the use of plants by the prehistoric population. Economic plants are domestic and wild plants utilized as food, having ceremonial or medicinal importance, or having other cultural significance (construction, tool manufacture, dyes, etc.). Through pollen sampling, the following taxa have been established as "economic" pollen types at the sites.

Taxa	Provenience
Zea	hearth, 5LP111 SF 1
Pinus	cist, 5LP111 SF 7
Opuntia	vessel 21, 5LP110 FS 31
High-spined	
compositae	vessel 23, 5LP110 FS 73
Artemisia	vessel 32, 5LP111 FS 46
Cheno-Am?	vessel 12, 5LP110 FS 46
	mortar fill, 5LP110 FS 83
	storage bin, 5LP110 SF 47

Because of the small sample size and lack of modern pollen data, the problems that arose during analysis cannot be resolved at this time. For this reason, the Cheno-Am group cannot be definitely stated, on the basis of the pollen data alone, to be of economic importance in 5LP110 and 5LP111.

Table 20. Chemical Processes Used to Prepare the Archaeological Pollen Samples

1. Crush sample in mortar.
2. Weigh in 400 ml beaker.
3. Add 50-100 ml distilled water.
4. Add concentrated HCl until evolution of gases ceases.
5. Swirl, rest 45-60 seconds, decant through screening into second beaker.
6. Second swirl, rest 60-90 seconds, decant through screening into weighed test tubes, two tubes per sample.
7. Centrifuge and decant until all decant is in tubes.
8. Save heavy fraction, dry, and bag.
9. Two HCl washes, one 15% wash and one concentrated HCl wash.
10. Distilled water wash, centrifuge and decant.
11. Add concentrated HF slowly; place in boiling water for one hour; let stand overnight, centrifuge and decant.
12. Add fresh HF; place in boiling water for one hour; let stand overnight, centrifuge and decant.
13. Two hot distilled water washes, centrifuge and decant.
14. Add nitric acid (50%); let stand ten minutes, centrifuge and decant.
15. Two hot distilled water washes, centrifuge and decant.
16. Add concentrated HCl; place in boiling water bath until liquid in tubes begins to bubble; centrifuge and decant.
17. Two hot distilled water washes, centrifuge and decant.
18. Add 10% NaOH, place in hot water bath 20-30 minutes, centrifuge and decant.
19. Distilled water wash.
20. Glacial acetic acid wash.
21. Add acetolysis mixture, place in boiling water bath 30 minutes, centrifuge and decant.
22. Glacial acetic acid wash.
23. Two distilled water washes, centrifuge and decant.
24. Dry residue; stain with safranin and glycerol.
25. Weigh sample plus tube; prepare three or more weighed slides per sample.

Table 21. Common Names of Pollen Types

Abies	fir
Alnus	alder
Amaranthus	pigweed
Ambrosia	ragweed
Artemisia	sagebrush
Betula	birch
Cercocarpus	mountain mahogany
Cheno-Am	goosefoot-amaranth group
Compositae - high-spined	
Compositae - liguliflorae	sunflower family
Compositae - low-spined	
Cruciferae	mustard family
Ephedra torreyana	Mormon tea
Eriogonum	Eriogonum (buckwheat family)
Euphorbia	spurge
Gaura	Gaura (evening-primrose family)
Gramineae	grass family
Helianthus	sunflower
Juniperus	juniper
Leguminosae	pea family
Liliaceae	lily family
Opuntia	prickly pear
Picea	spruce
Pinus	pine
Pinus edulis	pinyon pine
Pinus ponderosa	Ponderosa pine
Pseudotsuga	Douglas-fir
Quercus	oak
Rosaceae	rose family
Salix	willow
Sarcobatus	greasewood
Verbascum	mullein
Zea	maize

Paleo-Ethnobotanical Remains

by
Lorraine Dobra

Soil samples for flotation and paleo-ethnobotanical analysis were collected from vessels, cists, and architectural features at 5LP110 and 5LP111. Samples were floated after field excavation was completed. One-half of each sample was retained as a control in case of damage during flotation and for possible future investigations. When the amount of soil collected was less than one liter, at least .25 liter of soil was floated; in samples of more than one liter of soil, .5 liter was floated.

The flotation method employed was similar to that described by Streuver (1968). First, the sample was visually inspected for macroscopic organic remains. Next, two gallons of water were stirred with a large spoon, creating a centrifugal action. This action aided in separating the lighter fraction of the soil from the heavier fraction, as soil was poured into the bucket. Because of the different specific densities between organic and inorganic materials, the organic debris floated to the top of the water.

The organic remains were scooped from the surface with a tea strainer covered with 1/40 inch mesh screen. When all of the visible organic material was removed, the contents of the bucket were emptied over three screens of consecutively smaller meshes of 1/16, 1/40 and 1/80 inches. Following macroscopic inspection of the screened contents for additional material, the organic remains recovered were air dried.

When the samples were dry, they were scanned under a microscope at 16x power. Since the purpose of the study was analysis of the botanical remains, seeds were separated from bits of charcoal, bone fragments, and other organic debris, and were retained for identification. The use of Martin and Barkley's (1961) *Seed Identification Manual* aided in analysis of the seed material. Robert Bye, an ethnobotanist of the University of Colorado Biology Department, confirmed the identifications.

Most of the material recovered was charred and poorly preserved. Identification was possible to the family level and in some cases to the genus level.

Results

Organic remains at 5LP110 and 5LP111 include pinyon nuts, an immature juniper berry and seed material identified as ground-cherry, globemallow, chenopodium, amaranth, and grasses (Table 22). With the exception of the grasses, all of the seed

Table 22. Seed Remains from Durango South

Genus	Family	Common Name
	5LP110	
	Gramineae	grass
Zea	Gramineae	corn species: *mays*
Juniperus	Pinaceae	juniper
Physalis	Solanaceae	ground-cherry
Sphaeralcea	Malvaceae	globemallow
Chenopodium	Chenopodiaceae	chenopod
Amaranthus	Amaranthaceae	amaranth
Pinus edulis	Pinaceae	pinyon pine
	5LP111	
	Gramineae	grass
Zea	Gramineae	corn species: *mays*
Physalis	Solanaceae	ground-cherry

specimens were recovered from cists (Table 23). In 5LP110 Feature 1, charred fragments of corn cobs were found in three places: within a jar (Vessel 17, FS 64), on the floor, and in the partition wall bin; in 5LP111 Feature 2 a charred fragment of cob was uncovered in the lower fill.

Corn was the only domesticate found in the sites. Although there was no evidence of beans or squash, the other common domesticates of this area, they may have been present during occupation. Such factors as differential preservation and method of food preparation may explain their absence.

An "economic" plant is one utilized for food, medicine, construction, ceremonies, or any other cultural purpose. It is difficult to assign a definite economic value to the seed materials retrieved because of the small number of soil samples collected and seeds recovered. However, there is documentation that historic Southwestern Indians have used all plants represented by these seed remains.

Table 23. Proveniences of Seed Remains from Durango South

Provenience   **Seed Remains**

5LP110 Feature 1 - 13 samples, 9 with identifiable remains

Provenience	Seed Remains
SF 32 posthole	no identification possible
SF 33 posthole	grass, immature juniper berry
SF 34 cist	no remains
SF 35 cist	no remains
SF 36 cist	grass
SF 37 posthole	grass
SF 38 cist	grass, ground-cherry, globemallow
SF 39 cist	chenopod
SF 47 wing wall bin	corn - 11 rows
SF 52 cist	amaranth
FS 58 vessel 29	no remains
SF 62 cist	globemallow
FS 64 jar, vessel 17	corn

5LP111 Feature 2 - 7 samples, 6 with identifiable remains

Provenience	Seed Remains
SF 5 cist	grass
SF 6 cist	grass
SF 17 posthole	grass
SF 18 posthole	grass
SF 24 cist	ground-cherry
SF 30 posthole	no identification possible
SF 37 posthole	grass

V. Human Skeletal Remains

Introduction
by Edward J. Rowen III

Five burials, which include the remains of nine individuals, were recovered during excavations at 5LP110 and 5LP111. Location and orientation of the burials has been dealt with in Chapter II. The skeletal material was analyzed to describe metric (anthropometric), nonmetric (anthroscopic), and pathological and anomalous features of the population. The skeletal analysis adds to previous studies complied for the general region (Nickens 1974a, b, 1975a, b; Robinson 1974; Swedlund 1969).

The methods in this report follow those used by Nickens (1974a, b, 1975a, b) in establishing a standard for recording data in this region. For all notations and abbreviations used in the following text and tables, see the list of abbreviations (appendix).

Principle sources used in this study include the following: Anatomical features, sex, age and measurements - Anderson (1969), Bass (1971), Brothwell (1972), Warwick and Williams (1973), Krogman (1962), and Molnar (1971); stature - Genoves (1967); pathologies and anomalies - Brothwell (1972), Brothwell and Sandison (1967), Jarcho (1966), Saul (1972), and Wells (1964).

Only data from individuals complete enough to be measured are included in the tables.

Burial Descriptions

The five burials contained the remains of five adults

and three children, plus one isolated tooth found with one of the infants. Table 24 summarizes individual specimen data, i.e. age, sex, stature and cranial deformation. A brief description and inventory of each burial is summarized below.

5LP110

Burial 1: The burial contained the remains of one female individual. The general condition of the skeletal material is fair with most bones present, although many were broken postmortem. Missing bones include the sternum, patellae, left radius and ulna, and several carpals and tarsals. All the bones of the calotte are present although they have separated along suture lines and were deformed postmortem. The calotte was not reconstructed. Although both maxillae are present, they were not complete enough to reconstruct the face.

Burial 2: The remains of this child are in poor condition. Bones present include the right and left femora, right and left humeri, left ulna, left radius, right and left fibulae, rib fragments, skull fragments (calotte), vertebrae fragments, scapulae fragments, right and left ilia, and one deciduous mandibular molar. None of the epiphyses were present. One extra premolar (maxillary) was found in association with this material. The tooth was excluded from further analysis, since it does not fit with either this burial or the underlying burial (Burial 3), and shows no pathologies.

Burial 3: The bones of this male individual are in generally good condition. All skeletal parts are present except for the sternum.

Table 24. Individual Specimen Data

Site/Burial	Sex	Age	Stature (in cm)	Artificial Deformation of Cranium
5LP110 Burial 1	F	25-30	157.077_3.513 (R-L tibia)	none
5LP110 Burial 2	?	2-4	---	---
5LP110 Burial 3	M	25-30	158.813_3.417 (R femur)	none
5LP111 Burial 1	M?	20-25	---	---
5LP111 Burial 2				
Individual A	F	35+	150.821_3.513 (R tibia)	---
Individual B	?	1-2	---	---
Individual C	M?	Adult	---	---

Key: --- no observations possible.

5LP111

Burial 1: The remains of the primary individual contained in the burial were scattered and fragmentary. Material present included the mandible, left maxillary fragment, left petrous temporal bone, some cranial fragments, and one loose M^3. A second individual is represented by thin calotte fragments and is thought to be either an infant or young child. The second individual is not included further in the analysis because of the scarcity of the remains.

Burial 2: This burial consisted of scattered and fragmentary remains in poor condition. At least three individuals are represented as follows:

A: Represented by long bones (left and right femora, tibiae, and fibulae, and right humerus, ulna, radius), innominate, and three incisors and one molar. Fragments of scapula, sternum, ribs, vertebrae, carpals, and tarsals may also be included with this individual.

B: Represented by thin cranial fragments.

C: Represented mainly by a left tibial shaft. One M^3 and a right zygomatic fragment may be associated with this individual or with individual A from this burial. This may be the same individual as 5LP111 Burial 1. Since a positive identification is not possible, the two individuals are kept separate in this report.

Anthroposcopy

The nonmetrical macroscopic observations of this series are summarized in Table 27. In addition, 5LP110 Burial 3 has a parabolically shaped palate, a slight palatal torus, a concavo-convex nasal profile, and a medium degree of chin projection. 5LP110 Burial 1 and 5LP111 Burial 1 show pronounced and slight degrees of chin projection respectively. Other cranial characterisics are sexually differentiated; 5LP110 Burial 1 has a supra-orbital ridge and a median chin form. 5LP110 Burial 3 has a medium supra-orbital ridge and a bilateral chin form. 5LP111 Burial 1 also shows a bilateral chin form.

Anthropometry

Tables 25 and 26 present the cranial and postcranial metric variability measured in this sample. Although sexual dimorphism was observed between the three males and two females from these sites, it was not quantifiable.

Pathologies and Anomalies

Dental

Dental observations were difficult and in some cases impossible because of missing or damaged dentition in the adults of this series. The following are summaries of the available material.

5LP110

Burial 1 (Fig. 94a): Moderate wear (to dentine) is present except on the third molars. There is some alveolar resorption; however, the fragmentary nature of the maxilla makes judgement as to pre- or post-mortem loss difficult. The incisors exhibit slight shovelling and there is a light calculus formation. Interdental caries occur between the right M^2 and M^3 with another interdental carie present on the distal surface of the left PM^2. Some defects of the enamel are present, especially on the maxillary anterior teeth which may exhibit a slight case of enamel hypoplasia. Teeth present include: Mandible--left side PM_1, and PM_2, M_1 to M_3; right side M_1 to M_3; Maxilla--left side LI, C, PM^1, PM^2, and M^1 to M^3; right side PM^2 and M^1 to M^3. Two loose incisors are also present.

Burial 3 (Fig. 94b): Wear is beginning to erode the dentine. The wear pattern corresponds overall with Molnar's (1971:178) category #3, although the M^2 and M^3 show very little dentine. This wear pattern may be somewhat misleading because of premortem loss of both M^1s and subsequent resorption of the alveolar bone. The incisors are shovel shaped. There is medium resorption of the maxillary alveolar bone (other than at M^1) especially at the second and third maxillary molars, with associated peridontal disease. Interproximal caries occur between the left M^2 and M^3 with another interdental carie on the mesial side of M^2. The same situation exists on the right side of the maxilla. Slight calculus formation is present on the mandibular teeth. The teeth missing include: Maxilla--right side PM^1, LI, CI; left side PM^1 and PM^2; Mandible--right side CI, left side LI and CI.

5LP111

Burial 1 (Fig. 94c): The wear is slight with only minimal amounts of dentine showing on the incisors and canines and the third molars essentially unworn. There are advanced caries on both M_2s. Alveolar resorption has occurred at the left M^2 and

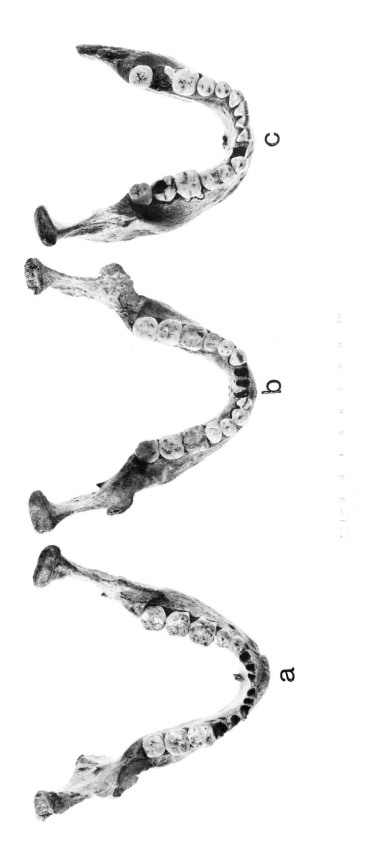

Figure 94. Occlusal view of the three mandibles from this skeletal series, showing tooth wear: a - 5LP110 Burial 1; b - 5LP110 Burial 3; c - 5LP111 Burial 1.

Table 25. Cranial Measurements (in mm)

Measurement	5LP110		5LP111
	Burial 1	Burial 2	Burial 1
maximum length	---	180	---
maximum breadth	---	133	---
minimum frontal	---	98	---
basion-bregma height	---	141	---
total facial height	---	118	---
upper facial height	---	71	---
bizygomatic breadth	---	139	---
nasal height	---	53.5	---
nasal breadth	---	26.3	---
nasion-basion length	---	105	---
basion-prosthion length	---	100	---
left orbital height	---	38	---
right orbital height	---	39	---
left orbital breadth	---	37	---
right orbital breadth	---	39	---
exterior palate length	---	47	---
exterior palate breadth	---	41	---
mandibular length	106.0	102.0	104.0
bicondylar breadth	118	114.1	---
bigonial breadth	87.5	101.5	---
ramus height	57.0L	55.0R	58.0R
ramus minimum breadth	33.8L	30.3R	33.4R
symphyseal height	31.3	35	31.5
interforaminal breadth	43.3	47.8	46.1
coronoid height	55.4	62.0	59.2
body thickness (M_2)	14.6	13.0	18.6
ramus angle (in degrees)	24°	23.5°	22°

Indices (x 100)

cranial	---	73.89	---
height-length	---	78.33	---
height-breadth	---	106.02	---
upper facial	---	51.08	---
total facial	---	---	---
nasal	---	49.2	---
orbital	---	97.44	---
external palatal	---	87.23	---
mandibular	91.53	91.59	---

Key: --- no observation possible

Table 26. Postcranial Measurements (in mm)

Measurement		5LP110		5LP111	
		Burial 1	Burial 3	Burial 2(A)	Burial 2(B)
humerus length	L	296.5	---	---	---
	R	---	---	---	---
maximum head diameter	L	38.2	---	---	---
	R	R	---	---	---
distal end breadth	L	51.6	---	---	---
	R	---	---	---	---
A-P mid-shaft diameter	L	18.6	17.2	---	---
	R	18.6	17.6	---	---
M-L mid-shaft diameter	L	20.4	16.2	---	---
	R	21.6	18.8	---	---
ulna length	L	---	---	---	---
	R	251	---	---	---
trochlear notch height	L	---	---	---	---
	R	28.6	---	---	---
distal end breadth	L	---	---	---	---
	R	17.1	---	---	---
radius length	L	---	---	---	---
	R	---	---	217.5	---
femur length	L	425	400	---	---
	R	421	406.5	378	---
bicondylar length	L	420	406	---	---
	R	417	402	---	---
A-P subtrochanteric diameter	L	20.8	22	---	---
	R	20.5	23.5	---	---
M-L subtrochanteric diameter	L	28.8	27.5	---	---
	R	28.7	26.4	---	---
A-P mid-shaft diameter	L	26.3	26.0	---	---
	R	24.6	24.4	---	---
M-L mid-shaft diameter	L	22.6	22.2	---	---
	R	21.3	23.0	---	---
maximum head diameter	L	40.6	40.3	---	---
	R	41	---	---	---
epicondylar breadth	L	70.5	---	---	---
	R	---	---	---	---

Table 26, cont'd. Postcranial Measurements

Measurement		5LP110		5LP111	
		Burial 1	Burial 3	Burial 2(A)	Burial 2(B)
tibia length	L	343.0	---	---	---
	R	343.0	337.0	320.0	---
maximum diameter proximal end	L	---	70.6	---	---
	R	---	73.5	---	---
nutrient foramen A-P diameter	L	26.5	33.5	---	29.8
	R	28.4	30.0	---	---
nutrient foramen M-L diameter	L	18.1	18.4	---	15.5
	R	21.4	19.0	---	---
fibula length	L	---	334	---	---
	R	335	---	---	---
innominate height	L	---	---	---	---
	R	---	---	178.0	---
innominate breadth	L	---	---	---	---
	R	---	---	129.5	---
Indices (x100)					
humerus-femur	L	69.76	---	---	---
	R	---	---	---	---
platymeric	L	72.22	80.0	---	---
	R	71.43	89.02	---	---
pilastric	L	116.37	117.12	---	---
	R	115.76	105.87	---	
platycnemic	L	68.30	55.01	---	51.84
	R	75.35	63.33	---	---
tibia-femur	L	80.71	---	---	---
	R	81.47	82.9	---	---
robusticity	L	11.51	11.78	---	---
	R	10.89	11.65	---	---

Key: --- no observation possible

Table 27. Non-metrical Variables

Trait		5LP110 Burial 1	5LP110 Burial 3	5LP111 Burial 1	5LP111 Burial 2(A)	Burial 2(B)	Obser-vances	Occur-rences
Os Inca		---	(-)	---	---	---	1	0
Lambdoid ossicles		(+)	(+)	---	---	---	2	2
Sagittal ossicles		---	(-)	---	---	---	1	0
Asterionic ossicles	R	---	(+)	---	---	---	1	1
	L	---	(+)	---	---	---	1	1
Tympanic dehiscence	R	(-)	(-)	---	---	---	2	0
	L	(-)	(-)	---	---	---	2	0
Supraorbital foramen closed	R	(-)	(+)	---	---	(-)	3	1
	L	(-)	(+)	---	---	---	2	1
Supraorbital foramen notch	R	(+)	(-)	---	---	(+)	3	2
	L	(+)	(-)	---	---	---	2	1
Multiple infraorbital foramina	R	---	(-)	---	---	---	1	0
	L	---	(-)	---	---	---	1	0
Multiple mental foramina	R	(-)	(-)	(-)	---	---	3	0
	L	(-)	(-)	(-)	---	---	3	0
Mastoid foramen	R	(+)	(-)	---	---	---	2	1
	L	---	(+)	---	---	---	1	1
Parietal foramen	R	(-)	(-)	---	---	---	2	0
	L	(-)	(-)	---	---	---	2	0
Metopic suture		(-)	(-)	---	---	---	3	0
Mandibular torus		(-)	(-)	(-)	---	(-)	3	0
Maxillary torus		---	(+)	---	---	---	1	1
Pierced olecranon fossa-humeri	R	(-)	(-)	---	(+)	---	3	1
	L	(-)	(-)	---	---	---	2	0
Third trochanter femora	R	(+)	(-)	---	(+)	---	3	2
	L	(+)	(-)	---	(+)	---	3	2
Squatting facets tibiae	R	(+)	(+)	---	(+)	---	3	3
	L	(+)	(+)	---	(+)	---	3	3
Pterion form		---	H	---	---	---	1	1H

Key:
(+) present
(-) absent
--- no observation possible
 H sutural form

M^3. If the M^3 that was present belongs with this maxillary fragment, it could only have been held in by soft tissue. Teeth present include: Mandible--all except the right LI; Maxilla--left M^1 and M^2 and possibly M^3 (loose).

Burial 2: Individual A had an isolated left $M_{2'}$, with heavy wear and heavy calculus formation on the distal-buccal sides.

Individual C (Fig. 99) had one M^3 with fused roots showing hypercementosis, a possible calculus or cementum formation between the cusps of the crown, and an interdental carie on the mesial side.

Skeletal

Skeletal pathologies or anomalies found in this series are summarized as follows:

5LP110

Burial 1: The left parietal bone (and parts of the frontal and occipital) of this specimen exhibits some pitting of the inner table of bone. This condition may be postmortem. However, this lesion may also have been caused by a meningioma, or tumor of the meninges in the parietal area (Fig. 96). According to Boyd (1961:1202) meningiomas are usually not malignant and may be related to local trauma. In most cases of this type of lesion, there is a bony thickening over the tumor area. In rare cases there may be erosion and perforation of the bone instead of thickening (Boyd 1961:1203).

Burial 3: There is a slight arthritic development of the left knee as evidenced by a bony exostosis of the tibia at the proximal fibular articulation (Fig. 97). The superior lateral corner of the patella is also resorbed (Fig. 98a). A lesion, probably periostitis, is located on the posterior surface of the left tibia, at midshaft. This lesion was possibly caused by trauma or infection (Fig. 100). The coronal and sagittal sutures of this individual exhibit a feature termed "lapsed union" (Krogman 1962:85), a suture that has begun to close but has failed to completely do so (Fig. 101). In this case, the sutures started to close prematurely, but have folded in on themselves. Sutures that have reached this state will not show further closure and are therefore useless as age indicators.

5LP111

Burial 2, Individual B: This individual showed a

definite development of a condition known as cribra orbitalis (osteoporosis) in the right orbital portion of the frontal bone (Fig. 98b). There is a possible involvement of the base of the occipital bone, although this may be due to postmortem thinning of the outer table of bone. Cribra orbitalia has been connected with possible anemic conditions during childhood and has been linked with weanling diarrhea (Zaino 1967; Carlson et al. 1974). Weanling diarrhea may have caused the death of this child at the age of less than two years.

Burial 2, Individual C: The tibia shows evidence of gnawing on the shaft.

The long bones of these individuals were examined radiographically for evidence of growth arrest lines or Harris Lines. A number of the bones were unsuitable for this analysis because they had been broken postmortem and appeared to be filled with dirt. Of those examined, the following results were noted.

5LP110

Burial 1: The left tibia showed three lines. The lines were 2.4, 8.7 and 10.5 cm from the distal end (Medial malleolus). On the right tibia, lines were located 7.6, 9.1, 10.8, 12.4, and 24.4 cm from the distal end. The right femur showed lines 12.5, 16.7, 20.0, and 22.1 cm from the medial condyle (distal end). On the right ulna, there were lines 4.8, 5.3, and 6.5 cm from the proximal end. The right radius showed one line 20.3 cm from the distal end (styloid process). This individual shows far more lines (16 total) than are usually seen in samples from Anasazi populations (Nickens 1975c), and possibly had a series of recurrent illnesses as a child.

Burial 2: This individual had a total of nine lines in the bones that were complete enough to be counted. The right humerus had six lines 2.5, 2.8, 3.1, 3.5, 4.0, and 9.0 cm from the proximal end. The left humerus had three lines 2.4, 3.4, and 3.8 cm from the proximal end.

5LP111

Burial 2, Individual A: The bones of this individual had only one line, located on the right radius 1.6 cm from the proximal end. Most of the other bones had been broken and filled with dirt and thus did not show any lines.

This individual from 5LP111 Burial 2 is the only individual in the sample which shows a pattern similar to the one that Nickens (1975c) reported for

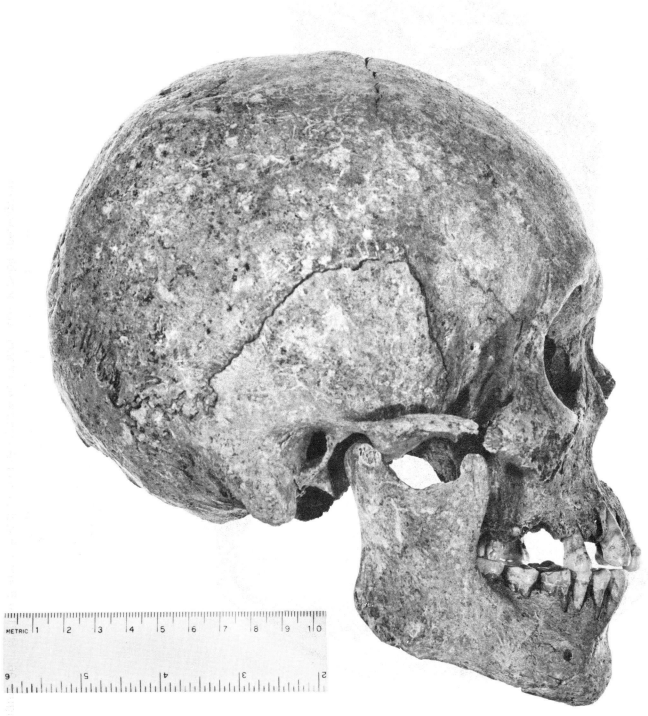

Figure 95. Side view of skull and mandible of 5LP110 Burial 3.

Figure 96.   5LP110 Burial 1: Basal view of skull showing interior, with possible meningioma.

Figure 97.   Left tibia from 5LP110 Burial 3, showing exostosis of fibular articulation.

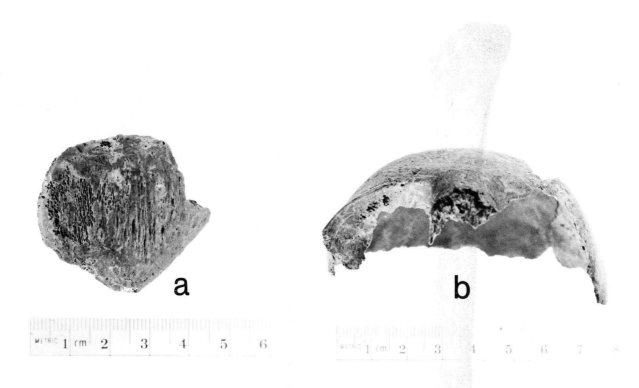

Figure 98.   a - Left patella from 5LP110 Burial 3, showing resorption; b - Frontal bone of child, 5LP111 Burial 2, Individual B. The right eye orbit shows evidence of cribra orbitalia.

Figure 99.   M³ with fused roots (hypercementosis) and an interdental carie on the mesial side, from 5LP111 Burial 2, Individual C.

Figure 100. Shaft of left tibia, medial side, 5LP110 Burial 3. Note lesion possibly caused by trauma or infection.

Figure 101.   5LP110 Burial 3: Top of skull, showing premature closure of coronal and sagittal sutures.

the Mesa Verde and Yellow Jacket areas: a generally low incidence of lines in individuals, with the number of lines decreasing from Basketmaker to Pueblo times. The observed frequencies of 16 (5LP110 Burial 1) and nine (5LP110 Burial 2) are more similar to the frequencies observed by McHenry (1969) on a series of California Indians. No definite interpretation of these data can be made at the present time due to the small size of this sample.

Summary

The skeletal remains of at least nine individuals have been described. The material is generally in fair condition. However, the postmortem breakage of many of the bones, especially the innominates, and the resulting lack of pubic symphyses, precludes accurate age analysis. Of particular note are the number of transverse lines in the long bones of Burials 1 and 2 from 5LP110, the presence of cribra orbitalia in the infant (5LP111 Burial 2, Individual B), and a possible meningioma in 5LP110 Burial 1. Information from this series adds to the data from Basketmaker III skeletal remains.

Acknowledgments

I would like to express my appreciation to Dennis Van Gerven for allowing me to use lab space and comparative collections and to David Burr for assistance with the radiographs. Thanks are also due to Curtis Martin for the photographs. In addition, several individuals gave of their time to assist in some of the identifications including: Dennis Van Gerven, David Greene, and Paul Nickens.

VI. Summary And Conclusions

The Durango District, geographically defined in Chapter I, was one of the focal locations of Basketmaker culture in the Northern San Juan Region. The number of documented Basketmaker II and III sites in the Durango District is substantial. In the immediate vicinity of the present city of Durango there are four documented Basketmaker III settlements: Hidden Valley (Carlson 1963), Griffith Heights (Daniels 1938), Bodo Business Ranch (Hibbets 1975, 1976) and Blue Mesa (Gladwin 1957:53-57). Although only tree-ring data are available (Dean 1975) it is most probable that other Basketmaker III settlements are located in Ridges Basin, along Florida Creek and along the Los Pinos River.

The data presented in this volume point out many similarities and some differences between 5LP110 and 5LP111 at Bodo Business Ranch and the other excavated Basketmaker III sites in the Durango District and throughout the region. Although two excavated sites provide a slender data base for anthropological interpretation, there is sufficient accumulated data from the above mentioned sites to warrant general interpretations.

Inferences into the nature of prehistoric social organization are difficult for three obvious reasons: 1) they must be supported solely by material remains that may have general associations with hypothesized aspects of social organization but not necessarily any known specific aspects of that organization; 2) it must also be assumed that in any synchronic analysis, the horizontal provenience of the artifactual remains accurately represents deposition relevant to some aspect of that social organization with no or very little subsequent disturbance; 3) they must be based on patterned, nonrandom behavior that must be demonstrated, quantifiably or otherwise, with sets of independent data.

The premises set forth by Dozier (1970:203-204) for making inferences into prehistoric social orginization delineate strict parameters for the methods of such studies and further illustrate the difficulty:

> First, the shorter the time gap between a prehistoric site and the living site, the more likely that the inference will be a reliable one.

> Second, the sociocultural level of the prehistoric and ethnologic group must be matched--at least roughly.

> Third, it is important to compare societies having the same type of subsistence economy.

> Fourth, inferences about societies widely separated in space can be made only with extreme caution.

> Fifth, in making inferences, language affiliation should be given low priority.

> Sixth, some measure of how conservative the ethnologic culture has been over time should be established, insofar as possible.

Dozier's (1970:204-205) demonstrations of the longstanding conservatism of the Pueblos lends credence to Dean's (1970:149) arguments, which rest on analogy with early ethnographic accounts of the Hopi, that Tsegi phase habitation units were lineal. Furthermore Dean's analogy is in line with Dozier's second, third, fourth and fifth premises above. Even given the 500 year time gap, that analogy seems reliable and is ethnologically valid (Aberle 1970:221). It has been repeatedly demonstrated that cultures change through time as a result of environmental, demographic and technological factors. Therefore in reconstructing prehistoric societies, it is the responsibility of the archaeologists to define those material aspects of social organization that can be traced to acceptable ethnographic analogies or to acceptable demonstrations of social organization in archaeological contexts such as those described by Dean (1970:140-174).

A recent study of Basketmaker III social organization on Wetherill Mesa by Birkedal (1976) proposes that "the band, rather than the lineage, was the basic residential unit during Basketmaker III" (1976:395). Birkedal's hypothesis is counter to the popular belief that the Basketmaker III residential groupings were based on localized lineages (Steward 1955:162; Chang 1958:322; Daifuku 1961:59; Martin and Plog 1973:266), but is in agreement with Carlson (1963:52) who argues for "autonomous households."

With Dozier's premises in mind, some questions arise concerning Birkedal's conclusions:

1. His definition of lineage, "a corporate group recruited by unilineal descent from a known common ancestor" (1976:398) cannot be demonstrated using archaeological data.

2. His definition of band, "an autonomous, territorially based association of nuclear families, normally consisting of twenty to fifty people, with affinal ties loosely allying it with one or a few other bands" (1976:401), hinges on the existence of the nuclear family as opposed to the extended family. Birkedal undertook a great deal of analysis in determining the number of occupants per pithouse; he arrives at the conclusion that this minimal residential unit was occupied by the nuclear family and that "this indicated degree of autonomy would be inconsistent with the idea that the Basketmaker III nuclear family was submerged within a tightly knit, corporate residential unit such as the localized lineage" (1976:469).

a. The above statement lacks any analogies that characterize localized lineages as "closely knit" and "corporate."

b. A nuclear family residence in a household does not preclude any lineage organization at the village level.

c. Unit village I and unit village II at 5MT1 strongly suggest occupation by more than a nuclear family utilizing a single principal pit structure (Wheat M.S.).

3. The question of the demographic composition of Wetherill Mesa populations during Basketmaker III times is a central feature in the analysis and interpretation of the settlement data (1976:406-407).

a. Birkedal's interpretations regarding settlement configuration and spacing of dwelling units may be valid for the sites he excavated. However, it is difficult to conceive of how hypothesized population numbers (1976:tables 82, 83, 84) can demonstrate the presence or absence of lineage organization as expressed in settlement patterns.

b. There are 17 documented Basketmaker III sites on the whole of Wetherill Mesa. This is equal to the number of pit structures at Shabik'eshchee Village, equal to the number of structures at Broken Flute Cave (Morris 1959:38-112), fewer than the number recorded at the Hidden Valley settlement, fewer than the number recorded at the Blue Mesa settlement, fewer than the number recorded at Bodo Business Ranch, and only slightly more than the number recorded at Griffith Heights. This leads to the conclusion that the Wetherill Mesa data cannot be considered representative of Basketmaker III demography and settlement without further analysis.

Attempts at new interpretations for the social organization of Basketmaker III populations in the Durango District would only further confuse the issue and would be predicated on ethnographic analogies spanning 1000 years. However, test implications have been established for localized lineages that are ethnographically derived and can be used with no alteration in the scope or direction of those tests. Vivian (1970:59-83) developed testable propositions relevant to localized lineages in analysis of social organization in Chaco Canyon. The first 16 of 20 test implications are used here in their original form. Propositions 5 and 6 are restated to address Basketmaker architecture as opposed to Pueblo architecture but are intended to retain the scope and direction of the original questions. It is assumed here that the differences between Basketmaker and Pueblo architecture are a reflection of change through time rather than a reflection of functional changes.

It is proposed that the settlement sites in the Durango District were residence groups reflecting localized lineages. If this proposition is correct, then one would expect to find the following evidence (after Vivian 1970:79-80):

1. "Villages should be of varying size reflecting the varying population numbers of lineages." Based on the accumulated data from the Durango District, none of the known settlements are of equal size. They range from approximately 12 pithouses at Griffith Heights (Helen Sloan Daniels, personal communication) to more than 40 on Blue Mesa (Hibbets 1975). This information is based on survey data.

2. "Villages should vary in length of period of occupation reflecting the fluctuating nature of lineage continuity." Tree-ring dates from Hidden Valley suggest an occupation spanning 30 years. The tree-ring dates from Bodo Business Ranch and the Durango South Project, as well as Blue Mesa and Griffith Heights, are inconclusive for definitive comment in the absence of cutting dates. The assumption from the few tree-ring dates that are available is that there were occupations of varying lengths at slightly different times for each village. If, on the other hand, one takes the opposite view that all were occupied simultaneously and for the same length of time, the logical conclusion would be a virtual population explosion at the middle of the 8th century at Durango. Such a phenomenon would seem extraordinary but is possible and has been documented in the Tsegi Canyon area (Dean

1970:140-174). Contrasting length of occupation with dendroclimatic data is useful in distinguishing environmental from social factors affecting population fluctuations.

3. "Villages should be composed of several contemopraneous household units." The tree-ring dates from Hidden Valley (Carlson 1963:Table 9) indicate that the four dated sites were contemporaneous. The excavated sites at Durango South and site 5LP115 were contemporaneous. Data from Griffith Heights and Blue Mesa are insufficient to determine coexistence of household units.

4. "The number of contemporaneous households should vary and some units within the village may appear to be abandoned or reoccupied through time." Stratigraphic data from Feature 1 at 5LP111 indicates that this structure was abandoned prior to the abandonment of Feature 2. The intrusive occupations at 5LP110 Feature 1 and at 5LP115 (Hibbets 1976:45-47) were unconventional but do represent some type of reoccupation. Data from other settlements are unavailable.

5. "Household units should be composed of two or three rooms connected by doorways." In application to Basketmaker III architecture this test implication could be rephrased, "Household units should be composed of a pit structure accompanied by one or more surface storage features or cists in the immediate vicinity of the structure."

The established definition of the Basketmaker III household unit embodies the following characteristics (Morris 1939:24-27): an irregularly circular pit is dug into the earth; it contains a superstructure of timbers which support upper walls and roof. The upper walls and roof are plastered with adobe. The structure usually has two doorways, one in the roof that also served as a smoke vent, and one in a slot in the earthen wall that also served as a ventilator. The structure is also characterized by a central firepit. Other common features are a bench around the periphery, a partition wall, and occasionally, niches and bins for storage. The definition goes on to include a description of storage bins "built adjacent to the sides of the house" (1939:26).

Every site excavated at Hidden Valley (Carlson 1963) embodies all or most of these characteristics. The sites excavated for the Durango South Project also embodied all or most of these characteristics. Data that are available suggest that this is also true for Griffith Heights (Daniels 1938) and Blue Mesa (Gladwin 1957).

6. "Household units should be separated from other household units by walls without connecting doorways."

For this test implication Morris (1939:26) provides a definition as well as a response: "Each of these very early dwellings was erected as a separate unit. Commonly they were placed a few steps apart; however if space were crowded they might be laid out almost touching but never joined or equipped with provision to pass directly from one to another." This spatial relationship holds true for the other Basketmaker III settlements discussed above.

7. "Architectural styles of household units should tend to be heterogeneous." The architectural styles at Hidden Valley (Carlson 1963) are heterogenous, as are the architectural styles of the Durango South Project and of 5LP115.

8. "Villages should contain at least one grinding room. If more than one exists, they may show temporal differences in use." Feature 1 at 5LP110 contains enough metates to be classified as a grinding room. Rooms with specific assigned functions such as grinding rooms have not been reported in Basketmaker III sites and are extremely rare if they exist.

Utilization of the available living space in Basketmaker III pithouses appears to be multifunctional. Artifactual remains recovered from the floors of such structures indicate that although functional areas may be defined within a pithouse (see interpretations, 5LP110, Chapter II), the distribution of artifacts is mixed to the extent that no hard and fast rules governed this phenomenon. For example, if all the metates on the floor and in temporary storage at 5LP110 Feature 1 were in use at the same time, they would have taken up the floor space of the entire structure. Their placement in the structure suggests their use in some type of parallel or sequential effort.

9. "Villages should contain at least one storage room for maize. This room may connect with the grinding room, or maize storage facilities may be present in the grinding room." This type of room or large facility for storage has not been identified in the sites associated with this project or any others in the vicinity of Durango. However, further excavations of surface rooms associated with Basketmaker III sites are needed to determine whether these rooms served this function.

10. "Household units should contain storage facilities for nonmaize foodstuffs." Pollen samples (Table 16, Pollen Analysis, Chapter IV) taken from vessels and architectural features indicate that these served as storage facilities for native plants as well as *Zea* maize. Seed remains from most of the cists (Table 23, Chapter IV) represented native vegetation. There is insufficient evidence that any of these storage facilities were exclusively for maize or other foodstuffs.

11. "Wild plant and animal remains, indicative of a major dependence on hunting and gathering should be present in the village sites." The exploitation of the natural environment is most clearly illustrated in Chapter IV. The pollen and seed analyses revealed the remains of a variety of native plants including grasses, sage, cactus, and possibly sunflower. The samples for the above analyses were small and were not collected or organized to reflect the total range of vegetal resources utilized by the prehistoric inhabitants. However, the data retrieved do reflect a dependence on gathering. The faunal lists (Table 10, Fauna, Chapter IV) for 5LP110 and 5LP111 include most of the native mammals in the Durango area; most of the species listed were found at both sites. It appears that the predation was not selective and that the relative abundance of species reflects availability rather than preference. The significant expansion of the recorded faunal list at these sites over previously recorded Basketmaker III sites probably does not reflect a difference in the exploitation habits of the prehistoric inhabitants but rather reflects excavation and analytical techniques designed to address the question of the material remains of a hunting and gathering economy.

Dogs were definitely exploited as a domesticated faunal resource. Although this species could not be separated from other canids when the bone was burned, cooked or made into tools, the total number of identifiable dog bones makes a strong case for a wide range of economic and ceremonial utilization of this occasional pet.

There is no substantial evidence for the domestication of the turkey in this area at this time. Previous accounts assign domestication of the turkey to Pueblo occupations (Wormington 1947:70). However, turkeys were the only bird

remains identified at the sites and their relative abundance represents either domestication or very effective hunting techniques.

12. "Tools associated with hunting and gathering should be equally distributed in all household units of the village." This test implication must be verified through further excavations of sites in the neighborhood of the Durango South Project. Based on the data presented in this volume there seems to be an even distribution of these artifacts between the two sites. Data from other sites are insuffucient to address this point.

13. "Villages should contain at least one ceremonial room or kiva. If more than one exists, they should show temporal differences in use." There is artifactual evidence and some architectural suggestions that 5LP111 Feature 2 may have served this function (see Interpretations, 5LP111, Chapter II). However, further test excavations must be conducted to verify that 5LP111 meets the criteria for Basketmaker III kivas in the area.

14. "Architectural styles of kivas, if more than one exists, should tend to be heterogeneous." There are no data on kiva architecture from the Durango District.

15. "Architectural modifications of a kiva through time should tend to show heterogeneous architectural styles." Data from the Durango South Project and the whole of the Durango District are insufficient to address this test implication.

16. "High status burials exhibiting marked differences in number and types of burial goods should not be found in village cemeteries." The number of burials recovered during the course of the project was small and none of them exhibited differential status. There is no information regarding status of burials at other sites in the Durango District.

Of the 16 test implications for localized lineages adopted for use here, nine have been affirmed on the basis of excavation of two sites and the accumulated data from surrounding areas: Numbers 1, 2, 3, 4, 7, 8, 10, 11 and 13. Two additional test implications, Numbers 5 and 6, have been affirmed by rewording of the test implications to address Basketmaker architecture. Five test implications, Numbers 9, 12, 14, 15 and 16, require additional data. The importance of 5LP110 and 5LP111 is in providing evidence that they functioned in communal integrative functions in the context of a known settlement.

In summary, some general observations drawn from the various types of analysis contained in this report provide some insights into the lifestyle of the prehistoric inhabitants of these sites.

In the chipped stone assemblage, there were no glaring omissions of tool classes. One would therefore conclude that a complete knowledge of techniques, functions, and limitations of lithic technology was available to the prehistoric inhabitants and the reduced percentages in this category are a reflection of the role this tool category played in the overall economy.

The size and morphological attributes of the projectile points suggest that the bow and arrow was a dominant weapon type. The seven morphological types of the projectile points suggest a range of variation for this particular implement rather than any change through time.

The ground stone assemblage exemplified a reliance on corn agriculture. Those implications are discussed above.

Analysis of the ceramics indicates a relative abundance of Lino pottery which is consistent with the findings from Hidden Valley (Carlson 1963:31-38). This verifies that at the end of the eighth century the cultural affiliation of sites in the Durango District was still Basketmaker III. The presence of Twin Trees Black-on-white, Moccasin Gray, and Abajo Red-on-orange pottery at the sites offers evidence of contact with areas to the west. The low percentages of these ceramic types in this time period has been interpreted by some as evidence that Basketmaker III in this area did not participate in the mainstream of cultural development (Hayes and Lancaster 1975:184; Carlson 1963:54). It seems more reasonable to assume that the indigenous population in the Durango District exercised selective acceptance of those imported cultural elements that were available to them. The shell beads that were recovered from Burials 2 and 3 at 5LP110 must represent trade relationships into this area that are part of a much larger network (see Shell Beads, Chapter III). Consequently the lack of receptivity to certain architectural features in households and to new ceramic technology or trade ware is more logically an expression of the conservatism of the prehistoric inhabitants.

A great deal of important information about Basketmaker architectural, ceramic, and economic development is readily available in the Durango District. However, since the death of Earl Morris 20 years ago, in-depth analysis and interpretation of the area during this important time period in Anasazi prehistory has all but ceased. The locale provides an outstanding laboratory for thorough study of any aspect of Basketmaker archaeology one would wish to address. The Durango South Project, like many others, came about because of an imminent threat of destruction to the sites, and the continued piecemeal data accumulation provided by salvage operations does not do justice to this episode of Southwestern prehistory.

Appendix

List of Abbreviations

Ad	adult	**Lt**	length
alv	alveolus	**Lt 19**	e.g. length 19 millimeters
A-P	anterior-posterior	**M**	molar
assoc	associated	**max**	maxillary
B	breadth	**MC**	metacarpal
C	canine	**misc**	miscellaneous
ca	about	**M-L**	medial-lateral
cf	near, close to	**Ms**	midsection
CI	central incisor	**MT**	metatarsal
D	distal	**N**	number in sample
DB	distal breadth	**No.**	artifact number
De	depth	**P**	proximal
F	Feature	**PB**	proximal breadth
frag	fragment	**PM**	premolar
FS	field specimen number	**R**	right
GB	greatest breadth	**SB**	shaft breadth
GLt	greatest length	**SF**	Subfeature
GP	Gila Pueblo	**sp**	species
H	Sutural form	**teeth:**	with superscript - upper tooth, e.g. M^2 PM^2
			with subscript - lower tooth, e.g. M_2 PM_2
I	incisor		
Indet	indeterminate	**W**	whole
Juv	juvenile	**w/**	with
L	left	**+**	present
LI	lateral incisor	**-**	absent
LSB	least shaft breadth		

References
Cited

Abel, Leland J.
1955   Ware 12A type 2, Ware 8A type 2. In Pottery types of the Southwest, edited by Harold S. Colton. *Museum of Northern Arizona, Ceramic Series 3.*

Aberle, David F.
1970   Comments. In *Reconstructing prehistoric Pueblo societies,* edited by William A. Longacre. University of New Mexico Press, Albuquerque.

Adams, E. Charles
1975   Causes of prehistoric settlement systems in the lower Piedra District, Colorado. Unpublished Ph.D. dissertation. Department of Anthropology, University of Colorado, Boulder.

Ahler, Stanley A.
1971   Projectile point form and function at Rogers Shelter, Missouri. *Missouri Archaeological Society, Research Series 8.*

Allen, G.M.
1920   Dogs of the American aborigines. *Bulletin of the Museum of Comparative Zoology* 63(9):431-517.

Anderson, J.E.
1969   *The human skeleton. A manual for archaeologists.* The National Museums of Canada, Ottowa.

Applegarth, Susan M.
1974   Archaeological survey of the Bodo Business Ranches. Department of Anthropology, Ft. Lewis College, Durango, Colorado xeroxed.

Armstrong, D. M.
1972   Distribution of mammals in Colorado. *University of Kansas Museum of Natural History, Monograph* 3.

Bartlett, Katherine
1933   Pueblo milling stones of the Flagstaff region and their relation to others in the Southwest: a study in progressive efficiency. *Museum of Northern Arizona, Bulletin* 3.

Bass, W. M.
1971   *Human Osteology.* Missouri Archaeological Society, Columbia.

Basso, Keith H.
1969   Western Apache witchcraft, an ethnographic study. *Anthropological Papers of the University of Arizona* 15.

Birkedal, Terje G.
1976   Basketmaker III residential units: a study of prehistoric social organization in the Mesa Verde Archaeological District. Unpublished Ph. D. dissertation. Department of Anthropology, University of Colorado, Boulder.

Bonnischen, Rob
1973   Some operational aspects of human and animal bone alteration. In *Mammalian osteo-archaeology: North America,* by B. Miles Gilbert, pp. 9-24. Missouri Archaeological Society, Columbia.

Boyd, William
1961   *A textbook of pathology: structure and function in disease.* Lea and Febiger, Philadelphia.

Breternitz, David A.
1963   Archaeological interpretation of tree ring specimens for dating Southwestern ceramic styles. Unpublished Ph.D. dissertation. Department of Anthropology, University of Arizona, Tucson.

Breternitz, David A., Arthur H. Rohn, Jr. and Elizabeth A. Morris
1974   Prehistoric ceramics of the Mesa Verde region. *Museum of Northern Arizona, Ceramic Series* 5.

Brew, John Otis
1946   Archaeology of Alkali Ridge, southeastern Utah. *Papers of the Peabody Museum of Archaeology and Ethnology, Harvard University*, Vol. 21.

Brothwell, Don R.
1972   *Digging up bones.* British Museum of Natural History, London.

Brothwell, Don R. and A. T. Sandison (Editors)
1967   *Diseases in antiquity.* Charles C. Thomas, Springfield.

Bryant, V.M., Jr.
1974   Pollen analysis of prehistoric human feces from Mammoth Cave. In *Archaeology of the Mammoth Cave Area,* edited by Patty Jo Watson, pp. 203-209. Academic Press, New York.

1975   Pollen as an incidator of prehistoric diets in Coahuila, Mexico. *Bulletin of the Texas Archeological Society* 46:87-106.

Bullard, William R., Jr.
1962   The Cerro Colorado Site and pithouse architecture in the southwestern United States prior to A.D. 900. *Papers of the Peabody Museum of Archaeology and Ethnology,* Harvard University 44(2).

Carlson, D.S., G.J. Armelagos, and D.P. Van Gerven
1974   Factors influencing the etiology of cribra orbitalia in prehistoric Nubia. *Journal of Human Evolution* 3:405-410.

Carlson, Roy L.
1963   Basketmaker III sites near Durango, Colorado. *University of Colorado Studies, Series in Anthropology* 8.

Chang, Kwang-chih
1958   Study of the Neolithic social groupings; examples from the New World. *American Anthropologist* 60 (2, part 1): 298-334.

Colton, Harold S. (Editor)
1955   Pottery types of the Southwest. *Museum of Northern Arizona, Ceramic Series* 3.

Cook, Sherburne F.
1972   Prehistoric demography. *Addison-Wesley Module in Anthropology* 16.

Daifuku, Hiroshi
1961   Jeddito 264: a report on the excavations of a Basketmaker III-Pueblo I site in northeastern Arizona, with a review of some current theories in Southwestern archaeology. *Papers of the Peabody Museum of Archaeology and Ethnology,* Harvard University 33(1).

Daniels, Helen Sloan
1938   Summary of NYA excavation at Griffith Heights. In Museum project of the Archaeological Department: material excavated, reconstructed, and filed by Durango Public Library Museum Project, National Youth Administration. Durango Public Library, Durango, Colorado.

1941   The NYA Project in 1938. In Sherds and points: the amateur's archaeological story of Durango, Colorado. *The Durango Herald* 1 (8).

Daniels, Helen Sloan, Frank C. Lee and James G. Allen
1938   Basketmaker III culture - Durango pre-kiva. *Durango Public Library NYA Museum Project, Bulletin* 1. Durango Public Library, Durango, Colorado.

Dean, Jeffrey S.
1970   Aspects of Tsegi Phase social organization: a trial reconstruction. In *Reconstructing prehistoric Pueblo societies,* edited by William A. Longacre, pp. 140-174. University of New Mexico Press, Albuquerque.

1975   *Tree-Ring dates from Colorado W - Durango area.* Laboratory of Tree-Ring Research, University of Arizona, Tucson.

Dean, Jeffrey S. and William J. Robinson
1977   Dendroclimatic variability in the American Southwest, A.D. 680 to A.D. 1969. Interagency Archeological Services, National Park Service, Denver. xeroxed.

Dimbleby, G.W.
1957   Pollen analysis of terrestrial soils. *The New Phytologist* 56:12-28.

DiPeso, Charles C.
1956   The Upper Pima of San Cayetano Del Tumacacori. *The Amerind Foundation, Publication* 7.

Dittert, Alfred E., Jr., J.J. Hester, and Frank W. Eddy
1961   An archaeological survey of the Navajo Reservoir District, northwestern New Mexico. *Monographs of the School of American Research and the Museum of New Mexico, 23.*

Dobyns, Henry F. and Robert C. Euler
1970   Wauba Yuma's people: the comparative socio-political structure of the Pai Indians of Arizona. *Prescott College Studies in Anthropology* 3.

Dozier, Edward P.
1970   Making inferences from the present to the past. In *Reconstructing prehistoric Pueblo societies,* edited by William A. Longacre, pp. 202-213. University of New Mexico Press, Albuquerque.

Eddy, Frank W.
1966   Prehistory in the Navajo Reservoir District, northwestern New Mexico. *Museum of New Mexico Papers in Anthropology* 15: Parts 1 and 2.

1972   Culture ecology and the prehistory of the Navajo Reservoir District. *Southwestern Lore* 38(1,2).

1977   Archaeological investigations at Chimney Rock Mesa: 1970-1972. *Colorado Archaeological Society, Memoir* 1.

Ellwood, P.B.
1973   Analysis of pottery from Stevenson Site Mt-1, Yellow Jacket, Colorado. University of Colorado Museum, Boulder. xeroxed.

Elmore, F.H.
1944   Ethnobotany of the Navajo. *University of New Mexico and the School of American Research, Monograph* 8.

193

Environmental Data Service
1977   Climatological data: Colorado 82(8). National Climatic Center, Ashville, North Carolina.

Findley, J.S. et al.
1975   *Mammals of New Mexico.* University of New Mexico Press, Albuquerque.

Flora, I.F.
1941a   A Durango home in 630 A.D. In Sherds and points: the amateur's archaeological story of Durango, Colorado. *The Durango Herald* 1(4).

1941b   Durango tree-ring dates: tree-ring weather records of Biblical times. In Sherds and points: the amateur's archaeological story of Durango, Colorado. *The Durango Herald* 1(16).

Genoves, Santiago
1967   Proportionality of the long bones and their relation to stature among Mesoamericans. *American Journal of Physical Anthropology* 26:67-78.

Gillespie, William B.
1975   Preliminary report of excavations at the Ute Canyon Site, 5MTUMR2347, Ute Mountain Ute Homelands, Colorado. Bureau of Indian Affairs, Albuquerque. xeroxed.

1976   Culture change at the Ute Canyon Site: a study of the pithouse-kiva transition in the Mesa Verde Region. Unpublished M.A. thesis. Department of Anthropology, University of Colorado, Boulder.

Gladwin, Harold S.
1957   *History of the ancient Southwest.* The Bond Wheelwright Company, Portland.

Guilday, J. E.
1971   Biological and archaeological analysis of bones from a 17th century Indian village (46PU31), Putnam County, West Virginia. *West Virginia Geological and Economic Survey, Report of Archaeological Investigations* 4.

Hall, Edward T.,Jr.
1944   Early stockaded settlements in the Gobernador, New Mexico. *Columbia Studies in Archaeology and Ethnology* 2(Part 1).

Hallisey, Stephen J.
1972   Site 1990, a Basketmaker III pithouse on Wetherill Mesa. In wetherill Mesa salvage archaeology, University of Colorado Research Center, summer 1971, by Stephen J. Hallisey, Larry V.Nordby, and David A. Breternitz, pp. 1-21. Interagency Archaeological Services, National Park Service, Denver. xeroxed.

Hansen, B.S. and E.J. Cushing
1973   Identification of pine pollen of late Quaternary age from the Chuska Mountains, New Mexico. *Geological Society of America Bulletin* 84:1181-1200.

Hargrave, Lyndon C.
1932   Guide to forty pottery types from the Hopi country and the San Francisco Mountains, Arizona. *Museum of Northern Arizona, Bulletin* 1.

Hawley, Florence M.
1936   Field manual of Southwestern pottery types. *University of New Mexico Anthropological Series 1* (4).

Hayes, Alden C.
1964   The archeological survey of Wetherill Mesa, Mesa Verde National Park, Colorado. *National Park Service, Archeological Research Series* 7a.

Hayes, Alden C. and James A. Lancaster
1968   Site 1060, a Basketmaker III pithouse on Chapin Mesa. *University of Colorado Studies, Series in Anthropology* 15.

1975   The Badger House Community. *National Park Service, Archeological Research Series* 7E.

Hibbets, Barry N.
1975   An archaeological survey of Blue Mesa, La Plata County, Colorado. Department of Anthropology, Ft. Lewis College, Durango, Colorado. xeroxed.

1976   1975 salvage excavations at Bodo Business Ranches: Site 5LP115, an early Pueblo I site near Durango, Colorado. Department of Anthropology, Ft. Lewis College, Durango Colorado. xeroxed.

Hill, J.N. and R.H. Hevly
1968   Pollen at Broken K Pueblo: some new interpretations. *American Antiquity* 33:200-210.

Jarcho, Saul
1966   *Human paleopathology.* Yale University Press, New Haven.

Kidder, Alfred V.
1932   The artifacts of Pecos. *Phillips Academy, Papers of the Southwestern Expedition 6.*

Kidder, Alfred V. and Samuel Guernsey
1919   Archeological exploration in northeastern Arizona. *Bureau of American Ethnology, Bulletin* 65.

Kilgore, L.W.
1955   Geology of the Durango area, La Plata County, Colorado. In Geology of parts of Paradox, Black Mesa and San Juan Basins. *Four Corners Geological Society:* First Field Conference.

Kluckhohn, Clyde, and Dorothea Leighton
1962   *The Navajo* (revised edition). Doubleday and Company, Garden City, New York.

Kluckhohn, Clyde, W.W. Hill, and Lucy Wales Kluckhohn
1971   *Navajo material culture.* Harvard University Press, Cambridge.

Krogman, W.M.
1962   *The human skeleton in forensic medicine.* Charles C. Thomas, Springfield.

Kurten, B.
1974   A history of coyote-like dogs (Canidae, Mammalia). *Acta Zoologica Fennica* 140:1-38.

Lancaster, James A. and Jean M. Pinkley
1954   Excavation at Site 16. In Archeological excavations in Mesa Verde National Park, Colorado - 1950, by James A. Lancaster, Jean M. Pinkley, Philip F. Van Cleave, and Don Watson, pp. 23-86. *Naional Park Service, Archeological Research Series* 2.

Lancaster, James A. and Don W. Watson
1942   Excavation of Mesa Verde pit houses. *American Antiquity* 9(7):190-198.

1954   Excavation of two late Basketmaker III pithouses. In Archeological excavations in Mesa Verde National Park, Colorado - 1950, by James A. Lancaster, Jean M. Pinkley, Philip F. Van Cleave, and Don Watson, pp. 7-22. *National Park Service, Archeological Research Series* 2.

Lawrence, B.
1967   Early domestic dogs. *Saugetierkunde* 32(1):44-59.

Lee, Frank C.
1938   Description, excavation, and the structure of Durango pre-kiva. In Museum project of the Archaeological Department: material excavated, reconstructed, and filed by Durango Public Library Museum Project, National Youth Administration, compiled by Helen Sloan Daniels, pp. 18-23. Durango Public Library, Durango, Colorado.

Leidy, L. Kent
1976   Archaeological resources of the Animas-La Plata Project - report on the 1975 season. Department of Anthropology, University of Colorado, Boulder. xeroxed.

Lister, Robert H.
1964   Contributions to Mesa Verde archaeology I, Site 499, Mesa Verde National Park, Colorado. *University of Colorado Studies, Series in Anthropology* 9.

1966   Contributions to Mesa Verde archaeology III, Site 866 and the cultural sequence at four villages in the Far View group, Mesa Verde National Park, Colorado. *University of Colorado Studies, Series in Anthropology* 12.

McHenry, Henry
1969   Transverse lines in long bones of prehistoric California Indians. *American Journal of Physical Anthropology 29:1-18.*

Maher, L.J., Jr.
1963   Pollen analysis of surface materials from the southern San Juan Mountains, Colorado. *Geological Society of America Bulletin* 74:1485-1504.

Martin, A.C. and W.P. Barkley
1961   *Seed identification manual.* University of California Press, Berkeley.

Martin, P.S. and W. Byers
1965   Pollen and archaeology at Wetherill Mesa. *American Antiquity* 31:122-135.

Martin, P.S. and F.W. Sharrock
1964   Pollen analysis of prehistoric human feces: a new approach to ethnobotany. *American Antiquity* 30:168-180.

Martin, Paul S. and Fred Plog
1973   *The archaeology of Arizona: a study of the Southwest region.* Doubleday/Natural History Press, Garden City, New York.

Martin, Paul S. and John B. Rinaldo
1939   Modified Basketmaker sites - Ackmen-Lowry area, southwestern Colorado. *Field Museum of Natural History, Anthropological Series* 23(3).

Mehringer, P.J., Jr.
1967   Pollen analysis of the Thule Springs Site. In Pleistocene studies in southern Nevada, edited by M. Wormington and D. Ellis. *Nevada State Museum Anthropological Papers* 13:130-200.

Molnar, Stephen
1971   Human tooth wear, tooth function and cultural variability. *American Journal of Physical Anthropology* 34:175-190.

Morris, Earl H.
1927   The beginnings of pottery making in the San Juan area; unfired prototypes and the wares of the earliest ceramic period. *Anthropological Papers of the American Museum of Natural History* 28 (Part 2).

1936   Archaeological background of dates in early Arizona chronology. *Tree-Ring Bulletin* 2(4).

1939   Archaeological studies in the La Plata district, southwestern Colorado and northwestern New Mexico. *Carnegie Institution of Washington, Publication* 519.

1941   Book review of: Archaeological work in the Ackmen-Lowry area, southwestern Colorado, and Modified Basket Maker sites, Ackmen-Lowry area, southwestern Colorado, by Paul S. Martin and John B. Rinaldo. *American Antiquity* 6(4):378-382.

Morris, Earl H. and Robert F. Burgh
1941   Anasazi basketry, Basket Maker II through Pueblo III. *Carnegie Institution of Washington, Publication* 533.

1954   Basketmaker II sites near Durango, Colorado. *Carnegie Institution of Washington, Publication* 604.

Morris, Elizabeth A.
1959   Basketmaker Caves in the Prayer Rock District, Northeastern Arizona. Unpublished Ph. D. dissertation. Department of Anthropology, University of Arizona, Tuscon.

Nickens, Paul R.
1974a   Analysis of prehistoric human skeletal remains from the Mancos Canyon, southwestern Colorado. Bureau of Indian Affairs, Albuquerque. xeroxed.

1974b   Additional human skeletal remains from the Mancos Canyon, southwestern Colorado. Bureau of Indian Affairs, Albuquerque. xeroxed.

1975a   Human skeletal remains from the 1974 University of Colorado Mancos Canyon excavations. Mesa Verde Research Center, University of Colorado. xeroxed.

1975b   Osteological analysis of five human burials from Mesa Verde National Park, Colorado. *Southwestern Lore* 41:13-26.

1975c   Paleoepidemiology of Mesa Verde Anasazi populations: lines of increased density. Department of Anthropology, University of Colorado, Boulder. xeroxed.

Nordby, Larry V. and David A. Breternitz
1972   Site MV 1824-71, a Basketmaker III pithouse and cist on Wetherill Mesa. In Wetherill Mesa salvage archaeology, University of Colorado Research Center, summer 1971, by Stephen J. Hallisey, Larry V. Nordby and David A. Breternitz, pp. 1-42. Interagency Archeological Services, National Park Service, Denver. xeroxed.

O'Bryan, Deric
1950   Excavations in Mesa Verde National Park, 1947-1948. *Gila Pueblo, Medallion Papers* 39.

Phillips, Phillip
1958   Application of the Wheat-Gifford-Wasley taxonomy to Eastern ceramics. *American Antiquity 24(2).*

Reed, Alan D.
1975   Bone artifacts from the Johnson Canyon area of southwestern Colorado. In The 1974 Johnson-Lion Canyon Project, edited by Paul R. Nickens, pp. 57-90. Mesa Verde Research Center, University of Colorado, Boulder. xeroxed.

Roberts, Frank H.H., Jr.
1929   Shabik'eshchee Village, a late Basketmaker site in the Chaco Canyon, New Mexico. *Bureau of American Ethnology, Bulletin* 92.

1930   Early Pueblo ruins in the Piedra District, southwestern Colorado. *Bureau of American Ethnology, Bulletin* 96.

1939   Archeological remains in the Whitewater district, eastern Arizona. Part 1: house types. *Bureau of American Ethnology, Bulletin 121.*

Robinson, Christine K.
1976   Human skeletal remains from 1975 archaeological excavations in Mancos Canyon, Colorado. Unpublished M.A. thesis. Department of Anthropology, University of Colorado, Boulder.

Rohn, Arthur H.
1971   Mug House, Mesa Verde National Park - Colorado. *National Park Service, Archeological Research Series* 7D.

Root, Homer
1965-67   Notes of excavations in Ridges Basin, Colorado. Center of Southwest Studies Archives, Ft. Lewis College, Durango, Colorado.

Saul, Frank P.
1972   The human skeletal remains of altar de sacrificios. *Papers of the Peabody Museum of Archaeology and Ethnology,* Harvard University 63(2).

Schaafsma, Curtis and John D. Gooding
1974   Archaeological survey of U.S. Highway 160-550: Durango South. Colorado State Highway Department Project Number F 019-2(14). *Highway Salvage Report* 8.

Schoenwetter, J.
1970   Archaeological pollen studies of the Colorado Plateau. *American Antiquity* 35:35-48.

Schoenwetter, J. and F.W. Eddy
1964   Alluvial and palynological reconstruction, Navajo Reservoir District. *Museum of New Mexico Papers in Anthropology 13.*

Schorger, A.W.
1966   *The wild turkey, its history and domestication.* University of Oklahoma Press, Norman.

Semenov, S.A.
1964   *Prehistoric technology.* Harper and Row, New York.

Shepard, Anna O.
1939   Technology of La Plata pottery. In Archaeological studies in the La Plata district, by Earl H. Morris, appendix. *Carnegie Institution of Washington, Publication 519.*

1968   Ceramics for the archaeologist. *Carnegie Institution of Washington, Publication 609.*

Shepardson, Mary and Blodwin Hammond
1970   *The Navajo Mountain Community: social organization and kinship terminology.* University of California Press, Berkeley.

Smith, Watson
1952   Excavations in Big Hawk Valley, Wupatki National Monument, Arizona. *Museum of Northern Arizona, Bulletin 24.*

Steward, Julian H.
1955   *Theory of culture change:the methodology of multilinear evolution.* University of Illinois Press, Urbana.

Streuver, S.
1968   Flotation techniques for the recovery of small scale archaeological remains. *American Antiquity* 33(3):353-362.

Swannack, Jervis D., Jr.
1969   Big Juniper House, Mesa Verde National Park - Colorado. *National Park Service, Archeological Research Series 7C.*

Swedlund, Alan C.
1969   Human skeletal material from the Yellow Jacket Canyon area, southwestern Colorado. Unpublished M.A. thesis. Department of Anthropology, University of Colorado, Boulder.

Tower, Donald B.
1945   The use of marine mollusca and their value in reconstructing prehistoric trade routes in the American Southwest. *Excavators' Club Papers* 2(3):3-5 (Cambridge, Mass.).

Tyler, H.A.
1975   *Pueblo animals and myths.* University of Oklahoma Press, Norman.

U.S. Soil Conservation Service
1976   *Classification of soil series of the United States, part 1.* Department of Agriculture, Washington, D.C.

Vivian, R. Gwinn
1970   An inquiry into prehistoric social organization in Chaco Canyon, New Mexico. In *Reconstructing prehistoric Pueblo societies,* edited by William A. Longacre, pp. 59-83. University of New Mexico Press, Albuquerque.

Warwick, R. and P.L. Williams (Editors)
1973   *Gray's anatomy* (35th British edition). W.B. Saunders Company, Philadelphia.

Wells, Calvin
1964   *Bones, bodies and disease.* Thames and Hudson, London.

Wheat, Joe Ben
1955   MT1, A Basketmaker III site near Yellowjacket, Colorado, *Southwestern Lore* 21(2).

M.S.   Unpublished notes of continued excavations of 5MT1. (1954-59) (1965-66).

M.S.   Unpublished notes of continued excavations of 5MT3. (1961-63) (1975-78).

Wheat, Joe Ben, James C. Gifford and William W. Wasley
1958   Ceramic variety, type cluster, and ceramic system in Southwestern pottery analysis. *American Antiquity* 24(1):34-47.

Whitehead, D.R.
1964   Fossil pine pollen and full-glacial vegetation in southeastern North Carolina. *Ecology* 45:767-777.

Whiting, A.F.
1939   Ethnobotany of the Hopi. *Museum of Northern Arizona, Bulletin* 15.

Woodbury, R.B.
1954   Prehistoric stone implements of northeastern Arizona. *Papers of the Peabody Museum of Archaeology and Ethnology,* Harvard University Vol. 34.

Wormington, H.M.
1947   Prehistoric Indians of the Southwest. *Denver Museum of Natural History, Popular Series* 7.

Young, S.P. and E.A. Goldman
1944   *The wolves of North America,* Vols. 1 and 2. Dover Publications, New York.

Zaino, E.C.
1967   Symmetrical osteoporosis, a sign of severe anemia in the prehistoric Pueblo Indians of the Southwest. In Miscellaneous papers in paleopathology:I, edited by W.D. Wade, pp. 46-47. *Museum of Northern Arizona, Technical Series* 7.

DATE DUE

JOSTEN'S NO. 30-505